ROSA · THE LIFE OF AN ITALIAN IMMIGRANT

ROSA

the life of an Italian immigrant

BY MARIE HALL ETS

FOREWORD BY RUDOLPH J. VECOLI

UNIVERSITY OF MINNESOTA PRESS, MINNEAPOLIS

Published in Great Britain, India, and Pakistan by the
Oxford University Press, London, Bombay, and Karachi and
in Canada by the Copp Clark Publishing Co. Limited, Toronto

Library of Congress Catalog Card Number: 70-110658

ISBN-0-8166-0574-2

Foreword

YEAR AFTER YEAR, decade after decade, they arrived by the
thousands, hundreds of thousands, and millions. From every corner of
Europe, and from other continents as well, they came in search of their
particular vision of America. Who they were, what they sought, and
what they found here is one of the grand themes and mysteries of the
American past. We see them in old photographs as they disembark,
carrying trunks, bundles, and valises, bewildered, anxious looks on their
faces. For a moment they stare out at us and then they are swallowed
up in the vastness of the American continent. To know the full meaning
of immigration for this country we should follow them to their new
homes and new jobs, observe them as they adjust to this strange land,
raise families, and seek to fulfill their vision. But this is difficult to do;
more often than not their tracks have been covered over by the shifting
sands of time. Only now and again are we able to retrace the steps of
one who lived this epic experience.

The year was 1884. The Statue of Liberty had not yet risen in New
York Harbor to greet the arriving shiploads of humanity. It was one
of the peak years of the nineteenth-century immigration; over a half
million entered the country. Among the jostling throngs who first set
foot on American soil at the Castle Garden immigrant depot (Ellis

Island was not opened until 1892) was a handsome and sturdy young woman. Who was she? What became of her? As if by a miracle she has been snatched from oblivion. In these pages Rosa relives her long and eventful life.

Rosa is almost unique in the literature of American immigration. Although immigrant records are voluminous, it is difficult to recall a more full and vivid account of the life of an "ordinary" person — and a woman at that. The great majority of the immigrants were Rosa's kind of people, peasants and artisans from the villages and fields of Europe. The historian who aspires to write the history of this inarticulate or silent majority is hindered by the paucity of sources. Although there are documents, such as "America letters," in which the voices of these common folk can be heard, they are hard to come by. Yet their motives, reactions, and destinies are at the heart of the meaning of immigration for America. Too often we have viewed the newcomers through the eyes of the official, the journalist, or the social worker. But even such a sympathetic observer as Jane Addams could not penetrate fully into the thoughts and feelings of the strangers in the land.

In *Rosa* we have an authentic expression of the immigrant experience. Its value is enhanced by the fact that the story is told by a woman. Historians have been accused of male chauvinism, of writing man-centered history. Certainly it has been the male immigrant who has dominated the pages of histories of immigration. *Rosa* presents us with the dramatic and poignant story of the young wife and mother who seeks to cope with the tasks of maintaining a household and rearing a family in a foreign land. From this volume we gain some sense of the heroic and important part played by the immigrant woman. Who will forget Rosa's account of giving birth unattended to her child in a mining village in Missouri?

In my judgment, *Rosa* has literary as well as historical value. It bears more resemblance to the fictional accounts of immigrant life than to immigrant autobiographies. The latter tend to be "success" stories, often with a personal or ideological ax to grind. Rosa has more in common with Willa Cather's Antonia or Ole Rölvaag's Beret than with Mary Antin or Bella V. Dodd. The charm of Rosa's story derives from the candor with which it is told. The reader feels that he is being

[vi

taken completely into her confidence. Although Rosa spares no grim details, it is all told without self-pity or self-justification. Uninhibited by prudishness, Rosa shares with us her intimate feelings and experiences. Endowed with a gift for language as well as something like total recall, she paints her story in vigorous, bold colors. From these pages, Rosa emerges an exuberant, vibrant human personality.

One of the merits of *Rosa* as a historical document is its richness of detail. We learn something about the texture of life in Lombardy in the nineteenth century. As Rosa recounts her girlhood in Bugiarno, we gain entry into the social world of this silkmaking village. We come to understand the web of relationships among parents and children, employers and workers, priests and laity, which constitute this particular community. Rosa's account of the culture of silkworms and of silk manufacturing will fascinate many readers. Her own days at childish play end early when she is put to work at silkmaking. Concerned with her precocious maturity, Rosa's foster mother arranges for her marriage to an older man from the village. Such an arrangement was not uncommon at that time. Rosa's husband shortly left to work in the iron mines of Missouri. When he sent for her, Rosa became a part of the historical phenomenon of American immigration.

Italy was one of the great hives of the European emigration. Between 1876 and 1926, more than sixteen and a half millions left the kingdom. Of these almost 9 millions came to the Americas, while 7.5 millions went to neighboring European countries. Migration was not a novel experience for the people of Italy. For generations there had been seasonal movements within Italy of grain harvesters, rice huskers, charcoal burners, and silk growers, while others migrated to work in the building trades, coal mines, and industries of Austria, France, Switzerland, and Germany. For many laborers and artisans, migration was an accepted part of the annual round of activities. Since their niggardly soil would not feed them, they had to seek their daily bread elsewhere.

When their horizon expanded beyond the Atlantic, the initial destination of the Italians was South America. The immigration to Argentina and Brazil was significantly greater than that to the United States until the turn of the century. Northern Italians made up the

[vii

greater part of the movement to Latin America, while those from the central and southern regions constituted the bulk of the immigration to North America. Both streams were predominantly male. Both were composed for the most part of sharecroppers and farm laborers, with lesser numbers of building tradesmen and other artisans. This was the key to the Italian emigration of these years. The pattern was to go abroad for a year or two to work and then return with a small hoard of savings. The common aspiration of the emigrants was to buy land in their native villages and so gain a measure of economic security and social status. These temporary emigrants were known as birds of passage. The rate of repatriation among Italian immigrants to the United States was estimated to have been over sixty percent.

Rosa's home region of Lombardy was one of the major sources of north Italian emigration. Although there were fertile plains in the lowlands, large estates owned by absentee proprietors were the rule. Tenants worked the land on a sharecrop or money rental system. In the mountainous and hilly areas, the soil was flinty and poor. While the peasants often owned land, the small stony plots yielded a meager return for their hard labor. Stingy soil, primitive methods of cultivation, and exploitative landlords, all kept the cultivators in a state of poverty. When drought, hail, or blight destroyed the crop it was a calamity. The staple in the peasants' diet was *polenta* (corn meal); dietary deficiencies resulted in a widespread incidence of pellagra. Under such harsh conditions, it is understandable why many chose to emigrate. As one of the *contadini* explained: "When it is a bad year there is no money and no wine. So we eat polenta and drink water. We don't die, because that is sufficient to keep us alive. The shops in the town give us credit. That is how we run into debt, and are forced to go to America."

In the hill towns of Lombardy such as Bugiarno where the silk industry provided an alternative source of employment the outlook was less bleak. During the latter part of the nineteenth century, increasing industrialization in northern Italy brought about a general improvement in living standards. Emigration did not abate, however, but appears to have been stimulated by rising expectations. Although the peasants of southern Italy suffered much more exploitation and misery than

[viii

did those of the north, the dead weight of an oppressive system stifled even hopes of escape. Change, however, came even to this backward part of the kingdom. In the 1890's the emigration from the southern regions increased gradually, culminating after 1900 in a mass exodus to America.

When Rosa arrived in 1884, there were but a few tens of thousands of her countrymen scattered about the country. By 1910 there were well over a million. While the majority of the Italians settled in the large cities along the eastern seaboard, they were to be found in every state of the Union. As had been true of the Irish, Germans, and Scandinavians before them, their first jobs tended to be as laborers in railroad construction and on public works. In New York, Chicago, and elsewhere, Italian labor agents known as *padroni* recruited gangs of laborers and shipped them out to isolated construction sites in the western and southern states. Living in boxcars and eating poor food, they worked twelve hours a day for a wage of $1.50, more or less. The ignorance of the immigrants exposed them to a variety of swindles, often at the hands of their more experienced countrymen. The experience of Rosa with a confidence man in New York was not unusual. That Rosa's destination was a mining village in Missouri was a reflection of the fact that an increasing number of Italians were finding work in the coal fields and iron and copper mines of the country. Italians came to make up a significant portion of the mine workers in such states as West Virginia, Illinois, Michigan, Kansas, and Colorado. Rosa's reminiscences of life in Union, Missouri, have a special documentary value for this phase of the Italian immigration.

Rosa gives us a particularly full account of her years in Chicago. These chapters constitute rich slices of immigrant life in that brawling, sprawling city. In its vivid reporting, Rosa's story rivals Upton Sinclair's *The Jungle*. We are assailed by the sights, sounds, and smells of the slum. What could be more graphic than Rosa's description of the swill box: "It was stinking so . . . Inside those boxes the wood was all rotten and juicy. One whole box of garbage was nothing but white worms." Through the eyes of Rosa we see Chicago as it was seen by the urban poor. What can equal her account of the impact of the depression of the 1890's upon the working people? Her tale of cold,

[ix

hungry women being attacked by the police is shocking even today. Through the years we share the pleasures, privations, and tragedies of the Cavalleri family. In the process, we learn a great deal about the family relationships, domestic economy, working conditions, religious practices, and superstitions of the Italian immigrants. Rosa's catalogue of "Miracles in Chicago" is a choice bit of urban folklore.

From this volume we gain a fresh appreciation of the strength of ethnic attachments and antagonisms in a city such as Chicago. As was typical of her generation Rosa thought in terms of nationality groups, some hostile, some friendly. She describes the discrimination which Italians encountered in housing and employment, but also the acts of kindness which sometimes came from unexpected sources. Rosa makes the most of comic situations such as the conflict between Irish and Sicilian women when the laundry of the former fell into the tomato paste of the latter. That the Italians were not themselves free of bigotry is evident from Rosa's discussion of regional antipathies among the Italians. In fact, she asserted, a north Italian would rather have his daughter marry even an Irishman than a Sicilian or Neapolitan! These prejudices based on the spirit of *regionalismo* were reflected in the geography of settlement, the social organizations, and even the churches of the "Little Italies" of Chicago. Rosa helps us to understand the strength of this sentiment, for example when the *Toscani* came to the assistance of her husband, Gionin, who was a *paesano*.

Beyond its value as an eyewitness account of certain historical events, *Rosa* stands as a personal document against which we can test certain ideas regarding the immigrant experience. While quantitative analysis may provide answers to certain questions, there are qualitative inquiries which numbers cannot satisfy. Subjective states of mind cannot be inferred with confidence from such "objective data." Unfortunately we have few autobiographical sources such as this which reveal in depth the effects of immigration upon particular human beings. Certainly in Rosa, we have no alienated, anomic type. Her journey from Bugiarno to Chicago was for her a high adventure in which even the hardships are relished for their bitter flavor. Rosa's zest for life which permeates these pages triumphed over adversities. In the end she can tell it all, without a tear in her eye or a tremor in her voice. What sustained Rosa in her odyssey were her high spirits and her simple faith. As she said: "In the old time there were more miracles than now, but I see lots of miracles — in Chicago too. The Madonna and the Saints, they all the time make miracles to help me out."

After a half century in America, Rosa appeared to have changed little in her essential character. Although she associated much more with Americans than did most Italian immigrants, her basic beliefs and attitudes seem to have remained those of the girl in Bugiarno. True, she found at the Chicago Commons a congenial environment in which her warm, loving nature flourished. Others were not so fortunate. The egalitarian spirit of America also suited Rosa's independent temperament. Strengthened in her sense of her own dignity, she refused to humble herself before the "higher" people. In her words, "in America poor people get smart."

We are indebted to Marie Hall Ets for this fascinating auto-biography. As Mrs. Ets tells us in her introduction, Rosa and she became fast friends at the Chicago Commons, a settlement house on the northwest side of the city. The cleaning woman and the young social worker found in each other kindred spirits. An accomplished storyteller, Rosa entertained her friend with folktales and stories about her own life. With great patience, Mrs. Ets meticulously wrote down these accounts. For Mrs. Ets and myself it is very gratifying to see this volume in print, but if Rosa were still with us she undoubtedly would be most thrilled.

Rudolph J. Vecoli

DEPARTMENT OF HISTORY, UNIVERSITY OF MINNESOTA

January 11, 1970

ROSA · THE LIFE OF AN ITALIAN IMMIGRANT

Introduction

ROSA CAVALLERI — Mrs. C. as everyone called her — was in her fifties and I in my early twenties when I came to live at Chicago Commons, a settlement house on the corner of Grand Avenue and Morgan Street, at the end of World War I. My husband had died in a war-training camp a few weeks after our marriage and friends had persuaded me to leave art and become a social worker. For this, they said, I needed to finish my degree at the University of Chicago and get training at the Graduate School of Social Service Administration. Also I must live in a settlement house. Hull House, where they had lived, they thought too sophisticated for me. They advised Chicago Commons, which was smaller and had a more familylike atmosphere.

I had just moved into the Commons and was in my little room at the top of the annex when Mrs. C. found me there weeping. I never mourned except when I was alone, but this time I was caught. She had come through from the men's side of the building where she had been cleaning and I had not heard her. Rosa's efforts to comfort me seemed strange at first — she just sat down and started telling me one of the folk tales she knew from her childhood in Italy. From that day on Mrs. C. and I became staunch friends. For the next thirteen years — with the exception of one year when I was away helping

[3

organize a child-health program in Czechoslovakia, and another period of some months investigating living conditions of miners in coal camps of West Virginia and Kentucky for the U.S. Coal Commission – Rosa and I saw each other almost every day. And even after I remarried and left the Commons in 1931 we visited back and forth until she died in 1943.

Mrs. C., as she liked to tell everyone, was the first neighbor Chicago Commons had helped. Dr. Graham Taylor, founder and head resident of the Commons, and his eleven co-workers, had just moved into the old brick building on Union Street in 1894 when Mrs. C. came to the door angry and weeping. She and her family, along with all the other families who had been living in the building, had been forced to move when the settlement rented it. The neighborhood at that time was mostly Norwegian, Irish, Dutch, and German – and no one wanted to rent rooms to Italians. The Cavalleris had had to move into the basement of an old saloon and it flooded every time it rained. This made Mrs. C. so angry that she went back to the new people scolding and weeping, and although she could only speak a few words of English, she made them come and see how she and her husband were scooping water out of the rooms by the pailful. She knew of a nice building a few blocks over that had empty rooms, big and sunny, and the rent was no more, but the landlord had refused to rent to Italians. The people from the Commons not only got her these nice rooms and moved her in the same day, they even paid the necessary month's rent in advance. "But I paid them back in two weeks," she would tell me. "I can't live with a debt! Never!"

From that time on Mrs. C. had been Chicago Commons' most devoted friend and neighbor. She came to their evening classes and social groups, and as soon as the Commons could afford hired help she stopped cleaning floors in the saloon and washing clothes for a group of plasterers and came every day to work in the Commons. Most days she cleaned the rooms of the residents, but soon she also substituted for the cook on the cook's day off. And it was here in the Commons' kitchen while eating lunch with the other cleaning women that she started telling her stories. The housekeeper heard her one day and told Dr. Taylor. And Dr. Taylor insisted on taking her into the residents'

[4

parlor one evening after vespers and having her tell a story to the residents. From then on Rosa's fame as a storyteller had grown so that by the time I met her in 1918 she and her storytelling were known to all the settlement houses in Chicago, as well as to various women's clubs downtown and to classes in storytelling at several universities in the area. She never went alone to these places—someone from the Commons always went with her. And she was never paid. She did it because she loved to.

Rosa liked to tell about one large gathering at Hull House where Jane Addams spoke first. Next Dr. Taylor spoke, and then "the big *somebody*" from Washington for whom the meeting had been called. But the audience was restless and didn't listen. Then she, Rosa, got up and started telling a story. For her the audience came to life. They sat up and clapped and laughed and shouted for more. Dr. Taylor told her afterwards that he wished he could make the people listen to him the way they listened to her. "Don't worry, Dr. Taylor," she told him. "You did good too."

After I came to the Commons Mrs. C. used my room for all her rest periods. "You're home, Mis' Mary? I disturb you?" I would hear her say as she came up the last flight of steps. She was always panting by that time, for she was very heavy — twice the size of an average woman. "When the residents give me their old skirts," she would say, "I have to sew two or three of them together to make one big enough for me." But she just laughed. Her weight and old clothes didn't worry her. For aprons she would patch together squares of their old gingham dresses. And nearly always she wore a neckerchief pinned with a safety pin, for in her girlhood in Bugiarno to expose a naked neck was a sin.

Once when Rosa was to tell a story to a large women's club downtown, her married daughter hired a seamstress to make her a dress. It was made of black broadcloth with a pink satin vest and belt. "And only when it was all made," Rosa would laugh as she told me, "I find out I have to pay for it myself. Me, I thought she was giving it to me." But Rosa didn't wear that dress very much. She felt more "comfortable" in her old clothes.

Rosa's big, beautiful eyes often looked sad when she was sitting alone, but sparkled with life when she was with anyone, and changed

[5

from one expression to another when she was acting out her stories. She wore her naturally wavy dark auburn hair in a simple knob on top of her head. Her shoulders were somewhat narrow and stooped from so many years of hard labor, but her hips and legs were so heavy that she found it hard to stand and walk. As she grew older she sat on a chair on the platform when telling her stories and used a cane when walking.

Evenings if I was in my room and had time she would tell me stories or talk about her early life. If I was not home or had studying to do she would sit by the window counting off prayers on her rosary and dozing. Days when she was staying for an evening club or was to tell a story at some gathering she would wash up in the bathroom down our hall and change her blouse and skirt there, for she had now moved too far out on Grand Avenue to go home and get back in time.

About 1927 or 1928, when ill health made me give up social work, I went back to art. I studied some more, this time at the Art Institute, and later under Frederick Poole, a member of the Royal Academy of Arts of London. One of my first assignments at the institute was to draw a picturebook for children. I had had some experience making up stories for a young nephew in Wisconsin, and I thought it fun, so for this assignment I not only drew the pictures, I wrote the story too. The result was *Mister Penny*. When this was published, Rosa was excited. She wanted to help me publish other books and offered to tell me more of her stories.

Most of the stories she told she had heard as a child in Bugiarno, a silkmaking village not many miles from Milan where she had been born. (The names of the Italian villages and of Rosa and her friends have been changed throughout this book.) She had been left at a hospital there the night she was born, and the hospital had farmed her out to a peasant woman in Bugiarno the next day. On winter nights the poor people would gather in a barn to be warmed by the animals. The men stayed way back in the straw with the animals, and the women knitted on a bench at one side with a single candle for light. It was the men who told the stories and they liked funny ones to make people laugh. Rosa liked the funny ones too, though she told me she

[6

sometimes feared Americans might think she and the peasants irreligious for telling jokes about the priests.

So, little by little, as she rested in my room I took her stories down. In the days of Rosa's childhood the poor could neither read nor write, so the stories they told were all traditional. Of course Rosa added new parts to make them more interesting, and she acted them out vividly, but when written down these stories held little that would interest moderns. It was the amazing story of her life and of the fears and superstitions and beliefs of the people of her village that interested me. These did seem worth taking down and passing on. And Rosa was anxious to have me do so.

Since Mrs. C. could read and write no English and very little Italian, she could make no notes. She just had to tell me things as she remembered them, and let me put them in order. First I took down her words in heavy dialect, as she spoke them. But this proved too difficult for the reader. Thus in this more recent version I have corrected and simplified the text, trying at the same time not to lose the character and style of her spoken words.

She loved telling me the story of her life and of the life in her village. The only thing she refused to tell was the name of her real mother, "a great actress," who lived in Milan, for she said everyone in the world would know that name. "I was born to do the acting like my mother," she would say — and I'm sure she was. "But God didn't want it. He wanted to save me for heaven in the end."

1

THERE used to be in the city of Milan a place that was called the *torno*. There was a hole in the wall of the hospital with that *torno*, like a cage that went around, in the middle. So all those new mothers who had some disgrace — they were not married or they were too poor to support it — they would go in the night and put their baby in the hole and turn the wheel. Then they would ring a little bell and run away. But in the year 1866, or 1867 (Mamma Lena told me but I don't remember for sure — she said it was the year Garibaldi brought the war to San Martino), the city hall said the hospital must take the *torno* off. Too many babies were getting hurt. Sure, it was the mothers' own fault when those babies got hurt! Probably they didn't know how, or they were afraid someone would see them, and they turned too fast. Or they put their baby on then changed their minds and tried to get it back. That's when most of the babies got hurt — when the mothers changed their minds and tried to get them back. That *torno* was a turnstile that only turned one way, and once you had given it your baby you could not change your mind and get it back.

But before they took the *torno* off, one other mother came and put her baby in the cage and turned. Maybe it was not the mother — maybe somebody else put it there for her — it was just that day born.

But in that time in the old country the mothers didn't have to stay in bed with the baby. They walked away the same day. Anyway, that new baby fell down to the cradle without harm and the sisters heard the little bell and came and found it. This baby had a card tied to its neck with the name "Inez." And on the string with the card was a half square of cloth which meant that the mother intended sometime to come back and get her baby. Those babies who were put on the *torno* with nothing around their necks belonged to the hospital entirely. The hospital could do what it wanted with them. But if a baby had a half square of cloth tied around its neck the hospital had to keep a record and know where that baby was even after it was grown. So the sister took the half square of calico — it was black-and-white checks on one side and all white on the other — and put it in the big book of records. Then she wrote down the name and the day — February 2, 1866, or 1867 — but instead of just "Inez" she wrote down "Inez Ignazius." She added the last name herself. People could always tell the children of the hospital by those names — Maria Margi; Luigi Luivanni; Inez Ignazius — the first letters of the names always matched. Then the sister picked up the baby to take care of it. And there, that Inez was me. I was the last, or the next last, baby to go on the *torno*. After then the mothers had to go to the door of the hospital face to face with the mother superior. But my mother didn't go to the door. She left me on the *torno* the night I was born.

Now in that time, if some poor woman in a village had the milk to nurse it, she liked to get a baby from the hospital in Milan and make a little money that way. So the next morning a poor woman from the village of Bugiarno, Visella her name was, came to the door of the hospital to ask if they had any baby. Her baby was dead. The hospital said yes and they gave her that Inez. So Visella took me. She took me on the *tramvai* — a kind of bus with horses — to Bugiarno, about eighteen miles from Milan. She took me home and nursed me.

But after not long Visella found that she couldn't nurse me anymore. She found she was in trouble again — she had another baby of her own on the way. She had no more milk, so she said, "I have to take this baby back to the hospital. It would take all the money I get from the hospital to buy milk from a cow. And I have too many children of my own to take care of another without pay."

But Visella had an old mother-in-law living there in the house — Marietta — and Marietta loved me so much she couldn't bear to let me go. I was such a pretty baby and so lively that Marietta was loving me better than her own grandchildren. So she told Visella that she would take care of me and feed me from a bottle. And she did. She kept me until I was about three years old. Then she began to worry. She said, "What am I going to do? I'm too old and the little girl is too young. I'm so old I can no more see the worms when I make the cabbage soup. I have to get ready to die. If I can't find some woman in Bugiarno to take my Inez I'll have to take her back to the hospital in Milan." And she was crying and sad because she thought I would be alone in the world. A rich lady heard about me and wanted me, but she was a schoolteacher and Marietta didn't trust her — an old maid like that. But then one day Marietta went to the fountain and met Maddalena Cortesi.

Maddalena Cortesi was crying because three weeks ago she had lost the daughter she had got from the hospital. The real mother and father had got married and had come back with their half piece of cloth to match and the hospital had to give them that Rosa. Eight years Maddalena had kept Rosa and loved her like her own. She was even angry with God and the Madonna because They had not listened to her prayers to let her keep Rosa always. She would no longer say the prayers for the other poor women when they went in the stable at night to keep warm. And she still wouldn't speak to her sister Teresa because Teresa had said she should get another baby from the hospital. As if any other could heal her broken heart!

So Marietta said, "You're brokenhearted because you've lost your little girl, and I'm brokenhearted because I have to take mine back. I'm too old and the little girl is too young. But oh, she's so pretty and so lively! And she's a daughter of the Madonna. The Madonna will bless the woman who takes care of that little girl. She was born on the *Purificazione di Maria*."

When Marietta's buckets were full, Maddalena started pumping to fill hers. Maddalena didn't want to think about me but the Madonna made her. "Born on the *Purificazione di Maria*," she said to herself. "Born on the day Maria was made clean after Jesus was born."

"Wait," she said to Marietta. "Don't take your little girl back today. I'm going to ask my husband. Wait until I can ask my husband if he wants another little girl."

"Oh, you're just the one! Just the one!" said Marietta. "You're such a religious woman! And not so poor, either! You're just the one!"

"Well, I'm not saying now," said Maddalena. "Come back at the ringing of the Ave Maria and I will be here and tell you then." So Maddalena went home and told her husband, Giulur.

Giulur, which is just the way we say Angelo, in the talk of Bugiarno, was more brokenhearted than Maddalena that they had lost that Rosa, but he was not angry with God and the Madonna. Giulur was never angry with anyone. When he heard about me he was happy. He said yes, he would love to have another little girl. "And instead of Inez," he said, "we'll call her Rosa, like the Rosa we lost."

Mamma Marietta was glad she had found such a good woman to take me, but she was crying to lose me, and I was crying because I didn't want to go. But Maddalena Cortesi made me. She took me home and little by little she made me stay there. But she had a lot of trouble with me in the first beginning, because I was all the time running back to Mamma Marietta. I couldn't get away from the love I had in my heart for my *nonna*.

(Why didn't Mamma Marietta keep me! She was only about seventy years old at that time and she lived to one hundred and four! One hundred and four years! I was loving her with my whole heart. I love her yet. But I guess she didn't know she would live so long and she was afraid I would be alone in the world. Everything comes from God. God wanted me to go with Mamma Lena so I would get the strong religion. Mamma Marictta was awful good but she couldn't say the prayers herself. God wanted me to go with Mamma Lena so I would learn all the Latin prayers. Probably I would not be so good if I had stayed with Mamma Marietta. She let me do more what I wanted. But Mamma Lena was too strict! Everyone said so. She made you go straight like a pin!)

[11

2

I WOKE up early in the bed Papa Lur had made for me out of planks and two wooden horses. At first I didn't know why I woke up early, but then I remembered — today was the *festa*! Yesterday me and Caterina and Toni had run to the square and watched the men from Milan putting up booths and colored lanterns and all kinds of things. The cornstalks in my mattress crunched as I climbed out of bed, but Mamma Lena and Papa Lur didn't wake up. Quiet, quiet I ran and opened the door and looked down into the court. There was no one around. Everybody was asleep. I went out on the landing and closed the door careful behind me. Mamma Lena always told me that even in the hottest weather you must never leave a door or window open at night. The night air would make you sick if you let it get in.

I went down the stairs, slow, slow, feeling the iron twists of the railing as I went. When I came to the bottom I pushed open the door to the *osteria* where Mamma Lena sold wine and polenta and went in. This room was darker and bigger than the room upstairs, and it was full of the smell of sour wine. Ugh, I didn't like that smell! I could smell the smell of men too, though there was nobody in the room now. The two long tables and benches where the men always sat were empty — they were just standing there waiting. There was a picture of God and a crucifix hung up on the wall, but I didn't look at them. I was feeling the cool, hard earth of the floor as I walked back to the fireplace. I looked in the two iron kettles, but they were empty. I put my hand in the hole of that little earth stove where Mamma Lena sometimes baked the onions and potatoes, but there was nothing in there either. So then I went on to the other side of the room. The chickens were waking up and clucking. I could hear them and I could smell them. I had come into the *osteria* just to see the chickens, but still I didn't hurry. And even when I reached their coop I stopped and looked up at the little Madonna on the shelf above. The Madonna was waiting for Mamma Lena to come down and light another candle. I tried to touch Her feet or the hem of Her robe but She was too high up — I couldn't reach Her. "O *Madonnina bella!*" I said. "*Madonnina bella!*" But the little Madonna just stood there smiling, holding the Baby in her arms.

So then I sat down and began talking to the chickens. A-Negrina and A-Pette pushed up against the wooden bars of the cage and talked back as fast as they could. A-Negrina started low and deep down, then her voice always broke and went up. A-Pette always talked high like a lady scolding. A-Pette was turning her head back and forth looking at me, first with one bright little eye, then with the other. Just to fool them I put my hand on the latch to the door. Then I took my hand away. I was not allowed to open the coop; if I did, Mamma Lena would whip me again. But then my hand went back and slow, real slow, I moved the latch up. The chickens were watching. They were pushing and squawking to get out. Suddenly I felt pins and needles up my back and in my hair. A devil inside of me had made me push the latch way up and the chickens had opened the door! Oh, those chickens were happy to be free! They flew over the benches and over the tables trying to get to the door. And I ran after them, clapping and laughing and shouting. Now there was life in the court. Now I was happy.

So then I was standing there by the door of the *osteria* near a big grapevine that was growing out of a tub, and pretty soon I started watching some ants in the tub. They were going in and out of a hole in the dirt making a big hill. Those little ants were smart, but they

[13

were so slow that I pushed them to help them along. Suddenly I heard Mamma Lena come out of the sleeping room upstairs. *"Santa Maria!"* she scolded and her wooden soles came clapping down on the cement of the steps. I knew she was angry with someone but I didn't know it was with me because I had forgotten all about the chickens until she grabbed me. *"Santa Maria!* Will you never learn to obey! How many times must I punish you for letting the chickens out before I can test them?" And she started beating we with one of her wooden soles. But she didn't get to hit me more than once or twice. I had on nothing but my chemise — my behind was all naked — and that wooden sole hurt! Like a flash I twisted out of her hands and was off up the stairs. Papa Lur was just coming down but he didn't stop me — he got out of my way. And once upstairs I was safe, under the big bed by the door. That big bed that Mamma Lena and Papa Lur slept in was built right into the wall, so no one could move it. Many times Mamma Lena had tried but she couldn't reach me under that bed.

For a little while I lay there crying. But then I remembered the chickens and how happy they were when I let them out. I should not have let them out until Mamma Lena had tested them for the eggs. Mamma Lena always stuck her finger up their behinds and if she felt the egg hard she would lock them up again and wait for the egg to come. The eggs of the chickens were precious. Rich people bought them and ate them. But anyway I was happy that I had let them out.

As I lay under the bed, I listened to the sounds in the court. About twenty guards of the district, all dressed like soldiers, lived in one long room in our building. I heard them laughing and talking and knew they had come out from their barracks and were going into the *osteria* for Mamma Lena to give them their breakfast. Then I heard Caterina and Toni. When I knew they were up I wanted to run down and play, but I was afraid to come out too soon — Mamma Lena might want to finish her beating. Me and Caterina were just the same age and were always playing together. Toni was younger, but we sometimes let him play too. And then as I was listening to all the sounds I heard two long deep chords of music. Beppo! It was Beppo and his concertina! But how could that be? Why hadn't Beppo gone to the fields? Then I remembered — today was a feast day! Beppo didn't have to go to work!

And now not even the fear of Mamma Lena could keep me away from the court. I climbed out from under the bed and ran to the landing and sure enough — there he was, sitting on his doorstep with the concertina on his knee.

"Come on, Rosa," he called. "Put your dress on and come."

I got my dress on backwards, but that was all the better — now the buttons were in front. "Play the *mumfrine*!" I called as I came down the steps. "Play the *mumfrine*!" *Mumfrine* was just a word I had made up myself but Beppo knew what I meant — I wanted the lively songs that made me dance.

So Beppo played and I sang the words of the songs with him and danced. Caterina and Toni tried to sing the songs too but they couldn't sing and dance the way I could.

"Bravo, Rosa!" Beppo would shout, playing faster and faster, and pounding time with his feet. "Bravo! That's a beautiful jig!" And neither of us would stop until I was all out of breath.

Beppo had a little room by himself on the court and used to hire himself out to work by the day in the fields. He was short and dark and more poor than the guards and other young men on the court, but no one in the world could play the concertina like Beppo. "I know I'm not pretty," Beppo would say. "I've got the big mouth and the broken nose, but Rosa loves me anyway. Isn't that so, Rosa?" Of course I loved Beppo! And I followed him everywhere. In winter I followed him into the stables when he played for the other men to sing their comic songs; in summer I followed him to the threshing floor when he played for the young people to dance on Sunday afternoons. We were always together. And when Mamma Lena knew I would be with Beppo she let me go.

A feast day was a busy day in the *osteria*. There was never enough room for all the men who came, so Papa Lur was carrying out planks and wooden horses from the toolroom and setting up extra tables in the court. But as he worked he was watching me dance and sing. The guards who had finished their breakfast were watching too. They were shouting and clapping and Papa Lur was pleased. He was proud that I could sing and dance like that — I could tell by the way he stood up straighter and smiled. After he had brought out the benches, he asked

[15

me if I was ready for some breakfast. Of course I was ready. I was always hungry. I started to run along beside him to the *osteria*, but at the door I remembered Mamma Lena and decided to wait on the wall.

In nice weather me and Caterina and Toni always sat on a low wall at the side of the court to eat our meals. That wall was there to mark off boxes to hold the dirt from animals and people. We didn't mind the smell. We knew that the dirt was precious — that it was needed to grease the fields. One man with a cart came every day and bought it. So I sat down on the wall and waited and Papa Lur brought me a wooden bowl half full of polenta and wine. Papa Lur had made the wooden bowl for me himself so that Mamma Lena couldn't punish me anymore for breaking the other kind.

"Why do you always put in the wine?" I asked. I didn't like that sour wine — ever!

"To help keep off the mad-hunger disease," he said. "Mamma Lena says you're too big to have milk, and the wine is good for you too."

I took my bowl, but I didn't eat. I waited to see what Toni got. Toni was smaller and he sometimes got milk. Sure enough, when Caterina and Toni came with their bowls, Toni had milk.

"Toni," I said, "you take my bowl and I'll take yours."

So he ate my polenta with wine and I ate his with milk. I was all the time eating his polenta and milk, but his mother didn't know it. And Toni didn't care.

After we ate Mamma Lena hung out her best shawl and her yellow silk bedspread and the sheet with the crocheted edge and everything pretty she had, to decorate the court. Then she called me to get me ready too. She washed me and dressed me in a nice red calico dress with a full skirt and no sleeves. Then she started combing and braiding my hair. When I cried and pulled away she gave me a slap and braided it all the tighter. She parted it down the back and pulled it forward into two tight braids.

"It's pride that you don't want your hair in the style of the poor!" she said. "You know your hair is beautiful and you want to show it off. Pride is a sin — a terrible sin! God and the Madonna will punish you

[16

for pride." What pride was I didn't know. I only knew that my hair was pulling and sticking out in my face.

When Mamma Lena had finished I ran back to the court and found Beppo and Caterina and Toni all dressed and ready too. Beppo had on his Sunday white shirt. Caterina had on a blue calico dress that matched her eyes, and her light brown braids hung down her back. Toni had on a white blouse and tight pants. He looked nice dressed up like today with his black hair and black eyes. We all danced around Beppo and I took his hand. "Hurry, Beppo! Hurry!" I said as we went out the gate and down the narrow roadway between the white-plastered buildings. I could hear shouting and laughing in the square and I couldn't wait to get there. Shawls and sheets and red-and-white tablecloths hung from all the roofs and high windows and other poor people coming from their courts shouted to us with jokes and laughing. Today everybody was happy. Today the Madonna would come out of the church and bless us.

In the square people were already crowding around the stalls looking at everything the men from Milan had brought. There were those wheels for gambling, and stands where you could knock the babies down, and tables full of snails. Those snails were still alive when the people ate them! There were show people walking tightropes, and there was a dog-and-monkey show. Beppo paid one *centesimo* each so we could see it. How cute the little dogs were, walking on their back legs and all dressed up! But the thing I liked best was a big wagon covered with black cloth with six holes on each side. You looked in one hole and there was a great big elephant. You looked in another hole and there was a great big tiger, or a man and woman getting married. In every hole there was something different, but everything big — bigger than the wagon! I wanted to stay there forever, but the man made me move on so someone else could see.

At noon Beppo took us home to eat. The tables in the *osteria* and in the court were full of men eating and drinking, all shouting and laughing and having a good time. Beppo went into the *osteria* but me and Toni and Caterina sat on the wall to wait for our bowls. As we were waiting, four men from the stalls came in to eat. They were poor workmen and their clothes were dirty, but they were men from the

[17

city and the poor men from Bugiarno all grew quiet and looked at their hands. When the workmen from Milan asked a question no one answered. But after those four men had finished and rushed off, the other men at the tables busted out laughing and everyone was trying to mimic the talk and the acting of the men from the city.

When Papa Lur brought my bowl it had the *minestra* in it. And the mother of Caterina and Toni brought them the *minestra* too. Oh, we were happy! We only got that good rice soup on Sundays and holidays. We examined our own and each other's and ate very slow to make it last longer.

"How come you have the *minestra*?"

It was *Signore*, the agent who collected the rent. We always called him *Signore* because he was higher than us. He was stroking his red moustache and smiling. We hadn't seen him come out and he was smiling to see how excited we were. I smiled back the way I did with everyone. When I was little I was not yet afraid of the high and the rich.

"Today is the *festa*!" I told him. "Today the Madonna will go through the streets and bless all the people!"

"The people who live in front — who rent the rooms on the garden — they eat the *minestra* every day," he said. "How will they know it's a feast day?"

Me and Caterina and Toni all looked at each other, then we looked back to *Signore*. Was he fooling us or not? Were there people so rich in the world that they could eat rice soup every day?

Some of the men at the tables in the court had started playing *morra*. "Five!" "Nine!" "Seven!" "Six!" they were yelling, banging their fists on the table with some of the fingers held out. But Mamma Lena heard them and came out and chased them away. "Pay your bills and get out!" she said. "There isn't room for you to play here today!" Those poor men fumbled for their money in their haste to get away, but I thought it was only natural that they were afraid of Mamma Lena. Everybody was afraid of Mamma Lena. Me too.

In the afternoon everyone from Bugiarno and many people from other villages too were in the square to see the Madonna come out of the church. I was crushed between Mamma Lena and Papa Lur just behind the rope, and I was so excited I couldn't stand still. Pretty soon a giant firecracker went off on the steps of the church and a skyrocket shot up to the sky. The women crossed themselves and the men took off their hats. Then there was silence. Everyone was waiting. And very soon, there coming out through the door was the big Madonna. A little boy and girl dressed like angels walked in front, and men with red ribbons across their chests walked at the sides and in back. The Madonna swayed a little as the men carrying the platform came down the steps. Oh, how beautiful She looked with the sun shining on Her blue robe! I shivered with joy and held Papa Lur's hand. She came nearer and nearer. Just opposite me She stopped. And then, as I watched, She turned Her head just a little and looked right at me! I couldn't breathe. I couldn't swallow. I held tighter to Papa Lur's hand. Then the Madonna looked down again to the Baby in Her arms. Now the men in the procession came to the ropes and took money from the people to pin on the Madonna's robes. I was wishing I had something to give Her. I loved Her so much and I had nothing to give Her.

(Maybe I imagined. I was only a little girl. Probably the Madonna didn't come to life for me, but I was sure She turned Her head and looked at me!)

While the Madonna was going through the streets — those two hours of the procession — everything was quiet and everyone was reverent. But after the statue had been carried back into the church there was shouting and laughing again. Mamma Lena and Papa Lur hurried back to the *osteria* and were so busy that Zia Teresa had to stay all the rest of the day and help serve the people.

At midnight came the fireworks. No one but the Italian people know how to make fireworks like we had them in Bugiarno! The last fireworks of all was the Holy Madonna Herself with the Baby in Her arms — all in fire across the sky. Some poor women were even falling on their faces to see such a beautiful thing.

3

NOW I will tell the story of Mamma Lena, the way she all the time told it to me. Maddalena Cortesi, her name was, but I called her Mamma Lena, so then everybody else called her that too.

When Maddalena Cortesi was a young girl — Maddalena Mateo her name was then — she was awful pretty and awful good. She was so good that she didn't want any man. She had the intention to go in a convent and be a nun. (She *said* she was awful pretty when she was a young girl. She always said so. But I don't know if she was. When I knew her she was big and skinny with tight lips, a thin nose, and pale eyes that were all the time scowling.) So she was a beautiful young girl and she lived with her mother and father and her big brother, Pep, and his wife and his children and a younger sister, Teresa, who was like eight years old. But then her father died and Pep became the head of the house. Maddalena and Teresa had to bring their wages from the silk mill to Pep, and Pep's wife was the boss in the house, telling Maddalena's old mother to do this and do that. Maddalena didn't like it.

So one day Maddalena said to herself, "Me and Teresa can support ourselves and our mother. I'm not going to bring my wages to Pep! I'm going to find a little room and me and my mother and Teresa can be our own boss!" So she did. She found a little room on another court and when it came time to go Pep let her take one or two pans and the cornstalk mattress and a bench and a table. But he wouldn't let Teresa go.

He said, "No. When the mother leaves her house the young children belong to the man. A woman can't take her young children." So Teresa had to stay with Pep and that cruel sister-in-law and all their children. Maddalena's mother was crying and didn't want to go, but Maddalena said it couldn't be helped — everything was arranged. So Maddalena went anyway and took her mother with her.

"I made three big sins in my life," Mamma Lena used to say. "That time I separated my mother and Teresa was one. But I didn't know until everything was arranged that I couldn't take Teresa." (What the other two sins were she would never tell. I was teasing and teasing to know, but I don't know yet. She would never tell.)

So Maddalena and her old mother were living there alone on another court and she had men going there all the time asking for her. Seventeen men she turned away in one season. She didn't even give them the chair. In that time if a girl liked a man she gave him a chair to sit down, but if she didn't like him she didn't give him a chair. Maddalena was so good she didn't want *any* man! Seventeen men in one season, she always said. And maybe it was true, because in that time a girl was gold. Not like now in America — six or seven girls to every man! In that time it was the girl that was valuable.

But then one day a beautiful young man came home to Bugiarno. He was a sailor who worked on the boats to America. For months he would be gone and then for one month he would be home. This time when he came home those young men who didn't get the chair from Maddalena thought they would have fun with him and play a joke, because he didn't know about her. "Lur, do you know that Maddalena? No? Oh, but she's beautiful! And good! And smart! She's so smart she can say all the Latin prayers just like the priest! And besides working in the silk mill she knows how to cut clothes, how to cook, and everything! She's the best, best girl you could find in Bugiarno! Do you want to see her? Come to the square by the church

Sunday morning, and when she comes out from mass we'll show you which girl she is."

So Giulur did. Sunday morning he went to the square and waited by the church with all those young men who didn't get a chair. And when he saw Maddalena he loved her right away.

"Go to her house, Giulur," the other young men said. "She is living all alone with her old mother on that court next to the threshing floor. You go there and talk to her. Sure, she will love you too! You're such a *beautiful* young man! Sure! Sure!"

So the other young men watched and when they saw Giulur going into the court where Maddalena lived — and right away that same afternoon — they busted out laughing. "That Maddalena, she won't give him a chair either!" they said. "She won't give any man a chair!"

But Giulur didn't know this and he went there by her door and talked so nice to the old mother that the old mother ran and told Maddalena. Maddalena said, "I don't want to see *any* young man!" But she came anyway. And when she saw that beautiful young man all dressed up in the clothes of a sailor she right away gave him a chair to sit down. And while they sat there talking to get acquainted, she was looking and looking and listening and listening.

Giulur — Angelo Cortesi, his name was — was tall and thin with dark, kind eyes and wavy hair that grew low on his neck. And his talk was gentle — not rough like the talk of the other young men of Bugiarno. It sounded different entirely. As Maddalena sat there looking and listening her heart started twisting inside of her and she forgot all about her intention to go in a convent and be a nun. Giulur was telling about himself and about his family. All of his family were dead but one sister, who was about twenty years old — Bunga her name was. Bunga was living all alone in one little room he had for her, but she was deaf and dumb and a stupid. She didn't know how to take care of herself and he had no one to take care for her. He didn't know what to do.

When Maddalena heard about Bunga she said she would go right away to see her. And so she did. Oh, that Bunga was terrible! Her hair was not combed and was full of lice and her face was all sores from dirt. She was terrible! Maddalena was so sympathetic that she said she would not make Giulur wait. She would marry him right away so she could take care of Bunga. So they were married, and Maddalena took Bunga home and cleaned her and made like a new woman out of her.

Always, when any of the women spinning and knitting in the court or in the stable started talking about marriage Mamma Lena would hurry to tell about hers. "When I was a young girl," she would say, "I was awful pretty and awful good. I was so good I didn't want any man. I only married Giulur so I could take care of Bunga. And I made like a new woman out of Bunga. I made her almost pretty enough to get married."

So they were all living there together in that one little room on the court next to the threshing floor: Mamma Lena and Papa Lur — whenever he was home from the ship — and Bunga and the old mother. But after not many years the old mother died, and Bunga died too. Then Giulur got to be too old to go as a sailor, so he and Mamma Lena started the *osteria*. They rented one big room for the *osteria*, and upstairs they had another room for sleeping. Then Papa Lur took all his savings and bought a little piece of ground in the country and planted grapes for his wine. Now Mamma Lena didn't have to go to the silk mill anymore. She just stayed home and took care of the *osteria* and was her own boss.

But still Mamma Lena was not content. She wanted to learn to read like the rich people. She knew all the prayers in the prayer book and she knew what the words meant too, so she began teaching herself to read from the prayer book. And when Don Domenic, our priest, saw how much she wanted to learn he helped her. Before very long she could read almost anything she saw in print, but she never learned how to write; if anyone owed her a bill in the *osteria* she had to put their names down in print. And then, because she knew many stories of saints and of miracles, she was helping Don Domenic by telling those holy stories to the women in the Sunday school. She told them so good that the poor women would come and fill all the benches and even sit on the floor to listen.

"Maddalena and Giulur, they never fight like the other husbands and wives," the old women would say as they sat spinning and knitting in the court.

But whenever Zia Teresa came in and heard them she would say, "No. Giulur is a saint, and that's why. He takes everything and keeps still."

Summers Papa Lur worked in his field, but when winter came he used to go to some nearby village and work. One year he was working in a factory that made whiskey stills. In that way he learned how whiskey was made and started making it himself to sell in the *osteria*. In that time there was not Prohibition, but the people were not allowed to make whiskey and sell it. But Papa Lur, he did. And he was making it so good that the poor men who came in the *osteria* bought more of that whiskey than any other drink. Mamma Lena was happy that they were making more money, but sometimes when she thought about all the whiskey she was selling she got a little scared. One day she couldn't stand it anymore — she *had* to know if it was a sin, if she was offending God. So she went to Don Domenic's house and asked him. But Don Domenic didn't scold. He said to watch out that she didn't get caught, that was all.

About this time Mamma Lena started getting babies from the hospital in Milan. Giulur loved babies so much and she had never given him any. Then too, she could make a little more money this way. The first baby, Lola, she kept three years before the hospital took it away. Then she got Rosa. And Rosa she kept eight years — just like her own. But the year Rosa was eight years old the real mother and father got married and took their half square of cloth to the hospital to match and the hospital said Mamma Lena must bring the little girl back.

So this was the time she got me. And in the beginning she had a lot of trouble with me. I was all the time running away — back to Mamma Marietta. Mamma Lena didn't like it that I loved Mamma Marietta better than her. She punished me and punished me. So, little by little, I had to learn to stay with her — that was all.

Then Mamma Lena didn't like it that I was so lively and so full of mischief and didn't obey. She no sooner took me out of one mischief than I was in another. And she didn't like all the loving and hugging I did. I would throw my arms around the knees of Papa Lur or around the knees of Zia Teresa and hug them so hard that I almost tipped them over. I was even loving the chickens. I would catch them when they were out in the court and squeeze them till they squawked to get away. I loved Papa Lur because he was always taking me with him when he went to work in the fields. "Today," he would say to Mamma Lena, "I'll take Rosa with me. She can play with the ants and the earth and at noon I will put her to sleep under a wine vine." And I loved Zia Teresa because she used to take me home with her and to her stable and was teaching me to suck the milk from the cow for myself. I just loved that warm milk. Then Mamma Lena didn't like it that I was all the time chattering and talking. She called me "a regular talking machine." When I was a little older, one time, she told me she would give me a *centesimo* if I could keep still five minutes. But me, I lost. I could never keep still five minutes — even now — if I have someone to talk to. Mamma Lena said I was a daughter of the poor and the daughter of the Madonna and I should be humble and quiet. But she didn't know how to make me. I kept right on laughing and shouting and running from one mischief to another.

4

THAT building where Mamma Lena was living, everyone used to call it the old *palazzo*. I guess it was an old palace lost for taxes. Most of it was empty. In front, in the main part, a few people who were not so poor rented rooms. *Signore* and his wife had a room in there too. Those people had a beautiful iron-bar gate like in a cemetery and they had an old garden with a broken-down fountain and rose bushes and tiger lilies. Us poor people who lived in the back had a wooden door in the wall for a gate and a big court with a hard dirt floor. On our court there was the *osteria* and over it our sleeping room. Next to us was the wall for the dirt from animals and people. Then came the barracks — just one long room where those young soldiers who were the guards of the district slept all in a row. On the far side of the court was the room where Mariana and Rocco, the mother and father of Caterina and Toni, lived. Beppo, who was about nineteen years old when I first knew him, had a room next to the empty stable. On the side nearest the gate was the toolroom, a long storing place where Papa Lur kept the tools and the frames for his garden. Some of the white plaster had fallen off the buildings and wall, showing the bricks underneath, and some of the round tiles had fallen off the roof, but it was nice in the court of the old *palazzo* anyway. There was a big vine over the door of the *osteria* and little trees growing out of tubs, and there were all those wooden benches where people could sit. Oh, I used to love all the courts in Bugiarno!

In the summer when the weather was nice, old women from other courts used to come to the court of the old *palazzo* to do their spinning and knitting and when Mamma Lena was not busy in the *osteria* she would sit down with them and say all the Latin prayers. As she prayed she kind of kept time with her hands — twisting the linen stuff from the distaff in her belt down to the bobbin below. I would sit there beside her and listen and listen. I had to sit there anyway because she was making me learn to knit. I would knit little pieces of old string on some wooden needles Papa Lur had made for me and I would listen and listen. I just loved the sound of those Latin prayers. The words were like music: *Ave Maria gratia plena Dominus tecum* . . . *Pater noster qui es in caelis sanctificetur nomen tuum.* . . . Pretty soon I was saying them with Mamma Lena. When she heard how good I said them she helped me — she taught me all the words and what the words meant too. The old women were so surprised. They thought I was wonderful. They couldn't say the prayers themselves; they could only say the responses.

Women in other courts heard about me and they started asking Mamma Lena to let me come and say the prayers for them. Mamma Lena was proud. She would dress me up clean and let me go. And me, I was not afraid or ashamed or anything. I would go into a court and kneel down in the middle of a circle of women and pray God or the Madonna just like I was talking to them — just like an actress. Then I would watch and if I saw tears in the old women's eyes I was happy for then I knew I had said the prayers good.

There was one old man, Old Benito, who had a long white beard and a little wooden shrine, who used to come to the different courts and say the prayers for the women knitting and spinning. The women used to tell him to say three Paternosters for this one sick, or five Ave Marias for another, and he would. (I remember now the Madonna in that little wooden shrine he would hold up when he prayed. She had a blue robe made out of real cloth.) When Old Benito had finished, the women would buy the prayer beads from him, or the *obetta* — a little square of cloth with the picture of Jesus on — to tie with a string around the children's necks. Old Benito was good; the women liked to hear him say the prayers, but they liked better to hear me say them. I was only four years old and I could say all those Latin prayers like a priest! The other children in the courts would stand around and look at me like I was something wonderful. And when I got through the women would give me a little cookie, maybe, or something sweet.

A lot of men used to come in the courts to sell things. Oh, I remember one man us children didn't like to see come — the hair man. We started shivering and shaking when we saw that man come in. He didn't holler like the other men. He came in quiet, quiet and would whisper to all the women, "Ladies, who's got the hair to sell? Who needs the money to buy a new shawl? Who needs the new wooden soles? Ladies, who's got some hair to sell?" Those women were not allowed to sell their hair. If their husbands found out the husbands would kill them! But some of them did anyway. (Me and Caterina and Toni didn't like that man, but we followed him into all the courts anyway. We wanted to see if any of the women let him take some hair.) When some woman would say she needed a new apron, that man would go there by her and start taking down her hair. He would take out all those long silver pins, like spoons, that the poor women wore in that time. Then he would take out the round pad and unbraid the braids and with his big scissors would cut one chunk out from the middle and put it on his scales. "One *lira*," he would say. "For one little piece more I will give you half that much again! You've got lots of hair. It won't show at all. Your husband will never know."

Once Mariana, the mother of Caterina and Toni, needed wool for a new shawl, so she sold some of her hair to that man. After he was gone the other women fixed her braids up on the pad again and put in all the silver pins, but I guess they didn't know how to do it like the *pettinatora* — that woman in the square who combed all the poor women's hair once a week for one penny — because when Rocco, the father of Caterina and Toni, came home from the fields, we followed him in to watch. "What is it? What is?" he said, looking at his wife. "You sold the hair? Let me see it! You sold the hair?" And there he was pulling out the silver and pulling down the braids. And when he saw, oh that poor woman! He beat her so hard we thought he would kill her. We started screaming and hollering. We screamed so much that that man stopped beating his wife and started chasing us. But he didn't catch us. We ran like lightning up my steps and under the bed. Caterina and Toni were afraid to come out and go home without Mamma Lena going with them. They thought their mother was dead or hurt bad. Mamma Lena went with them, but she didn't scold that husband. She said the man is the boss and he has the right to beat his wife. (But no man of the poor ever was the boss of Mamma Lena!)

Another man who used to come in the court was the frog man. We used to love to have that man come. He sold the frogs so cheap that everyone could buy. You could hear that man singing before he came in the gate. "*Rana! La bella rana!* Ladies, come buy the frogs! Nice pretty frogs! *Rana! La bella rana!*" And Mamma Lena used to come out with a big kettle and buy them to make soup to sell in the *osteria*. She would take the scissors and cut off their heads and they were still alive. Then at night us children would each get a bowl of that good frog soup and sometimes when Mamma Lena didn't see it some of the meat went in too. Mmmmmm! I can never forget that good frog soup! I even wish I had some now!

We were always hungry — me and Caterina and Toni. Sometimes when we thought of those people in front who ate the *minestra* every day we would run there and look through the iron bars of their gate and see if we could see them — people so rich they could have rice soup every day! And then we used to run to some of the other courts where there were pigs. In Italy pigs were not sloppy like American pigs. In Italy the people were feeding their pigs better than their children — they were throwing them boiled potatoes; so we used to run to some court where they were cooking potatoes over a little fire in the court and burn our hands trying to steal one from the kettle. But most always we got caught and chased away before we could get one.

Once I heard an old woman in our court telling about a poor widow who was crying and praying all night that God would send her a crust of bread so her children wouldn't starve. In the morning when she got up, there on her table she found a whole loaf of bread — one of those big round loaves of black bread! So then I told Caterina and Toni and we all started praying, asking God to send us something to eat. But we didn't ask for a crust — we asked for a whole loaf for each of us and a bowl full of soup besides. But God knew we weren't starving and He never sent us anything. (God and the Madonna know everything! God and the Madonna are always watching you!)

The time I liked best in the courts was the time of the worm camps. In the time of the worm camps the people were all cooking in their courts and sleeping in the attics or the stables or on the ground so the worms could have their rooms. All the beds and tables and benches — everything — had to be taken out and the walls and ceilings and floors had to be scrubbed and whitewashed so there was not one spot of dirt or any smell. Everything had to be just so for the silkworms. About three days before the eggs hatched, the silk mills closed so the women could stay home and make ready their rooms. Mamma Lena didn't have a worm camp — she needed her room and her time for the *osteria* — so me and Caterina and Toni used to watch Mariana and Rocco. When their room was all cleaned and ready they brought out the bamboo frames and long wicker trays from the toolroom and washed them and stood them in the sun to dry. Then they took them in and set them up like shelves — one above the other — along two sides of the room.

[*In Rosa's time in North Italy the eggs of the silkworms, which were called the "seed," were kept from one year to another by the silk owners in simple refrigeration in their basements or carried up into the Alps. Thinly spread out on cardboards they were carefully watched and protected from mice, rats, ants, or other pests. Then about May first when the leaf buds appeared on the mulberry trees and there seemed no more danger of frost, they were brought up to a well-aired room where the temperature averaged seventy-five degrees, but they were kept away from all direct sun, for the sun kills them. Eggs that had been well kept began to hatch on the fifth or sixth day, although they were still as small as mustard seeds.*

It has been said that "the races of silkworms almost equal those of the domestic dog." The mulberry silkworm that supplied the ordinary silk in Rosa's time was the larva of a small moth known as sericaria mori.

The women who worked in the silk mills raised the cocoons in their homes, which usually consisted of one large room. They had to

*stay home from their regular work two days to get ready for the worms.
All furnishings of the rooms were moved into the courts or barns and
the rooms were cleaned and whitewashed and sometimes even
fumigated. Then the shelves were washed and brought in, and while
the peasant men chopped the new mulberry leaves they had just
brought from the fields, the women brought home their worms from
the mills. Each woman had about two ounces of seed, enough to make
about two hundred pounds of cocoons.*

*As soon as she had her cardboard of seed home the woman would
put over them small pieces of gauze or net, which she then sprinkled
with finely chopped mulberry leaves. The worms immediately climbed
up through the holes to eat and were transferred with the nets onto
the paper- or cloth-covered trays on the waiting shelves.*

*Cleanliness was essential. The worm camps were often inspected
by the silk mill bosses to be sure the air was fresh and the shelves and
trays clean. The new worms had insatiable appetites and were fed the
chopped-up leaves five or six times during the day and two or three
times at night. But in preparation for each molt they rested and fasted
from two to three days.*

*The time from the hatching of the worm to the spinning of the
cocoon varied from thirty to forty days, during which time the larva,
or worm, usually molted, or shed its skin, four times. Within eight or
ten days of heavy feeding after the final molt, the worms lost their
appetites, shrank in size, became restless, and started throwing out silk.
Now the arches for the spinning of the cocoons had to be prepared.
These were made of twigs two or three feet long, set up over the
worms and made to interlock in the form of an arch above them. These
twigs, interlaced with dry brush, were set about a foot apart.*

*The temperature of the room now had to be kept above eighty
degrees, for the silk did not flow freely in a cool temperature. The
worms immediately mounted into the branches and began to spin their
cocoons. As they began to spin they had to be watched and kept far
enough apart so that two or three did not go together and make double
or triple cocoons. The silk is elaborated in a fluid condition in two
long, slender, convoluted vessels, one upon each side of the alimentary
canal. As these vessels approach the head they become more slender*

and finally unite in a spinneret from which silk issues in a glutinous state and apparently in a single thread. The glutinous liquid which combines the two, and which hardens immediately on exposure to air, may be softened in warm water. The worm usually takes from three to five days in the construction of the cocoon and then passes, in three days more, by a final molt, into the chrysalis state. The cocoon has an outer lining of loose silk known as "floss," which is used in carding. The inner cocoon is tough and compact, composed of one firm, continuous thread. Cocoons vary greatly, but are usually oval and yellowish.

The women who raised the cocoons carried them back to the silk mills before the chrysalises could make holes to come out. In the mills the cocoons were put in ovens or steamed to kill the chrysalises, then spread on shelves for about two months to dry. After this they would keep indefinitely, if protected from mice and rats.]

"It's a bad sign," Mariana would complain to Mamma Lena. "It's bad luck that they hatch the worms before the Day of the Santa Croce."

"It's these new times!" Mamma Lena would say. "Ovens for hatching the seed! The bosses watch the mulberry trees and hatch the worms when the leaves are ready with no thought of God and the Madonna!"

"It's true," Mariana would say. "It was better in the old days when the women hatched the seeds themselves — between their mattresses at night and under their breasts in the day. That way the seeds went to church and got blessed."

When the women brought the worms from the mills they looked like little black specks on the gray papers, but they were already alive. When Mariana brought hers from the mill, me and Caterina and Toni ran to the square to meet her and walked along beside her and opened the gate. She took off her wooden soles before she went into the room and she wouldn't let us children go in at all, but we watched from the doorway. She scattered the worms over the beds of fine cut-up leaves on the shelves. Then *Signore*, the agent, came in and inspected the room. "The air is stale," he said to Rocco, who was in the court cutting up more of the mulberry leaves from his field. "Open the window and make a little fire in the fireplace." Then he came and twisted my braid a little. "We have to take good care of those worms, isn't that so, Rosa? We want them to eat fast and grow strong."

So Rocco took the blanket from the iron-barred window and made a little fire. Then he picked up his empty sacks and started back to his field in the country for more leaves, because in the beginning the worms had to be fed every two hours with leaves cut up as fine as hairs. "Leaves for our *cavalleri*," Rocco said as he went. "More leaves for our little horses."

The summer I was five years old Beppo told me and Caterina and Toni that if we could find some of the weak worms that got thrown out with the trash when the women cleaned the shelves he would help us and we could have a worm camp in the court. He made us a little wood frame and said he would bring us some leaves from the country when he came from his work at night. We were so excited we could hardly wait for Mariana and the women in the other courts to start changing the worm beds. Sure enough, we found some of the weak worms still clinging to the old leaves. Gently we picked them up and carried them to the corner of our court and waited for Beppo. And after the first few days the worm beds were cleaned twice every day instead of once, and in the rush some of the strong worms hid and were thrown out with the weak. Then we *were* happy, and Beppo was happy too. But when Mariana found our strong worms she stole them away and put them back with hers.

Those worms grew fast and they were so cute. Soon they were firm and white and felt cool on our skin. I would put them against my lips and against my face. Then Caterina would feel them too. But when Toni wanted to feel them I said, "No, Toni. You're too little. You don't know how. The worms would be afraid of you."

That was the year Zia Teresa brought Pina to sleep in my bed with me. Pina was sick with the consumption and the sick were not allowed to stay in the rooms with the worms. So when Zia Teresa was getting ready for her worm camp Mamma Lena said she would take Pina and let her sleep with me. (Eight children Zia Teresa had and all of them died of the consumption. Her husband had it first but he was the last one to die. So much trouble my Zia Teresa had! But she was always happy — round and rosy and never complaining.) Pina was seventeen years old, but so thin and so sick that she couldn't walk anymore. Zia Teresa had to bring her in a wheelbarrow. Me, I was afraid at first to get into that little bed beside her. When Mamma Lena sent me up to bed at night I would stand there in my chemise listening to that poor girl cough and I didn't know what to do. "Don't be afraid, Rosa," Pina would say. And after a little I would lie down on the very edge of the bed, afraid to move.

While the worms were eating, Zia Teresa had no time to come and see Pina, because the worms have to be fed in the night and in the day. But when the worms had a *dormo*, one of those sleeps when they change their skins, she had a little time and she came. Once, on the hottest day in summer, when Zia Teresa came, Pina was crying and telling her mother to please take the featherbed cover off. Zia Teresa wanted to, but Mamma Lena said no. "It's the fever that makes her hot," Mamma Lena said. "It would be dangerous to change. The sick must be protected from the air." Then Mamma Lena complained that Pina hardly touched her polenta anymore — that she would take nothing but water. And I would run downstairs and bring up another dipperful from the bucket. (People were not particular in that time — everyone drank from the same dipper.)

On the twenty-seventh day in the evening the worms stopped eating for their fourth and last *dormo*. They would not have to be fed and must not be disturbed for a night and a day. So now the silk workers had a little time. Us children did too because our worms were sleeping just like the ones inside. So when the mother of Angelina from the next court came and asked Mamma Lena if I could go with Angelina to the country to gather wood, I was glad and asked if Caterina could go too. I didn't ask for Toni. Toni got tired too soon. In that time the landlords were allowing the poor to pick up the sticks and dead pieces of wood from the ground, and that little wood was precious to start the fires, so Mamma Lena was glad to let me go. Angelina was about sixteen years old and it was not allowed for young women to go to the woods alone — they might meet some man.

Angelina was barefoot like us but she had a nice full calico skirt over her chemise and a pretty flowered neck shawl. After she had filled her little jug at the fountain she walked on ahead of us and was singing as she went. As we passed the cemetery I saw some wild roses growing in the trash outside the white wall and me and Caterina ran and picked them. I knew at once what I wanted to do with them. I would take them to the little Madonna in the shrine near Papa Lur's field. We were all happy and Angelina was swinging her jug to keep time to her singing as we walked along between the poplars on the straight old Roman road to Milan. We had to walk two or three miles on that road before we turned off onto the narrow road to the river. The woods were on the other side of the river Ticino and we had to cross at one certain place where the water was not too deep.

When we came near Papa Lur's field I ran ahead so I could greet him and tell him where we were going. He was working with his spade around the grapevines. "Where did you get the flowers?" he asked. When I told him and told him that I was going to give them to the little Madonna, he nodded — he knew the Madonna I meant, in the shrine by the river. "May the Madonna bless you," he said, and went on with his work.

Just after we turned off onto the road to the river the sun disappeared and the sky grew dark. "It's going to storm," said Angelina. "We've got to hurry. There's no time for you to run to the shrine. Throw your roses away — they're all wilted anyway."

But I wouldn't listen. Even if my roses were wilted I loved them. The smell of them filled me with joy. I wanted to give them to the Madonna. And me and Caterina ran along the irrigation ditch till we came to the little shrine. We didn't stop to say a prayer. We just made the sign of the cross and laid our flowers at the feet of the Madonna and looked up into Her pretty face. "They're for You," I said. And we ran back after Angelina who was already wading into the river with her skirt tucked up in her belt. She went so fast that we couldn't keep up.

It grew darker and darker. It was almost like night. Before me and Caterina had reached the middle of the river a sudden wind bent the willow trees to the ground. Leaves and sticks flew straight up into the air like birds. The water came faster and faster and got deeper and deeper. First it came to our knees, then it came to our waists. In other

[35

storms the water had sometimes come to our necks. We were afraid to go on. Then came lightning and crashes of thunder.

"Hurry!" Angelina called back. "Let us hide under the big tree!"

"I'm afraid of the water!" I shouted. "I'm going back."

"I'm not afraid of the water," Angelina answered. "I can swim. But I'm afraid of the lightning." And Angelina ran on through the water and came up on the other side and stood under the big chestnut tree. The woods were still some distance away.

Me and Caterina started running back to the other side, but before we could get there the whole sky opened up with lightning and there came such a crash of thunder that we covered our heads with our arms and stood there trembling, afraid to move. You could hear that terrible thunder rumbling off in all directions. But gradually it died away in the distance and we took our arms from our heads and looked behind us. It was the big chestnut tree that the lightning had struck. That big tree was split in two down the middle. At first we didn't see Angelina. But then we saw her — we saw a naked body, all black and without any clothes. Then the rain came. The rain beat down in torrents, but we couldn't move. We couldn't go forward and we couldn't go back. We just stood there screaming and hollering and screaming and hollering.

Pretty soon a peasant going by with his oxcart on the road heard and came to see what it was. Then he started screaming too. Soon the storm passed on and the sky grew lighter and other people on the road and in the fields heard us screaming and they came and screamed too. They didn't know who that body was and they started asking questions of me and Caterina, but we were shivering so that they couldn't understand us at first. At last they did and they sent two young men running off to the village to tell the police and the parents of Angelina.

Then Papa Lur came. He saw the body and heard what had happened from the peasants and saw me and Caterina standing shivering in the river and he put down his spade and his jug and waded out to get us. As he took us by our hands and led us back to shore some of his warmth and calm entered into us and stopped our shivering and trembling.

[36

"How come," he asked, "that Angelina was under the tree and not you and Caterina?"

"She told us to come with her," I said, "but we were afraid of the water and ran back."

"It was a miracle," he said. "It was a miracle that you didn't go with Angelina when she told you! The Madonna put it in your mind to run back. It was the Madonna who saved you!"

Papa Lur looked back at the peasants. The peasants were all looking for the clothes of Angelina. He knew there was no use looking for the clothes — that the lightning had taken them away — but he said nothing, and he let them keep hunting. He picked up his spade and jug and started home with us. When we came to the irrigation ditch he set his spade and his jug down again and led us back to the little shrine. The wilted flowers, beaten down by the rain, were still there at the Madonna's feet. Papa Lur knelt and made me and Caterina kneel too. Then he made the sign of the cross. "*Grazie a Dio!*" he said. "*Grazie, Maria!*"

Papa Lur paid no attention to the other trees along the road that had been struck by the lightning. But when we came into the square at the side of the church and saw poor women coming from all directions wailing and weeping and running into the church to pray, he stopped to learn what had happened.

"It's the worms," the women wailed. "Our worms were just waking up when the lightning came. Half of our worms are dead and the others won't eat! Come to the church and pray. O Blessed Virgin, Mother of God, pray God that the worms not killed by the storm will start eating! Pray for the soul of Angelina, but pray first for our worms!"

That night when Mamma Lena sent me to bed I didn't go at once. I climbed the iron-rail stairs but stopped at the top and stood there in the corner against the wall. I was afraid. I was afraid of God and afraid of the Devil and afraid of death. I didn't want to go in by Pina. Pina was going to die too. I didn't want to be in the bed with Pina when she died. Suddenly I heard Mamma Lena in the court. I had to disappear somewhere, so I pushed open the door to the sleeping room and crawled under the big bed. For a long time I was just laying there trembling, thinking of Angelina. It was God and the Devil fighting that made the sky crack open like that. God was striking the Devil with the lightning when it hit Angelina. How would it feel to be dead like Angelina and the worms? The storm that had killed lots of the strong worms in the houses had killed all our poor weak worms in the court. God and the Devil were everywhere. There was no place you could go to hide from them. They stopped for no door. They were waiting for Pina now. Pina was coughing and crying and calling for someone to come and turn her because she couldn't turn herself. I wanted to do something for Pina but I was afraid to come out and go downstairs to get Mamma Lena.

After a while Pina's sobbing stopped — she must have gone to sleep. I began to breathe again and I stretched out the cramp from my legs. And as I lay there I began thinking of the Madonna. The little Madonna in the field had made a miracle to save me and Caterina from the lightning. The Madonna was the Mother of God. She talked to God. The Madonna prayed to God for all poor women and children. Me, I was a daughter of the Madonna — born on the Madonna's day. The Madonna would take care of me always, just as She had today. The pretty little Madonna was standing out there in the field now, alone in the dark. As I thought of the Madonna, love filled my heart. "O *Madonnina bella*, make the silkworms eat! Take care of the soul of Angelina, and make the worms eat!"

5

THE worms not killed by the storm did start eating again and made their cocoons, and when the cocoons were gathered the women went back to their work in the mills. But Pina was too sick to be moved, so she stayed in my bed until she died. Then Mamma Lena burned the cornstalks from the mattress and put the feather bed outdoors at night to get the air, and she made down Pina's skirts into dresses for me. But it was a long time before I could forget those two poor girls nailed up in wooden boxes and covered with dirt in the cemetery — Angelina and Pina.

That scare of the lightning never passed — I'm afraid yet. The electric storms in the old country — in Lombardy — were terrible. Here in America they are too, but not so bad. Mamma Lena told me that once during a storm, a young woman, just married, was pitching hay to her husband on his cart so the hay wouldn't get wet in the storm (every little grass was so precious in that time), and the lightning ran down her pitchfork and struck all the new silver pins in her hair and took off her head like it was cut. The people were looking and looking but nobody could find one piece of silver or one little hair from her head. The lightning had taken them completely.

Another story they used to tell— but I don't know if it's true or not

— was that one time there was a terrible storm and a whole row of priests — not priests, brothers I guess you call them — were all kneeling down saying their prayers in the church, and one of those big strings of lightning ran along the floor and pulled all the little nails from the soles of their shoes. Those monks got the scare and jumped up to run away and they all found themselves barefoot! That's just a story to laugh. I don't know if it's true or not. The men in the barns on cold winter nights used to tell a lot of laughing stories about the priests and the monks, but I don't tell those stories to the people in America very much — the people in America don't understand. They think we are not reverent to our priests if we tell those funny stories. Those poor men in the barns were reverent, but they liked to make the other men laugh, that's all. They didn't mean anything bad.

In my time in the villages of Italy the poor people had a little wood and coal for their cooking but they would never think of burning wood and coal to keep warm. When their day's work was done they would go in some barn to keep warm. Fifteen or twenty cows and horses and an ox and sometimes a few sheep made it nice and warm in those little white-plastered brick stables on the courts of Bugiarno, even in the coldest winter. Mamma Lena always went in the stable of Zia Teresa. That stable didn't belong to Zia Teresa — it belonged to the landlord in Milan — but everyone used to call it hers. (The Italian cows are not like the American cows — they don't have to have the fresh air all the time. They just stay in the stables.) And me, I used to love to go in those stables and listen to the stories of the men.

The women and children used to stay on the cement floor in the front part of the barn near the little oil lamp to do the knitting and spinning. The men all went back in the straw with the animals. They would laugh and joke and play *morra*. They had a little table made out of planks and they would bang their fists down with some of their fingers held out and yell the numbers. Who guessed the right number got the next droppings from the horse or the sheep or the cow to put on his field. When they made too much noise Mamma Lena would yell for them to keep still, so then they would tell stories instead. Those poor men had never been to school to learn to read and write but they were smart the way they told the stories. They made everyone bust out laughing. Me, I was listening and listening — I could never get enough of those stories. I was brokenhearted when Mamma Lena sent me home to bed. But Papa Lur was good. He would go with me and tell me stories himself to make me happy again. Papa Lur was better to me than Mamma Lena. He knew a lot of good stories too — animal stories, just made for children. The one I liked best was a story of the fox and the hens.

The poor people in the villages of Italy laughed and sang and told stories and the men played those games with the balls or with the round cheese or with the fingers, but they were all the time scared. In America the high people teach the poor people not to be afraid, but in Italy — in my time anyway, and I think now too — the poor people didn't dare look in the faces of the high people. And to ask the landlord a question about something they wanted to know — such *impertinenza* was never heard of in Bugiarno. All the poor people knew they got from each other in the courts or in the stables or at the fountain when they went to the square for water. And they were always afraid.

One time I remember everybody in the village was talking about two white horses and a carriage without a driver that came every night, one o'clock morning, on the road to the cemetery. The people were so scared they wouldn't even go down that little road in the daytime. But one night — they couldn't stand it anymore — about a hundred men and the priest came and told Papa Lur to go with them and they went there to see what it was. They took stones and sticks and the priest took his holy water and they went. And sure enough, about one o'clock, there came the white horses. The men threw their bricks and their stones and their clubs and ran and hid behind the trees. The priest too. He threw his holy water and hid. When the carriage came there it stopped. And there the son of the baker got out, Paulo. "What's all the commotion?" he said. "What's the big idea?" And when they told him, he said, "Sure I come home late every night, every night. Don't you know that me and that Margherita in the next village are engaged? We're going to be married, and I go every night to see her and it's a long way and I come home late."

Papa Lur was not *so* afraid like the other poor people. He was not so afraid because when he was a young man he was working on the ships going to America and he had learned a little more that way. He knew how to count and he could read a little and things like that, so he was not so stupid. One night when he was coming home from his field, it was already dark, and I was with him. When we were passing the cemetery he saw something moving in there, but he didn't say anything to me to scare me. He just told me to wait and he went to see what it was. It was a poor woman dressed all in black, and she kept raising up her arms and raising up her arms. When Papa Lur asked her why she was there and what she was doing, she said her husband was there under the ground. He had been dead two days, and she would never go away — she would never leave him. Papa Lur wouldn't let her stay there. He said it was not safe. If people came and saw her there, no telling what they would do, they would be so scared. So he made that poor woman come out and he took her home.

Mamma Lena could read, but she was more afraid than Papa Lur. There was one man in Milan, a butcher, who used to save the scraps of salt pork for Mamma Lena and sell them to her cheap to make soup for the *osteria*. So she used to go there to get them. And always when she went to Milan she would go and visit that other Rosa. She stayed a very good friend with the mother of the first Rosa and she used to go there all the time to see her. Mamma Lena could never forget the love she had in her heart for the first Rosa. So one day she took me and we went. It was summertime, and in summertime she didn't take the bus, she used to walk about six miles through the woods and take a boat on the river — it was cheaper that way. So we went there. (I remember yet the street and number of that other Rosa and of her mother, Zia Maria — Porta Romana, number 33. In Milan they had numbers on their houses and names on their streets.) When we were coming back through the woods it was getting dark already, and Mamma Lena started walking very fast. She had one big package and I was carrying a little one — I was just a little girl — and she kept saying, "Faster, Rosa! Go faster!" But I couldn't keep up.

I kept saying, "Why, Mamma Lena? Why?"

And finally she told me. She said that behind us was a man without any face! He was entirely black! He had no face at all! I looked and I saw him too. We went faster and faster, but however fast we went that man came just as fast. He was always right there behind us. By the time we came out of the woods even Mamma Lena had no more breath. Even if that man would catch us, she could no longer go so fast. So we stopped and looked back. And now here where it was not so dark we could see that man had a face like any other. And there it was Don Domenic, our priest! (But in a way I think he did wrong. He was a priest, but he was a man anyway and when he saw a woman and little girl in the woods like that he should have lost himself, instead of coming just as fast. But probably he was afraid too. All the poor people were afraid.)

One other time I had a terrible scare. There was a young woman not long married — Paola, her name was — who had to go to the country to cut grass, and she asked Mamma Lena to let me go with her because she was afraid to go alone. So we were there in the field and she was cutting grass, when all at once she dropped her scythe and started grabbing her belt. "Rosa!" she said. "Rosa! The scythe! Quick, give me the scythe!" I didn't know why she talked that way and why she didn't pick it up herself, but I gave it to her anyway. She grabbed it from my hand and started cutting her belt and cutting her shirt. (In Italy the poor women didn't wear all the clothes underneath like now in America. They wore only a shirt and a big skirt.) When I saw her face — how terrible it looked — and how she was sticking that knife into her stomach I thought she was killing herself and I started to scream. But when I looked again and saw her staring at the ground, I stared too. And there on the ground were two big pieces of a snake! That big snake had gone up her skirt and around her waist. Probably it thought it could squeeze her dead like that, and she had the nerve to take the knife and cut it in two! It must have been God who gave her the nerve to do such a thing! But she looked terrible afterwards. Terrible. She just wrapped her skirt around her and went home. She didn't live long afterwards. In two or three years she died. It's a wonder I didn't get the heart trouble and die too from all those scares I had when I was a little girl. I didn't get it, but I guess my blood caught and I passed it on to my Visella, because she got the heart trouble and died young. Probably she got it from me — from all those scares I had when I was a little girl.

[43

6

IN MY time, in Italy, there used to be more miracles than now in America. That's because the American people have not the faith and the strong religion. Oh, I remember so many miracles! And I know they are true because I saw them myself.

The greatest miracle that ever happened in Bugiarno happened when I was a little girl. There was a young man, Giovanni — "Gionin" we call it in Bugiarno — who didn't grow tall like other men. He was a man but he was no taller than me and he was a stupid. But he was good. He had a great devotion to the Madonna del Monte. (That's the Madonna without arms, and the Baby is without arms in the statue too.) Every year Gionin went to the *festa* of the Madonna del Monte in the village of Varese. One year he had a terrible sore foot, but he went walking on it barefoot to go to that *festa* — he had such a love for that Madonna.

Gionin had lived with his older brother but the brother died and Gionin stayed on in the house with his cruel sister-in-law. And because Gionin was a stupid, that sister-in-law made him mind her instead of her minding him. He was the man — he should have been the boss, but every day she sent him out with twenty-eight cows across the river Ticino where the grass was nice. So one night he was there minding the cows and there came a terrible storm. The water got so deep he couldn't get back across the river, and it got dark. The cows got scared and they all ran away — he lost every cow. Midnight came and Gionin was still in that place — he couldn't cross the river. He didn't know what to do, so he started to pray. As he prayed he saw a beautiful woman in a blue robe right in front of him. She took his hand and led him. He went in the water up to his stomach, but she stayed on top — he could see her feet. She was high up and holding his hand.

When they got across she said, "See, Gionin, here are your cows. Call them."

So Gionin started calling, "A-Morina! A-Carina! A-Mora! A-Negra! A-Bianca!"

And after all the cows were there she said, "Look at me, Gionin. I'm the Madonna del Monte." And he looked and saw a great splendor, and she disappeared.

Gionin was screaming and hollering when he came in Bugiarno. It was one o'clock night, but all the people woke up and crowded into the square to see what it was. Me too. I ran with Mamma Lena. We all gathered around him and listened. Then everybody was screaming. There in the square with Gionin were the twenty-eight cows to prove what he was telling. And he was telling it over and over. He stayed in the square until five o'clock morning. It was true. Oh boy, that was true! That man wouldn't holler like that if it wasn't! After that the people called him "Gionin del Madonna." And people were coming from all the towns around to hear him tell his story and to bring him gifts. So then his sister-in-law realized she had something wonderful in her house and she got good — she let him do what he liked.

Then there was a young woman in Bugiarno, not long married. Rosie, her name was. She was not one of the poor — she was rich. But everybody knew about her from her screaming. She got a terrible pain in her knee and she was screaming and hollering so much that no one knew what to do. Me, I was even holding onto the skirts of Mamma Lena when I heard Rosie screaming. The doctors looked but they could see nothing. They said they would take her the next morning to the hospital and make the operation on her knee to see what was wrong.

When the doctors went away Rosie said to her mother, "Mamma, take my silk shawl and all my jewelry and go right away to Milan, to the church of Maria Bambina. Give those presents to the priest in there and tell him to pray to Maria Bambina to make my knee well." In that church the Madonna is a baby. It's a wonderful church. People go there from all over the world and leave their crutches and walk away well. That Baby Maria is all covered with precious jewels from the people who got well. So the mother hurried and took the bus and she went to the church and gave the jewelry to the priest. The priest took a little piece of cotton and put it by the little statue's face. Then he gave it to the mother and told her to go home and put the cotton on Rosie's knee. So she did. It was night when she came home, but she put the cotton on Rosie's knee, and when the men with the stretcher came in the morning to take Rosie to the hospital, she was up washing herself and singing — entirely well. Some bad people in Milan make fun of the church. They say, "Yes, the people go by the church where the dolly is and they get well." But they do! I saw it myself!

Now I have to tell about Mamma Lena's arm, but I don't know if this was a miracle or if it was the great doctor. One day Papa Lur was up on those two-by-fours in the toolroom where he kept his tools and frames, and a frame fell down on Mamma Lena's shoulder and put that shoulder out of place. Mamma Lena was screaming and crying and screaming and crying. And she couldn't move that arm. Me, I was scared. I never saw Mamma Lena like that and I didn't know what to do. Papa Lur got the village doctor — the one who did everything for the poor for nothing, but that doctor didn't know what was the matter, and Mamma Lena wouldn't let him touch her shoulder to see. Then Papa Lur got the other doctor in the village — the one you had to pay — but he couldn't do anything either. And Mamma Lena kept crying and crying with the pain and doing all her work with one arm. Papa Lur had to put her dress on for her in the morning and take it off at night. She couldn't move that arm. Me, I couldn't even play, with Mamma Lena like that. She wasn't telling anyone what to do — she was just crying with that arm. But pretty soon the pain was not so bad and she started scolding again. One day one of the guards went off to another town without paying his bill and Mamma Lena took me and went after him. When that guard saw Mamma Lena coming, he quick took out the money and gave it to her. Mamma Lena was still the boss! She couldn't use her arm, but she was just like she used to be. So after that I ran home and started to play again.

Then one day the village doctor came and told Mamma Lena about a great professor — a wonderful doctor — who came to the hospital in Milan about once in five years. That doctor was a monk and did everything for the poor people without making them pay. He was going to be in Milan the next day and our doctor thought maybe he could help Mamma Lena's arm, but he said she would have to stand in line there a whole day. Mamma Lena said yes, she would go. She would stand in line a week, or a year, if anyone could cure her arm. So she took me on the *tramvai* right away that same afternoon. She thought that way she would be the first one in the line the next morning. But when we came to the court of the hospital early in the evening, there was a whole bunch of people ahead of us. Some of those people were on stretchers, and some were on crutches, and some were laying on the ground. For a long time I just stood in the line holding Mamma Lena's skirt and listening to all the groaning. The smells from the hospital and from the sick people made my stomach feel sick. But after a while I got so tired I laid down at Mamma Lena's feet and went to sleep.

It was noon the next day before it was Mamma Lena's turn to see the great doctor. He didn't look like a doctor at all, dressed up in his monk's robes. I was shivering and watching to see what he would do. Mamma Lena told him what had happened and before she could stop him, he put his hand on her shoulder and lifted her sore arm way up and gave it a twist and put it down again. Mamma Lena started screaming, but the monk paid no attention. He moved the arm around again and let it drop. "There's nothing more we can do for you," he said. "You can go. It was out of joint." But Mamma Lena didn't go — she just stayed there screaming and trying to make that doctor do something for her arm, even after he went on to the next patient. One of those sisters who wear the little bonnets had to put Mamma Lena out.

We passed back through the line of people in the court and Mamma Lena was screaming like insane. She wasn't ashamed before the people or anything. Me, I didn't know what to do, so I started to cry

[47

too. We came out into the street with all the people turning to look. Pretty soon we came to a church. It was the church of San Bernardino Dei Morti. And Mamma Lena ran into that church. That church is all decorated with the bones of dead people — the arm bones, the leg bones, and the heads with holes for eyes. But Mamma Lena didn't look at the decorations. She ran right up to the Madonna by the altar. "Madonna," she screamed, "if You don't make me well I won't ever go away! I won't ever leave! You've got to make me well." And so she was kneeling there screaming and praying. For a long time I was kneeling beside her and crying too, but then I couldn't cry anymore and I went back and laid down on the floor.

At six o'clock the janitor told Mamma Lena to go so he could lock up. Mamma Lena said no. She said the Madonna had to cure her arm or she wouldn't ever leave. So the man had to lift her and push her to make her go out.

By the time we came back into the square by the cathedral where we got the *tramvai* for home, I noticed that she wasn't crying so much anymore, but she didn't say anything. She didn't speak until we were out of the city and back on that old Roman road between the poplars. Then suddenly she said, "Rosa! I don't know for sure, but I think I can move it!" Still she didn't try to see if she could. She held her arm down like before. When we came back into the *osteria* and Papa Lur came to help her take off her shawl, like always, she said no — she could do it herself. And she did! She lifted up her bad arm the same as the other! When she found she could move her arm she started screaming again, but this time it was for joy. "It's a miracle!" she screamed. "The Madonna Addolorata in the Church of the Dead has made a miracle to cure my arm!" And she was showing the men at the tables how she could move it. Then she ran into the court to show the people there, and she went out the gate and down the narrow lane to the square to show the women at the fountain. I was running after her and listening. When the people heard her they all came out to see what it was. And she was telling it again and again and showing how she could lift her arm. "It's that Madonna with Jesus a man in her lap, in the church of San Bernardino Dei Morti!"

Some of the women told her that the Madonna had blessed her like that because she had taken care of me and taught me all the Latin prayers. And some said that maybe the pain would come back in bad weather. But the others said no, if the Madonna made a miracle to cure that arm She wouldn't let the pain come back. And some asked again and again where that church was so they could go there too. Mamma Lena herself thought the Madonna had blessed her for taking me and giving me the strong religion and she prayed to the Madonna not to let the hospital take me away and she promised to make me humble and meek.

At that time I believed Mamma Lena that it was the Madonna who cured her arm, but now I don't know. I think probably it was that great professor. That monk was a wonderful doctor — when he found that the shoulder of Mamma Lena was out of place, he just put it back again. Some of those doctors — those great professors — in Italy are wonderful! They don't have in America such wonderful professors. That monk at the hospital in Milan was the most wonderful doctor in the world. I am sure it was him that cured Mamma Lena's shoulder!

7

THERE was another young man a little older than Beppo that I
used to love to follow around too. That was Carlo, the mailman. Carlo
was not tall and not short — just right — and he used to wear a nice cap
from the city hall. But he was so dark we used to call him *Negro*. "All
right," Carlo would say when the people called him that. "Call me
what you want. I'm good-natured — I take everything and keep still."
I liked him because he was always making people laugh and because
he was always talking in such a lively way. He talked with his hands,
with his head, with his shoulders, with his face, with his eyes. Oh, that
man was good! So I used to follow him around to the different courts
and when I came home I would talk just like him. And that man was
always playing jokes. He made everybody die laughing. I remember
one time there was a young woman — she lived in the court next to the
silk mill of Signor Rossi — and she was nursing a baby for a rich man
in Milan. The family of that young woman was so dirty! They had
cobwebs all over their walls, and their floors were never swept, and
the sheets never washed. They were terrible. The other poor people
didn't like it, so they decided to play a joke. They told Carlo to write
a letter to say that on Saturday afternoon the rich father from Milan
was coming to see his son. So Carlo did, and he stamped that letter like

any other and he took it there and read it to those dirty people. And those people were so excited. They took everything out of their room and were scrubbing and cleaning like for a worm camp! They even cleaned their stable and washed the horse and the cow! One whole week they were cleaning. So then Saturday came and they were waiting and watching, but no rich man came from Milan. The same thing on Sunday too. Those poor people were even crying they were so disappointed and they told everyone in Bugiarno how hard they had worked and the rich man didn't come. All the other people were laughing and laughing to themselves, but they never let that family know it was a joke. They said, "Well, anyway, you got nice and clean in your house."

One day that summer when I was six years old I was playing in the court with Caterina and I saw Carlo coming in our gate. "It's *Negro*!" I called, and me and Caterina ran to meet him.

"Rosa," he said. "Go tell Mamma Lena that I brought a letter for her from Milan. I think it's from the hospital."

But I didn't have to tell Mamma Lena because she had heard me, and she and Mariana, the mother of Caterina, were coming out already. Mamma Lena took the letter, but she didn't know what to think. It was not the time in the month for the hospital to send the money for keeping me. "It's one of your jokes, *Negro*!" she said to Carlo.

"No, I swear!" said Carlo, and he made the sign of the cross.

And I knew he meant it too. Even Carlo wouldn't have the nerve to play a joke on Mamma Lena! So Mamma Lena broke the seal and opened the letter, but that letter was in writing and she couldn't read it. She handed it back to Carlo and waited for him to tell her what was in it.

"It's from the Mother Superior," said Carlo. "She says the real mother of Inez — of the little girl you are keeping — has come back to the hospital with her half piece of cloth to match and you must bring the little girl back there tomorrow."

For a long minute Mamma Lena just stood there staring at Carlo and at the letter in his hand. Then she started to cry. "No!" she said. "I won't let that real mother take her! That real mother can't have my

Rosa! I'm not going to take Rosa back to the hospital!" And Mamma Lena cried louder than ever.

So then me and Caterina and Mariana, the mother of Caterina, we all started to cry too. Even Carlo was almost crying himself. And I was holding onto the skirts of Mamma Lena and telling her that I wouldn't stay with that real mother — that I would run away and come back.

The next morning, Sunday, I was waiting in the square with Mamma Lena to take the *tramvai* to Milan. Papa Lur was there too and Beppo and Caterina and Toni and Mariana and Zia Teresa and Zio Tomaso, the husband of Zia Teresa. And everybody was crying. I looked up and saw the brown crooked fingers of Papa Lur wiping the tears from the wrinkles in his cheeks and I started to cry too and I was telling Mamma Lena not to take me — not to make me go.

This time when we came to that big hospital in Milan, where the great doctor fixed Mamma Lena's shoulder, there were no people in the court and the sister who answered the bell led us down a long hallway to take us to the Mother Superior. My wooden soles made an awful noise as we went down that hall past all those rooms where you could hear the groans of sick people and the crying of new babies. The crying of the babies made my heart start bumping, because I didn't know what was going to happen to me either. We all belonged to the hospital and had to go where the hospital said. And the smells of the medicine in that hospital made my stomach twist.

Mother Superior sat behind a big desk in a little office and took the letter from the sister that brought us in. Then she turned to a beautiful young woman who was sitting on a bench at the side. "Diodata," she said. (I won't tell the real name of my real mother because she was only fourteen years old when I was born, so she can be living yet. And everybody in Italy would know her name.) "Diodata," Mother Superior said. "This little girl is your daughter. This is the baby you left on the *torno*." Me, I was looking and looking at that beautiful young woman. Oh, she was pretty! And she was all dressed up like the city, with a little plume hat and the full, long skirt covered with ruffles and a little parasol covered with ruffles too. She was a wicked woman, though — she didn't have a neck shawl! You could see her naked neck way down low! In that time it was a sin not to wear a neckerchief, even in the hottest weather in summer. But now no more — they took that style away.

As I was staring at that beautiful young woman she jumped up from the bench and started waving her hands and waving her parasol. "Impossible!" she cried. "It's impossible! A child that large! And this is the child of a peasant! She's got the brown skin of a peasant! *Gesu Giuseppe Maria*! I don't want some other! I want my own!" And she was even scolding the Mother Superior.

So then Mamma Lena stepped up to the desk and looked straight into the eyes of Mother Superior. "Please, *Superiora*," she said. "Let me keep her. Let me take the little girl back to Bugiarno. The real mother doesn't want her. I will keep her myself — and without pay from the hospital. I will adopt her and bring her up for my own."

Mother Superior just turned to the big book of records on her desk and looked at a card and a half square of cloth. "February 2, 1867," she read (or maybe it was "1866"). "That makes her six, going on seven years old."

So then Diodata opened her little bag and took out a half square of cloth and laid it beside the one in the book. And those rags were just matching. I was watching and watching and hoping they didn't match. But they did — they were exactly fitting to make one square, and both black-and-white checks on one side and white on the other.

Then Diodata looked at me again and she began to laugh. "Well she looks like a peasant, for sure!" she said. "I'm afraid to hear her talk. Does she talk like the country too?"

Diodata was talking like a *Milanesa* and I couldn't understand every word, but I knew she was laughing at me and I could feel my face getting red. I hated her! I hated her, just as I knew I was going to! But as I looked at her and smelled the flowers in her perfume I felt a little bit happy anyway. If I had to have another mother I was glad she was so pretty.

"Let me take the little girl back to Bugiarno, *signora*," said Mamma Lena. "Let me keep her for you."

Diodata threw her parasol and her little bag to the bench and came over and knelt down beside me and took the headkerchief off of my head. And there I had the same curly chestnut hair and the same brown eyes — big, rogue's eyes just like hers. "She's mine!" she exclaimed. "Mine! She looks so much like me I can see it myself! No, no one can take her from me again!" And she threw her arms around me and squeezed me so hard that she almost knocked me over. I had to push with all my strength to get away. Then she tied that headkerchief back on my head and laughed again, "I never thought I would have a peasant for a daughter!"

When Mamma Lena saw that she could do nothing — that my real mother wanted me after all — she asked Diodata if she could go with her just to see where I am going to live. And Diodata didn't care — she said why not, there was plenty of room in the carriage. So then we were all going out together and riding through the streets of Milan and I was holding on to Mamma Lena. But Mamma Lena's mouth grew tighter and tighter. As we passed the big cathedral in the square the driver up in front lifted his hat to say hello to God, and me and Mamma Lena made the sign of the cross. Diodata had to change her parasol from one hand to the other before she could cross herself, so it looked like she was greeting God with a wave of her parasol. "I don't stay in Milan all the time," she said to Mamma Lena. "I'm an actress — I act and sing on the stage — and I have to go all over the world making plays. But now in summer we have the vacation so I have time to come and get my daughter." And this time Diodata did wave her parasol. She was waving to some young men in another carriage who had taken off their high hats and were waving to her. "The little peasant is my daughter," she called out, pointing to me and showing all her pretty white teeth.

"Well, if you're an actress," said Mamma Lena, when the other carriage had passed, "why do you want the little girl? She will only make you trouble. Let me take her back to Bugiarno and keep her for you."

"If you want," said Diodata, "I will let you keep her two weeks more. I didn't know when I sent for her that I have to go to Paris the day after tomorrow and I have nothing arranged. And when I come back I will come and get her from Bugiarno myself. I'm going to take her to Rome, to live with my mother in Rome."

When I heard that I could go back to Bugiarno and see Papa Lur again and Zia Teresa and Beppo and Caterina and Toni and everyone, I was happy! And Mamma Lena was happy too. I could tell. She said, "Yes, I will be glad." But she was thinking that maybe that actress wouldn't come back — maybe she would leave me in Bugiarno. A lot of rich people in Milan leave their children in the village.

Diodata lived in one of those tall buildings that have nice balconies and awnings on the windows. She lived on the top floor and had to let herself in with a key. In Milan the people all had locks on their doors because they have thieves in the city — I knew, Papa Lur had told me. She had just two rooms up there — one big, big room — bigger than the *osteria* — with one side all windows and the ceiling all made of windows too. Then she had a bedroom with a big bed in, and a cubby room, like a big closet, to store things in under a little stairway to the attic. The bedroom was not high like the big room and it had that attic above. So when we came into that big room with all the windows I was looking at everything. There was one of those big pianos on three legs, like at the other Rosa's, and beautiful furniture, and rugs with red roses. Me, I was always stepping around those rugs on the floors in Milan. It didn't seem right to step on them. Then there was a white marble fireplace, but there wasn't anyplace to hang kettles, and instead of pans up above there were two gold-covered angels and some vases with flowers. "Where do you cook your polenta?" I asked Diodata. I was always hungry— always interested in the food and I wanted to know if I was going to get something to eat if I came to live in this place.

That was the first time Diodata had heard me speak and she threw back her head and laughed. "Where do I cook my *polentur*?" she said, and I knew she was making fun of me because I didn't talk like a *Milanesa*. In Bugiarno we always said *ur* on the end of a name instead of *a*. The people in Bugiarno didn't call me "Rosa," they called me "Rosur." But then she stopped laughing and talked nice. She said she didn't have any place to cook — that a woman downstairs did the cooking, or else she went out and ate in a restaurant.

Mamma Lena had gone to the end of the room. That part of the room looked like Papa Lur's toolroom. There were all kinds of wood frames standing around — easels I guess they were — and the frames for paintings. And the paintings were there too. Mamma Lena was standing there like she was frozen — like she had turned into a statue — and her mouth shut so tight you couldn't see it. "What's the matter?" said Diodata, when we came there too. "Don't you like it? The small one in front is my little boy, Carlo. He's out with his father now or you could see him too. Nicolo, my little boy's father, is a great artist. He's always painting pictures of me and of my Carlo. My Carlo is three years old."

But Mamma Lena wasn't looking at the little boy. She was looking at the big painting of a woman without any clothes — a woman all naked except for a red sash she was holding in front of her. And the woman was Diodata herself.

"They should be coming home any time now," said Diodata. "If you want to wait you can inspect them too."

"And is this artist the father of your little girl too?" asked Mamma Lena when at last she could speak.

"No," said Diodata.

"Well, is he — is he your husband?"

When Mamma Lena said that, Diodata began to laugh again. This time she was laughing at Mamma Lena and I didn't like that either! What she said I couldn't understand. But I don't think he was. I don't think so. And Mamma Lena didn't think so either. She told me after.

Mamma Lena didn't say anything to Diodata after that. She just turned and took me by the hand and told me to come. So we went out and started down the stairs and Diodata followed. "Wait," Diodata said. "The carriage is waiting. I'll take you to the square to get the *tramvai*."

"It's too early to get the *tramvai* back to Bugiarno," Mamma Lena said. But she said it to me — not to Diodata. "We'll go and see the other Rosa." And when we came down to the street she started to walk. But I guess she didn't know the way and it was a long way, because in the end she listened to Diodata and got into the carriage. So me and Diodata got in too. And when Diodata wanted to know where to, so she could tell the driver, Mamma Lena wouldn't answer. I had to answer for her. I said, "She wants to see the other Rosa. We're going to Zia Maria's — to Porta Romana, number 33."

When we came there and started to get out, Diodata said, "I'm letting you go now, Inez. But in two weeks I will be back from Paris. Then I'm coming to Bugiarno to get you." And she almost knocked me over, throwing her arms around me and kissing me. "Kiss your mother good-bye!"

"You are not my mother!" I said, and I pushed her away and climbed out after Mamma Lena.

"All right," she said, and she was laughing — she liked seeing me mad like that. "But in two weeks I'm coming to get you."

When we came into Zia Maria's Mamma Lena dropped down on that sofa Zia Maria had and started crying and telling Zia Maria that she wouldn't let Diodata take me — that Diodata was a *diavola* and she wouldn't let her take me — that I was a daughter of the Madonna and she wouldn't let an actress get me and give me to the Devil — and she not even married. And Zia Maria was just standing there and looking at me and at Mamma Lena and trying to understand what had happened.

"Diodata?" said Zia Maria at last. "Diodata, the actress, is the mother of Rosa? *Mamma Mia!* Everyone in Italy knows Diodata — and in other countries too! A daughter of Diodata!" And Zia Maria looked at me like she had never seen me before. "No wonder she can act and sing like she does!" And Zia Maria was so excited that she almost forgot to give us some coffee with cream and sugar and those nice white rolls she always gave us when we went there. The other Rosa — she was about ten or eleven years old in that time — she came in and listened too. Zia Maria knew all about Diodata because her husband, Zio Cesco, was playing in the orchestra in the theater. Zio Cesco had told her that Diodata was the most wonderful actress — only twenty or twenty-one years old, but she was better than any other. He said she could make you die laughing but when she got angry even the directors were afraid. She was a wonderful actress but she was a *diavola* too. And Zia Maria gave me more rolls and more coffee with sugar and cream. She gave me all the rolls and all the coffee I could eat.

And so Mamma Lena took me home to wait until that Diodata came back from Paris to get me. And she was telling all the old women in the court how bad that real mother was — an actress on the stage and standing all naked in a picture and the artist was the father of the little boy but was not the father of me and she didn't even think that artist was the husband. And all the time Mamma Lena was crying and praying the Madonna not to let that devil of a Diodata come and get me and give me to the Devil too. And the more I listened to Mamma Lena and the women the more scared I got. The Devil was always waiting to catch you. If I went with that Diodata he would get me for sure. I began praying to the little Madonna over the chicken coop in the *osteria* that She wouldn't let my real mother come back, that She wouldn't let Diodata take me and give me to the Devil. So when two weeks went by and Diodata didn't come, I thought the little Madonna had heard my prayers. Mamma Lena thought so too. And we began to feel happy again because we thought she was not coming.

Sunday morning in the third week came and Beppo was there in the court with his concertina and I was singing and dancing. Caterina and Toni were there too, and the guards who had just finished breakfast were standing around us shouting and clapping. "*Bravo! Bravo*, Rosa! Sing it again! Sing it again!" they were saying when I had finished, and they were all laughing. "Sing it again!"

And right then, when they were all laughing and shouting, here came running in between them that Diodata. She was laughing and shouting too, and waving her parasol and a little satchel she was carrying. "*Bravo*, Inez! *Bravo! Bravo!*" And the way she grabbed me and kissed me, with her satchel behind my knees, I sat down on the ground. "Sing it again!" she said. "Sing it again!" And she let go of her parasol and the satchel, letting them fall where they wanted, so she could take my hands and help me up. "You are better than I was when I was your age! You will be on the stage in no time at all!"

No one had seen her come in the gate — they had all been watching me — and so she had been standing there listening too. I pulled away and went over to Caterina and took hold of her hand. "It's my real mother," I said. "She's come to take me away!"

Papa Lur had just been coming out with my bowl of polenta. When he saw Diodata he stopped right where he was and looked. Then he turned and went back into the *osteria* to tell Mamma Lena.

Probably if my real mother had been old and ugly me and Caterina and Toni would have run away when she came to take me. But Diodata was so young and pretty in her big floppy hat with roses on it, and her flowered dress with lace ruffles, that we just stood there and looked. "That kind of comical peasant song is just the kind I can do best too," she said to Beppo, who sat there looking at the ground. "What are the words? I can't understand all the dialect." But Beppo was afraid to look up or answer. So I had to tell her myself. The guards just stood there looking down too — the ones not sitting on the benches. The ones on the benches picked up sticks and started to whittle.

"It's the song of a poor peasant and how that poor man is so afraid of the landlord. The poor man is so afraid of the rich that he even has to bow down to the cow and the sheep and the horse in his stable because those animals belong to the landlord. But in the end the poor man's ox butts the rich man's horse right out of the barn." And I was so interested in telling her the words of the song that I forgot she might laugh at the way I talked. But she didn't. She just listened, careful like, and then asked me to sing it again. "Play it, Beppo!" I said. "Please play it!" because I liked it so much and was happy that she liked it too. But just then Mamma Lena came out.

Mamma Lena came straight over to Diodata, but instead of greeting her she just told her that she invited her to stay one week in Bugiarno and that she would show her the church and the cemetery and that Diodata could talk to the priest and to the other women and see how nice I had it.

"If you think I am going to leave such a child in the village, you are mistaken!" said Diodata. "This child is better than I was when I was her age! I am going to have my old *maestro* in Rome teach her and she will be on the stage herself in no time at all."

When Mamma Lena heard that — that Diodata planned to put me on the stage — she just stood there staring, her mouth open. Then all to once she turned and started running to the gate. "No!" she cried. "No! I won't let you! I'm going to tell Don Domenic! Don Domenic won't let you!"

When Mamma Lena was gone Diodata picked up her parasol and closed it, and then she picked up the satchel. Then Papa Lur came out and invited her into the *osteria*. She sat down at one of the tables and he served her a big bowl of the Sunday *minestra* and wine. Caterina and Toni and me had followed her in and stood by the door. Two men playing *morra* at the first table stopped yelling the numbers and looked in surprise to see such a beautiful young woman from the city. Papa Lur refilled Diodata's glass. "We will feel sorry to lose the little girl," he said sadly. "We love her like our own."

So then Diodata explained to Papa Lur how she had come to get me because it was time I started school. She had planned to send me to a convent school to let the sisters teach me, but now that she had discovered that I was born to be an actress she would send me to a great teacher in Rome. I was going to live with her mother in Rome and a great *maestro* and some others would teach me and I would be on the stage like her in no time at all. She was so excited and so happy that I could sing and dance like I did that she couldn't get over it. She was still talking about how wonderful I was going to be, when Don Domenic, our priest, came in followed by Mamma Lena. She didn't see him until he spoke to her.

Don Domenic was thin and short, but he had a big nose and a deep voice and when he spoke he made everyone listen. Me and Caterina had to go closer to listen because at first his voice was too low to hear. He was calling Diodata his child and asking her if it was true that she planned to put me on the stage and while I was still a little girl.

"Yes, Father! Yes!" she said. That Diodata wasn't afraid of anyone — not even the priest!

Then Don Domenic's voice got louder and he started to scold her. He said it would be a sin for her to take me away from the good people who had been taking care of me in Bugiarno. He said here I had been brought up to fear God and love the Madonna, and God would punish her if she took me away and gave me to the Devil. He told her to leave me in Bugiarno with Mamma Lena and Papa Lur. But Diodata said no — that her mind was made up. Then she asked Mamma Lena if she could have some clean clothes for me, because she would have to wait until she came to Rome to get some others made. But Mamma Lena just stood there beside Don Domenic and didn't answer.

"Better you get them for her, Lena," Papa Lur said.

So then Mamma Lena went off upstairs and came down with a little bundle. Diodata said thank you and put my clothes in her little satchel. Then she came over and tried to take me by the hand. "No!" I said. "No!" and I ran and grabbed Mamma Lena by the skirt. "Don't let her take me!" I cried, and I was trembling and shaking. "Don't let her take me!" But Mamma Lena did nothing. So then I looked to Don Domenic, and then to Papa Lur. But they did nothing either. And Diodata came and took my hand and she pulled me away from Mamma Lena and out through the door. "No!" I cried. "Don't make me go! Don't make me go!" But somehow I knew that I had to. This young woman was my real mother and she had the right to take me. She was taking me away from everyone and everything I knew and loved and there was no one who could help me. Such a hurt filled my chest that I couldn't stand it! I burst out screaming and crying as she dragged me across the court and out the gate.

On the road in front of the old *palazzo* a carriage with three horses was waiting. We were just going across to get in, when there from behind came a scream, "Wait! Wait!" It was Mamma Lena, but she didn't try to stop us. She just had something to give me. She put something in my arms. "Here, Rosa," she said. "Take it! Take it!" And I was wiping the tears from my eyes and trying to see. At first I couldn't believe it! It was the little Madonna from over the chicken coop. Mamma Lena knew how much I loved that little statue and she was giving it to me! "Take it, Rosa," she said. "Take it! And when you get in trouble you pray the little Madonna. The Madonna is going to help you."

8

AND SO Diodata took me to Milan and we came back to the top
floor of that building where she was living. When we entered that big
room with the windows there was a bunch of young men, and a few
young women too, standing around the piano and having a good time.
But they all stopped their singing when they saw Diodata and I could
tell by the way they crowded around her with shouts and kisses
that they liked her best of all. And they all listened when she told them
about me and how I was better than she was — the way I could sing
and dance and imitate the people — and only six years old. Then here
came the artist — Nicolo his name was — with the little boy, Carlo.
Diodata took the little boy up in her arms and kissed him. Then she told
me to kiss him too. She said he was my little brother. And he came
over and stood there waiting. But me, I wouldn't kiss that little boy I
had never seen before! And I knew right away that I didn't like him. I
didn't like him at all! Diodata started scolding to make me, but Nicolo,
the father of the little boy, said to give me time — that I needed time
to get acquainted. But acquainted or not acquainted, I would *never* kiss
that little boy! Nicolo, the artist, he was a pretty young man with the
nice clothes of an artist and a little beard coming down in a point from
his chin, but he was a *sordomuto*. He was not *muto* — he could talk —

but he was *sordo* — he couldn't hear. He had to watch the people's lips to know what they said. Once later I asked him what was the matter with him and he told me. He was not cross — he was kind to me — but he made me understand that he was not my father.

A woman called Anna came up and washed me and gave me a nice white roll and a mug of sweet chocolate. Anna was the wife of the janitor or something; she was round and rosy like Zia Teresa and she wore a pretty white apron. So then Diodata took me over by the piano and tried to make me sing the song of the peasants — that song she had heard me sing in Bugiarno. She said she wanted to learn it herself. But me, how could I sing and act before all those strange people from the city and without Beppo to play the concertina and help me! I couldn't, that's all! A lump filled my throat and I held my little Madonna tighter and tried to pray. Diodata took the Madonna away and laid it on the table behind her. She wanted me to forget the statue and think about the song. But I wouldn't look away from my Madonna. I could see Carlo, who had been playing with paper and pencils, on a little platform. He had left the platform and was coming toward my statue. I got there just in time to grab it away and hold it up so he couldn't reach it. Carlo started crying and Diodata came and scolded and told me to let him hold it. But I wouldn't! I wouldn't let that little boy hold my Madonna! Never! The young men and women at the piano all laughed and said I was the daughter of Diodata for sure — the same temper and the same eyes. And Diodata took her little boy off to give him a sweet and stop his crying.

When it came time for me and Carlo to go to bed, Diodata put him in the big bed in the bedroom — he was going to sleep with her and the artist. But me she put on some blankets on the floor of that little cubby room under the stairs. She said she had nothing prepared, but it was just for a night or two until she could take me to Rome. Then she wanted to take off the dress for me, but I wouldn't let her. I was no baby. I could get myself ready for bed. So she left me alone and started to get herself dressed to go out with those other actors. And I was thinking of Mamma Lena and Papa Lur and my own bed in the room over the *osteria* and I wouldn't lie down. And pretty soon the tears were running down my face and I couldn't stop them. I stood there praying to my little Madonna and crying. Then Carlo started calling for water and Diodata came in with an empty bottle and told me to run down to the pump at the foot of the stairs and fill it. She said that would give me something to do. She took my Madonna and laid it down on the blankets, then put the bottle in my arms and I had to go.

It was night already, but I was not afraid. Those gas lights they had in Milan made it not so dark like in Bugiarno. I would not be afraid to go anywhere in the night in Milan. There were thieves in the city. Maybe the thieves would come and steal me away. But I wouldn't care if they did! I wished they would! I looked all around, but I didn't see any thieves. So then I stood up at the fountain that was under a little piece of roof and held the bottle to catch the water. The water was coming out of the mouth of a dog, but it was not a whole dog, just his head. When the bottle was full I put my hand over the dog's mouth and the water came out all around and hit my face. I wiped it away with my skirt and went back up the stairs. And there when I came back up into the bedroom I saw Carlo coming out from the cubby room with my Madonna in his arms! Diodata didn't see him — she was by her dressing table combing her hair. I dropped the water bottle and ran to grab it away, but he held on. He didn't cry — he knew he shouldn't have it — but he held on with both hands. I had to bend his fingers to make him let go. Then I grabbed hold of his thick black hair and pulled with all my might. I held up my Madonna with one hand so he couldn't reach it and with the other I pulled his hair. So then he started screaming and Diodata had to come to make me let go. She kissed him and put him back in the bed and then put me in the cubby room, and this time she locked the door. When I heard her locking the door I couldn't believe it. I began to shake it and pound and cried for her to unlock it. But she said no — she had to leave it locked so me and Carlo couldn't fight when she was gone.

The next morning Diodata told me she was going to take me out to see somebody and she wanted me to look nice. So she was combing my hair and she let it hang loose in a natural curl with a little piece of velvet ribbon around my head. But me, I was pulling the ribbon off and telling her to make it the way Mamma Lena always did. I didn't want it in the style of the city! And I was even crying. So in the end she

[64

had to comb it like always with two tight braids sticking out in front. Then I felt better and went into the big room to wait for her to get dressed.

Nicolo, the artist, was in there painting. And there standing on that little platform was a live woman without any clothes. Never in my life had I seen such a thing — a naked woman! What would Mamma Lena say? Maybe it was a sin just to look, but I kept looking anyway. I wanted to see all there was to see. When the woman saw me looking like that her face got red. Then mine got red too. Carlo was sitting on the edge of the platform playing with his blocks and paying no attention to the woman. Pretty soon Nicolo told the woman to rest and she sat down on the chair and pulled a kimono around her. So I sat down beside Carlo and watched him. His pile of blocks got so high that he had to stand up to reach them. If I gave the bottom block a little shove the whole pile would fall over and Carlo would cry. I knew Carlo was littler than me and I shouldn't tease him, but my hand reached out anyway and touched the bottom block. The crash was better than I had expected. And Carlo was so surprised that for a minute he just stood there staring. Then he started screaming and hitting out at my head with both fists. I put my arms up over my face and let him hit. He was too little to hurt very much and it made me happy to know how mad I had made him.

Diodata came running in and pulled Carlo away. Then she gave me a magazine full of pictures and made me go and sit down on the floor behind the easel where Nicolo was painting. I had never had a magazine to look at before and this was a fashion one — full of rich young women dressed in pretty dresses. And there were some rich children in there too, playing with hoops. The young women all looked like Diodata and the little boys looked like Carlo. I wanted to punch their faces and make them cry.

The house where Diodata took me was the house of a rich man. There were all those nice striped awnings and iron balconies and a nice garden for a court. And in the middle of the court there was a fountain. The fountain was a little girl no bigger than me made out of stone and pouring the water from her pitcher. I ran over and looked at her and tried to catch the water in my mouth. The water splashed in my face and I wiped it off on my dress. "Come, Inez!" called Diodata. She had gone on to the door of the house and was standing there with a rich-looking man who was much older than she was. The man had been watching me and he was laughing. When I came up he put his hands on my shoulders and looked into my face. "What beautiful, beautiful eyes!" he kept saying. "But beautiful!" And he leaned down and kissed the top of my head.

But me, instead of looking at the man, I was looking at the big marble stairway and the pretty iron-curl railing and at the big lamp hanging down from the ceiling that was sparkling like diamonds. So then we went up the stairs and into a big room, and I was staying behind a little so I could look at everything. The furniture was made of gold, like for a palace. And there were so many flowers in the big rug that I had to walk around the edge, to not step on them. Diodata and the man had gone over and were sitting down by one of those door windows with a balcony. "Come, Inez!" called Diodata.

"My name isn't Inez!" I said. She had been calling me that name ever since she took me from Bugiarno, and I didn't like it!

So then the man was asking her about it and she was telling him that I didn't know my right name because the mother and father I had in Bugiarno had always called me Rosa.

"Inez," she said to me when I had come up and was standing there between them. "This man, he's your father." And she spoke very slowly to make me understand the talk of Milan.

People had always told me that I had another mother, so I could understand a little about my real mother. But nobody had ever told me about another father, so I was not prepared.

"This man is not my father!" I said. "Papa Lur in Bugiarno is my father!"

Diodata tried to explain. She said that this man, who was my real father, and she, who was my real mother, had left me on the *torno* the night I was born so the hospital would give me to some nice people until I was old enough to go to school. And now that I was old enough to go to school they had come back to the hospital and had taken me. And from now on they were my mother and my father.

[66

"If this man is my father," I said, "why don't we live here with him, then, instead of with the *sordomuto?*" But Diodata didn't answer.

Then suddenly the man reached out and took me on his knee and started hugging me and kissing, and hugging and kissing. Me, I was not used to hugging and kissing and I didn't like it. I pushed him away, wiped my face with my hands, and climbed to my feet. And I stood far enough away so he couldn't reach me. But he got up and caught hold of my hand and sat there holding it, so I couldn't run away. "Your mother, Diodata, is a great actress, Inez," he said. "And she tells me you are too. She wants to take you to Rome to your grandmother and in Rome a great *maestro* will teach you so you can go on the stage while you are still young and entertain the people. You would like that, wouldn't you?"

"No!" I said. "No! Don't let her take me to Rome! Don't let her give me to the Devil! I don't want to go on to the stage to sin against God and the Madonna! I want to go back to Bugiarno!" And as I thought of Mamma Lena and Papa Lur and Beppo and Caterina and Zia Teresa, tears filled my eyes and rolled down my cheeks. Maybe I would never see all those people I loved again. And suddenly I was crying with all my heart.

My father tried to put his arm around me and he looked to Diodata. "We want her to be happy more than anything else," he said. "Our taking her has only made her unhappy. Maybe we should let her stay there in the village with the people she loves."

"Leave a child like that in the village!" said Diodata. "Never! She's unhappy right now but she'll get over it. She'll be happy in Rome when she gets used to it. I wish you could see the way she can sing and act and imitate the people! But she's stubborn and won't do it here. It takes a little time, that's all."

And so they kept talking, while I stood there crying. In the end the man they called my father gave a whole roll of money to Diodata, but he didn't give anything to me. And when we were down the stairs at the door to the garden he said good-bye to Diodata and kissed her hand. Then he put his hand on my head. "*Addio* – Rosa," he said. When I heard him calling me that I looked up and smiled.

[67

"*Addio, signore,*" I said, and I ran out after Diodata, letting my wooden soles clap like horses' hoofs on the stones of the pavement.

The next day, or the day after, I was on the train with Diodata and Carlo, and that train was going to take me to Rome. I had my statue Madonna in my arms and I was sitting in one corner of the seat crying and praying. Diodata and that little boy sat on the other end of the seat and they were looking out of the window. (Diodata didn't want us to fight, I guess.) Other people came in and sat on the seat facing. Then just when the conductor was calling, "All aboard, *signori!*" a fat old lady came climbing on and pushed herself between me and that Diodata. She had one of those little bonnets they used to wear and a black shawl with long fringe. At first she was all out of breath and didn't say anything. But after a while she started looking around. And last of all she saw me sitting there in the corner beside her, crying and saying the Latin prayers and she didn't know what to think.

"Little girl," she said. "Why are you crying? Who are you with? Where's your mother?"

"Mamma Lena's my mother," I said. "Mamma Lena is in Bugiarno. But another lady stole me and she's taking me to Rome."

Just then Diodata turned around and said, "She's with me. I'm her mother." But then Diodata looked back out the window with Carlo.

"She's not my mother!" I said. "She stole me! She took me away from Mamma Lena and she's taking me to Rome."

And that old lady didn't know what to think — I could see it. She looked at Diodata all dressed up like the city in a nice black velvet suit and a little black velvet hat and talking like a *Milanesa* and at Carlo with his lace collar and white-buttoned shoes. Then she looked at me in my headkerchief and wooden soles and heard me talking like the village and she looked to the people opposite and shrugged her shoulders. And those people didn't know what to think either. They were shrugging their shoulders too. When I saw how interested the old lady was I thought maybe she would help me. So I began to pray harder than ever, telling my little Madonna not to let the lady who said she was my mother steal me away from Mamma Lena and take me to Rome. "Stop her, *Madonnina bella!*" I prayed. "You stop her!"

The old lady patted my knee but she didn't say anything anymore. Then the train stopped at one station and the old lady got off. So she wasn't going to help me after all! There was no one to help me! I stopped praying and began crying more than before.

At last we came to the city of Piacenza and everybody was getting off. And here came up two *carabinieri* and arrested Diodata. Diodata started scolding and arguing and those policemen didn't know what to think. They said they were sorry, but it couldn't be helped. They would have to make an investigation.

"Little girl," they said. "Is this woman your mother?"

"No!" I said. "She's not! She's not! She stole me from Mamma Lena and she's taking me to Rome!"

"Inez!" cried Diodata. "Will you keep still! In the name of heaven! I'd like to twist your neck! I could tear you in two!"

"My name isn't Inez!" I shouted. "My name is Rosa!"

And I don't know now why those *carabinieri* came and arrested her. At first I thought maybe she hadn't paid for her ticket, but then they kept asking me if she was my mother. But how could the old lady who got off the train at another station tell the *carabinieri* in Piacenza about me! I don't know! I was only a little girl, and I don't know now.

So the police took Diodata to the jail and me they let stay with one old woman overnight. And the next morning we were all on the train again going back to Milan. One *carabiniere* went with Diodata and the little boy and another went with me. And there when we got off the train in Milan was a police wagon waiting. The *carabinieri* helped me and Carlo up, but when they tried to help Diodata she wouldn't let them. She told them to let go her arm and she would get on by herself. And she did. With one hand she held her long full velvet skirt around her, and with the other she took hold of the iron bar and stepped up like a lady getting into her carriage. Oh, but she was mad! She wasn't even speaking to me and I stayed as far away from her as I could get.

And this time we all had to stay in the jail. Diodata and Carlo they put in one part and me they put in a big room full of women. There was a big lock on the door and bars on all the windows so you couldn't get out. Some of the women were lying on the floor and some on benches and some were just sitting at the tables with nothing to do. After a while some of the women told me to come by them so they could see my Madonna. So I let them see the little statue but I didn't let them take it. Instead I stood it up on the end of one table and I knelt down and started saying the Latin prayers. And some of those women were even saying the responses. And some had tears in their eyes too.

But then one young woman said, "Better you have a doll than you play all the time with that little statue!"

And another woman said, "Let us make her a doll!" And everyone said yes, they would make me one.

Those women — oh, I wish you could see them! — they were cutting pieces off their petticoats, tearing the ruffles off their skirts, raveling yarn from the top of their stockings, pulling some stuffing out of their mattresses to get what they needed. And each made one part. One made the hands and sewed in all the little fingers. One made the hair with two braids sticking out in front. One made the head and put on the face. "Come here, Rosa, and let me look at your eyes!" "Come here, Rosa, let me see how your dress is made!" "The hands are bigger than the feet!" "What difference? Rosa doesn't care, do you Rosa?" And so they were all talking and laughing and telling me to come by this one, then this one. Everyone was happy and helping. And I went all around watching. I had never in my life had a doll before and this one was going to be a beautiful doll. They were making it look just like me. When they had finished they put it in my arms and I sat down and played with it. But I didn't give up my little Madonna. I still loved my little Madonna best.

The next morning me and Diodata and Carlo had to go in a court — I guess it was a court — and there waiting was Nicolo, the artist, with his nice little beard. I didn't know what it was all about but the judge was asking me if Diodata was my mother and I kept saying no, that Mamma Lena in Bugiarno was my mother. But in the end he told me that I must go with Diodata and do what she said. He said she was my mother and I must obey her. And so we went and we came back to that big room with windows. Diodata was so angry she wouldn't talk to me. But she told me one thing. She said, "All that acting you did,

Inez, made a lot of trouble, but it did you no good, because in a day, or in two days, you are going to Rome anyway!"

So then that night Diodata had a big party. But me, I was locked in that cubby room again so I couldn't fight with Carlo. Diodata and the artist loved that little boy. They let him sleep in their bed and sent me down to get water when he was thirsty. They didn't love me. Why did they want to keep me then? Why didn't they let me go back to Mamma Lena and Papa Lur? I could hear Diodata in there in the big room singing and laughing and entertaining the people. But with me she was so angry she wouldn't even speak. And I began crying and praying my Madonna.

I must have fallen asleep because I was just dreaming that I was back in the court of the old *palazzo* with Caterina and Toni, when here came in Diodata with a candle. She didn't say anything to me — she just got something off the shelf under the stairs and went out. And when she went out I noticed that she forgot to lock the door. So I was free! I could get out! Why didn't I run away? I couldn't run away now, but when everyone was asleep I could. And I began listening for the people to go. Probably it was the Madonna that put it in my mind to run away. The Madonna didn't want me to stay here and let Diodata give me to the Devil. If I didn't run away now before she took me to Rome I could never run away. And I could never see Mamma Lena and Papa Lur again — and Caterina and Toni and Beppo and Zia Teresa and Don Domenic. "Help me, *Madonnina!*" I prayed. "You've got to help me!" And I crept over to the crack by the door and sat there listening.

At last the people went. Then in a little while I could see that everything was dark and I knew that Diodata and the artist had gone to bed. I pushed the door more open, then felt around in the dark for my doll and put that in my arms with the Madonna. The *sordomuto* couldn't hear me, but I must wait until Diodata was asleep. I pushed the door way open and stood up. Before very long I could tell by her breathing that Diodata was asleep. So then I went slow, slow, across the bedroom and into the big room with the windows. My bare feet on the floor made no noise at all, but when I turned the key in the lock to the door by the stairs it made a noise. I waited a little but nobody came, and I went out and started down the stairs. And I came down the third stairway into that little hall and was ready to run, when here behind me stood the *sordomuto*! He had come down behind me! How in the world that deaf man had heard me I didn't know. But there he was in his nightshirt and I thought he was going to stop me, but he didn't. He just gave me a little rolled-up painting and told me to go. "Run, Inez!" he said. "Run!" And so I did. I went out the door and I started running. I didn't know where I was going but I was running and running, alone on the streets of Milan. (I remember that painting yet. I kept it a long time. It was Saint Lawrence with a pot of boiling oil and all the martyr babies in.) And when I could no longer run, I was walking and crying. I was not afraid of the night but I was afraid of the silence. And all that silence made me run again.

At last the *alba* came — that first false light before the morning. And a few early workmen started coming out on the street, and some men with satchels were coming from the depot. One of those men from the depot saw me and stopped. And he was asking me why I was crying and why I was out on the street alone and if I was lost. I didn't know what to say so I didn't say anything.

"Are you lost?" he said. "Do you know the street and the number where you live?"

And right away I answered, "Porta Romana, number 33." That was the only street and number I knew — the address of the other Rosa.

"My, you're a long ways!" he said. "You are really lost! If I give you the money can you get on the *tramvai* and go there?"

"No, *signore*, I don't know how. You take me. You take me there and my Madonna will bless you." And I showed him my little statue.

"Yes," said the man. "I will. I will take the time and take you there myself." And so he did.

It was still early, early morning when we came to the house of the other Rosa and rang the bell. But at last Zia Maria stuck her head out to see who it was. "*Mamma Mia!*" she said, when she saw me. "Rosa! Where did you come from? Where have you been?" And she came and threw her arms around me and kissed me.

"She was lost," said the man. "She was lost entirely. I found her crying way over there in the other part of the city near the railroad station. But she knew the address where she lived so I brought her here."

"Oh yes, *signore!*" said Zia Maria. "Thank you very much! Thank you very much, *signore!*" And she didn't say anything more because she wanted the man to go away.

So when the man was gone she took me in the house and heard my story. Then she woke up Zio Cesco and the other Rosa came too. And they all listened.

"*Per l'amore di Dio!*" said Zio Cesco. "For the love of God!" That Diodata is a devil! But it's not safe for Rosa here! They will look for her here the first thing!" And suddenly Zio Cesco ran off and came back pulling up his trousers over his nightshirt. "I'm going to take her back to Bugiarno," he said. "We can still catch that first *tramvai* to Bugiarno. Then let that Diodata try to get her! In the name of God, I'd like to see Diodata try to take her again from Mamma Lena!"

Back in the court of the old *palazzo* the first person I saw was Papa Lur. I saw him but he didn't see me. He was in the wine vat by the toolroom, treading the early grapes. I ran over and stood there looking up into his face. And at last he saw me.

"Rosa!" he said. "Rosa!" And the tears started rolling down his cheeks. He wiped them away with his crooked fingers and looked to Zio Cesco. He had never seen Zio Cesco before and so didn't know who he was.

"She has such a sad story!" said Zio Cesco. "Such a story! Wait till you hear!"

"Lena!" called Papa Lur. "Lena!"

Mamma Lena came to the door of the *osteria* with a wet rag in her hand. When I saw Mamma Lena I ran over and stood in front of her, smiling up in her face like I had with Papa Lur. But Mamma Lena didn't say a word — she just busted out crying. For joy — just for joy. Then she went over to hear what Zio Cesco was telling to Papa Lur. Papa Lur had climbed out of the vat and was wiping his feet on a rag. "Tell them, Rosa," said Zio Cesco. "Tell them how you were locked in a closet and put to sleep on the floor! And how the *carabinieri*

[73

arrested Diodata for something and took you all to the jail! And how you ran away in the night — all alone on the streets of Milan!"

"*Santa Maria!*" said Mamma Lena, when she had heard my story. "*Santa Maria!* But it's not safe for her here either! That devil Diodata will come and make trouble and try to take her again. Better we go right to the city hall. We must tell her story to the city hall before that real mother comes and finds her. You come too," she said to Zio Cesco. "You can help tell her story." And as Mamma Lena spoke she pulled off her gunnysack apron and threw it on the ground. "I will go to the mayor himself," she said. "I won't let that Diodata take our Rosa again!"

"Well," said the mayor to Mamma Lena when he had heard our story. "You take the little girl home and we will send to Milan and investigate that real mother."

So then after two or three weeks he sent a man to bring me and Mamma Lena down there again. And he didn't say what they found in Milan. He didn't tell us anything about that Diodata. He just asked Mamma Lena if she wanted to be the real mother by law — if she wanted to adopt me. And Mamma Lena said yes. So he gave her some papers or something to show and he said, "Now you are the mother. If ever that other one comes back you call the police — she can't take her."

So then I was no longer a daughter of the hospital and I was no longer a daughter of Diodata. I belonged to Mamma Lena entirely. Mamma Lena could do what she wanted with me now. So I was six, going on seven, and she sent me to work like all the other little girls of the poor in Bugiarno. She sent me to work in the *filatoio* — the silk factory — of Negrina.

9

THE *filatoio* was not the mill where the silk was made. In the *filatoio* we were winding the silk from one spool to another. Each little girl had about seventeen spools to watch and when the thread to one of those spools broke we had to quick catch the ends and tie a knot. We had to stand there between the big belts that turned the wheels and watch. There was one spool above that was so big it took my two arms to reach around it. Then there were all those little porcelain spools below — the *rocchetti*. When the silk was awful good we even had twenty *rocchetti*. And when all the little spools were full we had to pile them on the table and put in new ones. One woman used to go back and forth behind us to watch and if we didn't tie fast enough she would hit us.

Me, I didn't know why we were all the time winding that thread on the spools, then taking it off again. And I was asking everybody, but nobody knew. So then one day when me and Caterina and some of the other little girls had run back from our lunch early and were waiting in the court, Arturo, the head man who watched the machines, came out and stood near us.

"Caterina," I whispered. "Probably Arturo knows. I'm going to ask *him*."

[75

"Oh, no, Rosa!" she said, and all the little girls started shivering. "You can't talk to Arturo! He's higher than us! He will slap you in the face!"

But I did it anyway. I ran over and looked up in his face and asked him if he knew. "Yes, Rosa," he said — there he even knew my name! — and he told me. He said that when the silk came from the silk mill it was too thin to use for weaving — it would all the time break. So here in the *filatoio* we were doubling it and twisting and stretching. And he didn't even take his hands from the belt to his trousers. He just turned and went into the mill. So then I knew and was happy and was the first one in to my place.

Once when the silk was so poor that it kept breaking everywhere, that woman, Agnese, came along behind and saw all my spools stopped and she slapped me. It wasn't fair! I had tied as fast as I could! "The silk is no good," I said. "The threads are all breaking at once. It's impossible to tie all the knots at once!"

That woman, she grabbed hold of me and such a shaking she gave me! She made me so dizzy I couldn't see what I was doing and when I reached to put back some spools the big belt beside me caught hold of my braid. I didn't even have time to pray. But the Madonna helped me anyway. She made my head go all around with the wheel so it would come out again at the end. (Sure, it was the Madonna! I didn't know myself to do such a thing! The Madonna is the best friend I have!) And all afternoon I was trembling, thinking how I had almost come to my end. Other little girls had got their hands crushed, or their fingers, and I wasn't even hurt. But it was all the fault of that Agnese that I had almost been killed. Mamma Lena would fix that Agnese!

That night when I got home and told Mamma Lena, she just scolded and started to slap me some more. But Papa Lur stopped her. He said, "No, Maddalena! You're too strict! Rosa is one of the best workers — Arturo told me. And she's so young — not yet seven years old."

"So young!" said Mamma Lena. "*Santa Maria*! In my time we were working when we were five! She's got to learn not to talk back to the bosses! She's impudent like that real mother, Diodata!"

[76

Most nights when I came from the mill I would fall asleep before I could finish my polenta and Mamma Lena would have to wake me up to make me wash my feet and go to bed. But this night I couldn't go to sleep even after I was in bed. I was only a little girl and one of the poor, but if Agnese was wrong why shouldn't I tell her! It would have been her fault if the machine had killed me! It was the Madonna who had saved me! And I was just saying my prayers to the Madonna when in came Papa Lur. He came in in the dark and pulled a bench over by my bed and sat down. He didn't say anything. He just started in telling the story of the fox and the hens. That old fox was smart but he wasn't smart enough. I knew — but he didn't know — that in the end he was going to get caught. And so I went to sleep smiling.

We had no whistle — no certain hour to go to work — in my time. So long as we could see we worked. In the summer we started at four or five o'clock in the morning, in the winter not so early. With the daylight we came and with the daylight we went. About nine in the morning our mothers or someone would bring us our breakfast. It was not the style in my time to have breakfast before going to work. Our mothers would leave our little pails at the door with the *portinaia* and she and her husband would bring them to us. And at twelve o'clock we ran home for our dinner — a cooked onion or a potato or whatever there was. Sometimes when Mamma Lena wasn't going to be home she would give me a *centesimo* to buy something. So I used to run to the square and buy some of those spotted pears that the rich people won't eat. One old woman was cooking them in a big boiler. I would buy one for me and one for Mamma Marietta and then I would run there by her court and give it to her. Mamma Marietta was crazy for those pears. And I could never forget the love I had in my heart for that poor old woman.

Me and Caterina worked in the *filatoio* of Negrina watching the spools until I was seven. Then in February when I was seven — Caterina was seven before me — our mothers sent us to work in the *filanda*. We went to work in the *filanda* of Signor Rossi. They could get more money for us there. Forty *centesimi* — about eight cents — a week I earned. Mamma Lena said it was just enough to pay for the salt in the *osteria*.

The *filanda* is the real silk mill. In the *filanda* big girls and women unwind the silk from the cocoons. Those women used to sit four in a square — two facing two — and at each corner of the square was a big wheel to turn the reel. But there were no belts and no machines to turn those wheels. The machines were us little girls. All day we had to stand there by our wheel, turning and turning and watching the thread as it unwound from the cocoons. And we had to do it just right. When the cocoons were good we had to turn fast and when the cocoons were poor we had to be ready to stop as soon as the thread broke. Each woman had a basin of water in her table and underneath a little fire to keep the water hot. That big room of the silkmakers was so full of steam you could hardly see. And in summer we were just sweating bullets. So each woman had a little girl to keep the fire going and to turn the wheel. In the *filatoio* we went to work with the daylight, but in the *filanda* we had to go before the daylight. We had to make the fires and have the water boiling before the women came. And at night we had to stay after it got dark and throw out the *roccia* — that dirty water with the old worms and moths in. Pew, how that water used to stink!

But Papa Lur was good to me — better than the fathers of the other little girls. In the morning he used to watch and call me so I would not be late and get the punishment. And he used to make me a little bundle of twigs to help start my fire. We were supposed to start the fires with the big wood, but that was impossible. The boss he knew it — he knew that some of our fathers would have to give us the kindling. And I was proud and happy that I had that fagot every morning and could help the other little girls when my fire was burning.

Some of those women used to come even before it was daylight. They didn't get more money. They just wanted the honor of making more silk. But the other women didn't like it. The other women used to call those early birds names. Not "scab" like now in America, but something not nice.

My silkmaker was not one of the early birds — she only came when she had to. She was fat and jolly — a bride just married. Berta, her name was. She was strict, though. If I didn't do just right she would take off her wooden sole and biff me. She would come running in the last minute and plunk herself down on her stool, throw a handful of cocoons in the water and pick up her little brushbroom. And when she had brushed the fuzz off the outside of the cocoons she would stick her hands down into the scalding water and catch the heads of the threads. If the silk was poor maybe she would have to get five heads to get the right thickness, and when it was good maybe only three. Then she twisted the threads together, threaded it through the eye on her basin, and fastened it to the reel above. Then it was time for me to start turning. But even when the silk was good I had to watch every minute, because near the end the thread got thin and Berta would have to put in new heads. And so I would stand there turning and turning and turning. When one arm got too tired to go I would help it out with the other. And sometimes as I stood there my arm would keep right on turning by itself. It was aching and aching but I couldn't stop it. I would see one of those stubborn cocoons following the thread right up to the eye on the basin, instead of unwinding in the water. But my arm wouldn't stop. So then the thread broke and Berta would give me such a blow that I couldn't go to sleep like that again for the rest of the day. I had to stay awake and watch what I was doing.

The little boys of Bugiarno used to go to some other village and work in the cloth mills, but they never worked with the silk. The silk was the work of the women and girls. Only when the silk mills closed for the worm camps — only when the new cocoons were being made — we could do something else. One summer I went with other little girls, and boys too, to work in the rice fields. We had to go a long ways on a wagon and sleep in a big barn that was there. In the rice fields we had to stand with our legs in the water and pull up the weeds. For food we got a big bowl of rice three times a day and we slept all together on the floor of that barn. (But we were not like the American boys and girls together. We never thought anything bad. We were too tired at night — we all fell asleep. All but one boy. That boy was never too tired to make fun. He used to go up and down the rows tickling all the feet.) For pay, our mothers got each one a big bag of rice after the harvest. But only once I worked in the rice. The next summer old Maria, the mother of Don Domenic, asked Mamma Lena to let me come and help her with her worm camp. And oh, I was happy!

I just loved to take care of the worms. And I did so good that she asked me to come every year. Those worms grew so fast and were so cute. Their noses were just like the noses of little pigs. I just loved holding them and looking in their faces. "You watch out that you don't handle those worms too much!" Maria would say. But she never scolded. She was always kind. And Don Domenic helped. He used to gather the leaves himself. He had some mulberry trees right there in their court and he would pin his skirts up like a lady and climb the ladder.

When me and Caterina got a little older we used to carry our piece of hard corn bread, or whatever our mothers gave us, and stay in the court of the silk mill at noon so we could listen to the talk. There was one girl, Carlotta, who made everyone laugh before she opened her mouth. I used to follow her around and watch how she mimicked the people. And I was wishing that when I got older I could be just like her. One noon she climbed up on a mountain of packing boxes and was preaching like the missionary when Pietro, that terrible strict boss in the mill of Signor Rossi, came out into the court. The women stopped laughing and covered their mouths. If Carlotta saw Pietro she would fall down and break her neck! But Pietro knew it too — he stood behind a post until she had climbed down, then went on to the gate. Then all the women started telling again how once when Pietro's wife had talked back to him he had broken her arm with a chair. And when the doctor had come for his pay — five lire — Pietro had taken out ten lire and said, "You keep it all, doctor. Then when my wife talks back to me again I will break her other arm and have the doctor already paid."

So then I began to think about the man and the woman — how Rocco, the father of Caterina, had almost killed Mariana the time she sold some of her hair. And of another time when he came home in a storm all wet and she had asked him to get the water from the fountain, because he was wet anyway. He had taken the buckets without a word and gone down to the square. But when he came back he lifted them up and poured all the water on her. "Now you are all wet," he said. "Now you can get the water."

"Why are the men always so mean?" I once asked Zia Teresa.

"The woman is made to be the servant of man," said Zia Teresa. "The man is the man and the woman must obey him, that's all."

"Papa Lur never fights with Mamma Lena."

"No," said Zia Teresa. "Papa Lur is a saint."

After that wet night Mariana started asking the women if they hadn't noticed that Rocco didn't fight with her so much anymore. Then she told them why. She had gone to Don Domenic, crying and asking him what to do. And Don Domenic had given her some magic water. But he had told her it was a secret and she must not tell or it would spoil the magic. And all those women were teasing and teasing to know the secret. All the women wanted some magic water. But right then they had to stop for the worm camps and had no time to go to Don Domenic and ask him. At the end of the camp, though, when the worms had had their last *dormo* and were ready to make their cocoons, all those women started to come there by Don Domenic's house. Me and Maria had just finished making a little forest of oak twigs on our shelves when the women started to come. (You can always tell when the worms are ready to make their cocoons. They raise their heads and start feeling around for a place. So then we have to hurry and stick up the little branches — in rows to look like trees.) There was nothing to do while the worms were making the cocoons — those seven or eight days — so the women had time and they came. And I would follow them down to the arbor to hear what they said. None of them told on Mariana but they were all asking for some magic water and the secret to keep their husbands from fighting with them. "The magic is not in the water," Don Domenic would say. "The magic is in filling your mouth quickly, whenever your husband starts to scold, and letting not one drop fall out until he has finished. The water I gave Mariana was just plain water from the fountain. So you go home and try it. But remember, it's a secret."

"Why do you tell them all the same thing and then say it's a secret?" I asked him one day.

"Don't you know, Rosa?" he said, and he was smiling at me. "No woman can keep a secret. As soon as she knows it's a secret she will tell all the other women. And when the women can no longer talk back the husbands will stop fighting."

"But why shouldn't the woman talk back?" I asked him.

"God gave the man the right to control the woman when He made him stronger, Rosa," said Don Domenic. "It's a sin for the wife not to obey. Only God and the Madonna come first. Only when the husband wants his wife to sin against God and the Madonna she must not obey him. Remember that, Rosa."

"Yes, Don Domenic," I said. "If ever I have a husband who wants me to sin against God and the Madonna I will not obey him even if he kills me!" And I made the sign of the cross.

Most of the worms crawled up on our branches like they were supposed to do and started making the cocoons. But one or two crawled up the walls or into corners and made webs instead. Even when we caught them and put them down they would go right back again. "You see?" said Don Domenic. "Worms are like people. There are always some who won't do the right thing." Some of the others did wrong too — they went two together and made the double cocoons. The silk in the double cocoons is thick and wrinkled and has to be undone in a special room in the *filanda*. And while I was watching the worms spin I discovered one thing. I discovered that whatever color his front legs, that was the color cocoon he made — all different whites and yellows and greens.

Signor Rossi himself came to inspect the cocoons and tell Maria when to pick them. (One year he had a Japanese silk merchant with him and they had their two children — the son of Signor Rossi and the little girl of the Japanese. Those children were older than me but they did nothing but play!) Signor Rossi would shake the cocoons by his ear to tell when they were ready. Then I had to run and tell all the women who were going to help pick to come the next morning. And early, early before they came Maria and I spread sheets in the court and carried out all the little branches with the cocoons. Then I sat down and helped pick with the women. And I was so proud. I was as proud as if I had made the cocoons myself. And I was even sorry when the men from the mill came and weighed the baskets and carried them away.

So then when all the new cocoons had been gathered, me and all the other little girls had to go back to the mills. And for about one week we had to work all night and all day — we couldn't go home at all. The time of the *giornata longa* we called it — the time of the long day. Me, how I hated the *giornata longa*! But it couldn't be helped. If the worms in the cocoons stayed alive too long they would start making the holes to come out and spoil the silk. We had to hurry and kill them. We carried the big trays to the furnaces in the basement and the men who watched the furnaces put them in and roasted them. And once every hour for fifteen minutes, while the cocoons were in the ovens, us little girls could lay down on the floor and sleep. Me, I was such a sleepyhead I never heard the bell to wake up. But I was lucky. Beppo was one of the men to tend the furnaces and he always watched and woke me to save me from that terrible boss Pietro. Beppo was always saving me from punishment in the time of the *giornata longa* — from the kicks of Pietro. And one other time he saved me too.

It was so hot in the room with the furnaces in the middle of summer you couldn't stand it. So us little girls wore nothing but our long chemise. And me, I was getting kind of big and I was ashamed to go to sleep like that on the floor by the men at the furnaces. So one time I saw an empty bag for the cocoons laying there and I crawled in that. The bell rang but Beppo didn't wake me because he couldn't see where I was. So then the men came for their sack and found me in it, still sleeping, and they decided to play a joke. They carried me up and dumped me in the tank of water in the court. I woke up under water with that sack over my head and I didn't know what had happened. But Beppo saved me. He heard the men laughing and found out what it was and jumped in after me. Oh, he was mad at those men! He was scolding and scolding and telling them they would have drowned me. But me, I didn't stop for my choking or anything. I just ran for my trays. Pietro would kill me if he found out I had slept through the bell! And that good Beppo helped me and put my trays in with the others and never told. As I stood there looking at him with his hair down over his face and at his crooked nose and big mouth I thought he was the most beautiful man in the world and decided that when I grew up I would marry him. (Probably the worms in those trays made the butterflies and came out and surprised the boss after the cocoons had been put away. But nobody ever knew why, huh? There *was* one tray

[83

the boss didn't roast — that he saved and let the moths come out so they would make the seed for the next year. But that tray he kept in a special place and watched.)

That summer, after the work in the fields was done, Beppo could find no more work in Bugiarno, so he joined one of those gangs that were going to America. When I heard that Beppo was going to America I was sad to lose him, but I was a little happy because I thought then I would go to America too someday. Those men going over, the company paid their tickets, but then the men had to work one or two years to pay it back and to save enough money to send back for their families or wives or for some girl to marry. So Beppo would send back for me. But then one noon I was in the court of the silk mill and I heard the women talking. They said Beppo was going to get married before he went. He had some money saved up from playing for the dances and he was going to marry a young woman from Zia Teresa's court. Lisetta her name was. He didn't know Lisetta. He had sent someone else to ask the mother for him. How could Beppo — *my* Beppo — desert me like that! When the bell rang I went back in the mill and started turning the wheel. But I didn't know what I was doing. No! Beppo couldn't marry Lisetta! He didn't even know Lisetta! He had to wait until I grew up and marry me! Berta's wooden sole struck my head. I had turned too fast and broke the thread. I had to watch what I was doing. But all afternoon I had a sick feeling in my stomach and as soon as I was through emptying the stinking water at night I ran for home without even waiting for Caterina.

Beppo was not in the court. I found him in the *osteria* eating his polenta. I crowded in between him and one of the guards. "Beppo!" I said, and I was even crying. "You've got to wait and marry me! I love you more than Lisetta loves you! You don't even know Lisetta! You've got to wait and marry me!"

The guards at the table all started laughing, but I didn't pay any attention to them. I was just watching Beppo and looking in his face.

"But Rosa," he said. "I can't marry you. You're only a little girl. The men going to America need a woman to do their washing and cooking."

"But I will grow up sometime!" I said. "And I love you so much! I will love you always, Beppo!"

Look how bold I was! Telling that young man he had to wait and marry me! But, heck, I did love him! I loved him with my whole heart!

On the day of the wedding the people all came back to the *osteria* from the church and were eating little cakes and drinking and laughing and joking and having a good time. And I couldn't stand it — I started to cry. The women sitting along the wall were laughing at me. "She's stubborn and wants her own way," said Mamma Lena. "And she's jealous of Lisetta. And look how bold — telling Beppo he must wait and marry her! Already you can see she's a *diavola* like her real mother!"

"Oh, *per l'amore di Dio!*" said Zia Teresa. "Let her alone! She's only a little girl! What does she know about marriage? She and Beppo have been together singing and playing and dancing all her life. She loves him like another father, that's all!"

But I was brokenhearted entirely. I ran upstairs and got under the bed and cried all the rest of the day.

10

GIRLS were not allowed to speak to boys. The boy and the girl, they were like the rich and the poor together, like the man and the woman, like the North Italian and the South Italian — the boy was so much higher than the girl. You didn't dare do anything to a boy. But me, I was a devil. If some boy smiled at me I would smile back. I was nine years old, so I was going Sunday afternoons to Don Domenic to learn the catechism for first communion. And in that class only one boy did better than me. But that boy was older and had gone to school like the rich when he was young. He could read and write and everything. Remo his name was. But then his father died and Remo had had to go to work like the poor children and his mother had put up a little stand in the square and was selling fruit. Remo was so much higher than us that even the other boys didn't speak to him unless he spoke first. But I used to catch Remo looking at me and when I looked he would smile. It made me happy that he liked me and I would smile back.

One Sunday in winter some of us girls had come to the church early — Don Domenic had not opened the door yet — so we were throwing snowballs. And there at the side I saw Remo watching me, and I got the nerve and threw one at him. I was really a devil! I don't know how in the world I had the nerve to do such a thing to a boy! If

Mamma Lena had known she would have killed me! But Remo didn't care. He just laughed. "Rosa!" he said. "What I'm going to do to you now!" And he came and threw me down in a snow bank and covered me up entirely. But then he got the remorse and uncovered me and pulled me up again. And we were both laughing.

When I got to be ten, going on eleven, I was no longer flat and skinny. I started to get nice round breasts. I was big for my age and pretty. Those guards and other young men who came to eat in the *osteria* started talking sweet to me and making love when I served them their wine. And Mamma Lena, oh she got mad! I was not allowed to talk back to those young men, but I smiled at them with my eyes. How could I not smile when they were liking me so much! Mamma Lena scolded and scolded. Then she started beating me with a stick or with her wooden sole. And once when one young guard followed me down the steps to the wine cellar and blew out the candle and kissed the top of my head Mamma Lena almost killed me. She didn't see what that boy did but she saw him come up and saw the light out. She dragged me upstairs and pulled off my dress and beat me with a stick. She beat me until the blood came. But then the next day when I was in bed with a fever she got the remorse and was putting linen cloths soaked in oil on my back. And Zia Teresa was scolding her. Zia Teresa said Mamma Lena was too strict. "It is cruel to beat a young girl like that!" Zia Teresa said. "Rosa is innocent and good. What harm if she smiles at the young men? It's not her fault she's so pretty and the young men all like her and make love."

"Not her fault!" said Mamma Lena. "They wouldn't like her the way they do if she didn't smile at them with those rogue's eyes of hers! She's just like her real mother! She's just like that devil of a Diodata! And it's not safe for her here!"

So then — I don't know from where or how — Mamma Lena heard about the convent at Canaletto. It was not a convent, it was an institution for orphan girls. A rich man in Milan had a silk mill on Lago Maggiore near Canaletto and the girls that made the silk for him were the girls of the *istituto*. He didn't pay the girls but he let them live at the *istituto* and he paid for the food and for the sisters to teach them and take care of them. When Mamma Lena heard about the *istituto* she

[87

thought that was just the place for me. She thought there I would be safe from the guards and other young men in the *osteria*, and with the sisters as an example I would learn to behave like them. Then too I would get the stronger religion and I would get a little education — I would learn to read and write. And without waiting for anything she took me right away on the *tramvai* to Milan to see the boss of that silk mill. Signor Adolfo, his name was.

Signor Adolfo said, "Well, your girl is younger than the other girls, and I like better to have the orphans — with no parents to take them away when they know how to make the silk. But your girl is big for her age and she knows already how to work in the silk. If you want to promise to let her stay three years she can go there now — this morning — on the wagon with the baskets of food."

And Mamma Lena said yes.

So there I was on my way to Canaletto — to a place I had never heard of before — and I would have to stay three years. I could not even say good-bye to Papa Lur. But in a way I was glad. I wouldn't be getting any more of those terrible beatings from Mamma Lena. And it would be nice to see the mountains and the lake — to see everything new. But whether I liked it or not, I was going, that was all.

The sisters who received me were those sisters with white boats for hats and blue robes and big white collars. Sisters of San Vincenzo they were and they were French, from France. To themselves they talked in French, but they could speak perfect in Italian too. Sister Teresa received me and took me up to the dormitory to show me where I was going to sleep and give me the red-and-white striped dress of the *istituto*.

The dormitory was one big long room with a passage down the middle and a big crucifix hanging up at the end. And on each side of the passage were low walls to mark off smaller rooms. And in each little room were eight beds, four facing four. Sister Teresa showed me the bed where I was going to sleep and told me that I was number 74. She said, "Some girls wear the little velvet corset over these red-and-white calico dresses for every day. But if you want the corset you have to pay for it yourself." Me, I didn't have money to buy anything, but I didn't care — I was too young to think about the style. So then she started to measure me for the gray sailor dress with the blue braid for Sunday. "Rosa!" she said. "You're not yet eleven years old and you have such big breasts! I don't like it! It's not nice — it's not modest — to have the breasts standing up under the dress like yours!" I had never thought about my breasts before and she made me feel ashamed, but I didn't know what to say. So for once I kept still. But I was glad when she had finished and let me go.

About six o'clock the girls of the *istituto* came marching home from the silk mill. It was still daylight when they came in two by two and took their places on the benches at the long tables. So then Sister Teresa came and gave me a place. She gave me a place next to a kind-looking girl, Annina. And there in the tin pails at our places we each found a little polenta. No wine, no milk — just a little polenta in the bottom of the pail. But I was lucky. Annina was sick and couldn't eat all of hers, so she let me finish hers too. She had the consumption and was coughing like Pina. "When the figs in the court get ripe we will each have a fig by our place at night," she said. I was sorry that kind girl was sick, but I was glad that I could get a little more food. The sisters — there were six of them — sat at a separate table and had their own food. And every night while we were eating, *Superiora* would pick one girl to do some reading from a book. That little book was full of stories about saints, and the girl reading had to know all the words and say them loud enough so everyone could hear and just so. Some of those stories weren't interesting but we had to listen anyway. So then after the girls were through eating they went out to the court and sat down on the edge of the porch and one started telling a story. The girls listened because they were too tired to do anything else, but that girl didn't know how to tell a story and she didn't know any good stories. I knew a lot of good stories that I could tell, from the men in the stables, but I didn't have a chance that first night. *Superiora* came out and made everyone dance so they would learn how. We were supposed to dance every night, but no one wanted to dance after working all day in the mill.

When it was dark everyone had to march up to the dormitory and to bed. And as soon as we were under the quilt Sister Teresa came up and started marching up and down the passage in the middle and

[89

saying the prayers. Up and down. Up and down. "*Pater noster qui es in caelis, sanctificetur nomen tuum. Adveniat regnum tuum. Fiat voluntas tua, sicut in caelo, et in terra. . . .*" She was saying them in Latin and we were saying the responses in Italian. And when she heard no more responses — when she thought all the girls were asleep — she went.

As soon as she was down the stairs Beata, the captain in our room, would sit up and say, "Now let's say one paternoster to San Antoni so he will make us the matrimony. I don't want to be a sister in a convent! I want to get married!" (Saint Anthony, he was a monk. How could he be the protector of matrimony? That was just Beata's idea. But he helped her anyway.) Beata said, "Rosa, if you don't want to get married yourself say a prayer for me. Every night all the girls in my room say a prayer to San Antoni for the matrimony. I want San Antoni to send me a husband."

"Beata's crazy for the boys!" said one of the girls.

"Sure," said Beata. "And why not? I love all the pretty young men!"

"The sisters make Beata work in the *filanda* so she won't see any young men, but Beata is all the time running to the *filatoio* to laugh and talk with the men who work the machines."

"Yes," said Beata, "and I'm all the time getting the punishment — all the time bread and water. But I don't care. When *Superiora* scolds me I say, 'Don't they look like Jesus?' And that makes her happy again. She always tells us we must think of Jesus when we see a pretty young man."

Beata was about fourteen years old and pretty and lively. I loved her right away and was glad she was the captain in our room. I was too young to think about the marriage, but I said an extra prayer every night anyway to please Beata. And then I learned why Beata wasn't afraid of the sisters like the other girls. She had been left at the gate of the *istituto* when she was a baby and the sisters had found her and they had been her mother and her father.

Early in the morning Sister Teresa came up again and hollered, "*Viva Gesu! Viva Gesu!*" And everybody jumped up. Then Sister Teresa blessed us and started saying the prayers and we sang the answers while we were dressing. Then we ran into the washroom and each one had a place to wash with a little string of water coming down from a box above. The first morning I went in there two sisters from downstairs had just finished filling the boxes and were climbing down the ladder. Then they went away without saying a word.

"The dormitory is Sister Teresa's job," said Beata. "The other sisters can't talk to us up here."

After we had washed we marched two by two downstairs to the chapel and said the rosary, then into the dining room and again found a little bit of polenta in the bottom of a pail. When we had eaten and were waiting two by two to march to the mill, here came *Superiora*. You could tell by the way that sister walked that she was the boss! She came up with a sheet and pinned it around the back of Filomina, a poor homely girl who had the bed next to me in the dormitory. She pinned the sheet so it would show the big wet spot and she said, "That will teach you to stop wetting the bed! Every time you wet the bed you're going to wear the sheet to the mill so everyone from Canaletto can see — the men in the mill too." All of the girls looked one to the other. Everybody felt so sorry for Filomina, but nobody spoke.

"March!" said *Superiora*.

It was just getting light as all of us girls in our red-and-white striped dresses marched down the road to the mill, with Sister Teresa and Sister Giuseppina marching behind. On one side were those beautiful hills and mountains covered with trees and flowers, and on the other side the lake. It was like fairyland in the half light of the morning.

At twelve o'clock we all came out from the mill and marched back to the *istituto* and had onion-and-water soup. Then we went back to work until two. I was standing next to that sick girl, Annina, in the *filatoio*, tying the knots and watching the spools — like I had done first in Bugiarno. On other days, the girls said, we would go to school from two until four, but this day was Thursday and there was no school, so we were going to walk up the mountain to a little village in Switzerland to buy food for the sisters. It was cheaper over the border. Sister Maria, the cook, and Sister Paolina, the housekeeper, were waiting for us when we came out. Only Beata was not allowed to go. "Beata is never allowed to go with the sisters when they shop," said the girls. "In

Switzerland or in Canaletto she flirts with the young men and makes them ashamed."

Oh, it was pretty walking up the road in the mountains! Down below you could see the little islands in the lake and the castles standing half in the water and little boats. And all the hills and mountains ahead with snow on their tops and flowers down the side. But we had to hurry. We had to be back in the mill at four o'clock. We couldn't stop to look around.

When we came to the border there was a little house with Swiss soldiers and Italian soldiers standing guard. But they didn't stop us. They just smiled at us. And we all lowered our heads like we were supposed to do, but we were smiling back anyway.

In the village the sisters bought sugar and coffee and beans and butter and that kind of cheese with the big holes, and they had everything put in little packages so each girl could carry one in her blouse. So we were marching back past those guards and they never even thought to stop us. They just smiled like before. But Filomina — that poor girl! — she got in trouble again. She had taken some butter and it was so hot that all the butter had melted and was running down her stomach. She didn't dare stop until we had passed the soldiers or they might catch us and the sisters would kill her. So she waited until we had gone around a bend. Then she stood to one side and when Sister Maria came up she told her. Oh, how the sisters scolded. They took Filomina behind some trees and tried to catch some of the butter in a big leaf. But they didn't get very much. But why did Filomina choose butter on such a hot day? Me, I took some beans.

That night after the girls had eaten and we were sitting on the step in the court, some of the girls started telling stories again. But none of the stories were any good. So then I had my chance. I told the little story of the monk who by mistake one day wore another monk's pants. And when he put his hand in his pocket and found five lire he thought God had made a miracle for him. I was talking like the people in Bugiarno, but I was acting everything out so the girls could understand me anyway. And they almost busted their sides laughing. So then I had to tell another and another. I told them a lot of funny little stories from the men in the stables. And I was happy that I could make the

[92

girls laugh. After that I was always thinking of other stories I could tell. I was the youngest one there but I knew how to entertain the others better than any. "Rosa, you tell us a story! Get Rosa Cortesi to tell us a story!" they were all the time saying.

No man was allowed to come in the *istituto*. The sisters did everything themselves, and each one had her own job. Sister Teresa had the job to take care of the girls in the dormitory and she went in the silk mills too and watched how we did. She was worse than the watchdog woman who walked behind us. She knew how to make silk perfectly herself and if the ones learning to make silk didn't do it right she would hit their sore hands with her crucifix. And she was the doctor. She had great courage, that sister, the way she could take a knife and cut open a boil on a girl. She said in the wartime she had gone out on the field with the soldiers and helped the doctors. Once she had seen a soldier with all his guts shot out and she had stood there and watched the doctor put them back and sew the man up. Sister Maria, the cook, she was fat with a red face and she always had a lot to say. She did a lot of talking to us when we were helping her in the kitchen. Sister Giuseppina was little and thin and she had the job to take care of the chapel and tell the priest when to come for the services and like that. And she was the one who loved Beata so much. She had taken the most care of Beata when she was a baby. Sister Paola, the tall boney one, was the man. She plowed the corn in the garden and nailed the boards to make shelves, and she was the housekeeper too. She made the lists of food and all like that to give to the boss in Milan. But she did her own work and didn't have much to say to the girls. And then there was Sister Vincenza, the most beautiful sister in the world! She was our teacher — our *maestra*. Oh, how I loved that sister! I could never take my eyes from her face.

Sister Vincenza was the newest sister in the *istituto* and she was young. She was not much older than some of the girls, and she always took the girls' part. But she was high-educated. She knew more than any other sister in Canaletto. Her father was a count or a duke or something, and rich. And he had three sons but only one daughter — only her. So that rich father and mother wouldn't let their only daughter go in a convent and become a sister. But she did anyway.

[93

And they were so angry they would never forgive her — they would never speak to her again. (Oh, I hope they forgave her before they died! I hope they did! But when I was in Canaletto they had not.) And there when she first came to the *istituto* the other sisters were so mean to her. She had never had a broom in her hand before and they made her sweep the whole building. And *Superiora* was giving her the oldest robes and hat — all patched and worn. The girls said that once when Sister Vincenza came down with her robe on crooked or something, *Superiora* pulled it off and made her go back and put it on all over again. And *Superiora* used to punish her because when they went to mass in Canaletto on Sunday morning all the people would stand outside just to look at her face — she was so beautiful. But after a little the other sisters and *Superiora* herself — they couldn't help it — had to like Sister Vincenza. And they listened to her too. Her real name was Carolina, but the other sisters thought that name was too pretty so they made her take the name of the order — Vincenza.

One Sunday afternoon when all of us girls were sitting in the court a beautiful carriage with eight horses stopped at the gate. And there were all those servant men dressed up like for a king. We couldn't imagine who it could be. And there it was the brother and sister-in-law of Sister Vincenza come to call. Sister Vincenza went off to the stone bench on the other end of the court to talk to them. That sister-in-law was dressed up in the latest style with gold spangles and lace — everything. We were all looking and looking how she was dressed!

And when they left and Sister Vincenza came back we all crowded around her and we were saying, "Oh, Sister Vincenza! How beautiful she dressed! How beautiful!"

It was a hot, hot day in summer and Sister Vincenza had on that blue wool robe like in winter. The sweat was falling down her face. But she just smiled and picked up her robe and kissed it. "I like better these clothes," she said.

The first night Sister Vincenza came out in the court to dance with us we were all so surprised. All the girls were saying, "Can *you* dance, Sister Vincenza? Can you dance?"

"I just love to dance!" she said. "Do you think I never danced

[94

before I went in the convent?" And she was dancing beautiful and beautiful and teaching us girls how to do it. When she danced with me I was so happy I didn't know what I was doing. And she was laughing and having a good time.

It was almost too good to believe that me, a poor girl, was going to school to learn reading and writing and counting and geography — and from such a wonderful teacher. Every day as I worked I kept thinking of those two hours in the afternoon when I could come out from the mill and go into the classroom with the other girls and have Sister Vincenza to teach me. Sister Vincenza made us learn good, but she was always kind. And me, I could never get enough of the learning.

Once Sister Vincenza said to me, "Rosa, why are you always looking in my face like that?"

"Oh, Sister Vincenza," I said. "You have the prettiest face in the world! You look like an angel from heaven!"

"No, no, Rosa," she said. "You mustn't talk like that. My face is homely."

That sister she could read my heart like a book and she was always saving me from a punishment from *Superiora*. Sister Vincenza used to listen when I was telling the stories to the girls and she was laughing just like them. So one time I was telling that story of how Saint Peter tried to make a miracle like Jesus and he burnt up the blacksmith's mother-in-law. Nobody saw *Superiora* behind the pillar. When she heard that story she came out and grabbed me by the shoulders to shake me, but Sister Vincenza saved me. She came and put her hand on me and said, "No, Mother, you make a mistake. Rosa is reverent and she is very religious. The story is one of the old stories of Italy, told in all the villages." And so *Superiora* let me go.

Another time the boy from the priest in Canaletto came in with a message and I was standing there on the steps of the chapel. "Rosa," the boy said. "You tell Sister Giuseppina that the priest is coming for mass at eight o'clock in the morning." I smiled to let him know I understood. I was not allowed to speak to a boy — I should say not! When *Superiora* heard how the boy knew my name and saw me smile she came out with a terrible face. But Sister Vincenza put her arm around me to save me.

[95

"Rosa is innocent and young," she said. "I know her well from the school. She means nothing. She is friendly and smiles at everyone, that's all."

Superiora, she was the one to punish us girls. And when she punished she punished for sure! Sometimes she punished the innocent ones too. Maybe when she said her prayers she asked God to forgive her for punishing the innocent ones. But maybe not too! That woman, she knew how to make herself respected. We were not allowed to speak to her — to say good morning or anything. She thought that way she would make the girls respect her. And oh we did! She was smart though — she knew wonderful stories about saints and miracles that she used to tell us on Sunday afternoons. Some of the miracles she had seen herself.

Every year on her birthday instead of going to school when we came from the mill in the afternoon we used to run up the mountain and gather daisies and all kinds of white flowers. Everything had to be decorated with white flowers for *Superiora*'s birthday. The other sisters would cover a platform with gold paper and we would put those flowers all around. Then *Superiora* would come in and go up on the platform and we would sing the songs we had learned just for her. In one song we called ourselves her "heart children." And on that day we each got by our place at night an orange and a paper of candy. *Superiora* bought them for us herself. But we deserved them — all those songs we were learning a month before, and all the punishment we had to take.

Most of the time I was getting punished because I talked too much. One Sunday afternoon us girls were sitting on the step of the porch and someone started talking about Maria when she was young. And one girl said she didn't think that the Blessed Virgin was born like other babies. And I said, "O yes, she was born like other babies, but her mother gave her to the temple and made her a saint."

Nobody had seen *Superiora* behind the pillar. When I said that, she came out and grabbed me by the shoulder. "Rosa!" she said. "How dare you say such a thing!" And her face looked terrible with anger. I had just been talking because I never could keep still. I didn't know how Maria was born. I didn't know how any baby was born. I stood up when *Superiora* grabbed me but I didn't know what to say.

"Who told you that?" she demanded, and she gave me a shake. "Where did you get it?"

I didn't know why what I had said was bad, but since it was I didn't want *Superiora* to think that I got it from Mamma Lena. "From a book," I said.

"From a book? What book? Where did you get the book?"

"I found it."

"You see!" said *Superiora*, turning to the other girls. "That just shows! There are wicked men — Protestant men — who put books where people will find them and read those terrible lies about the Blessed Virgin! Where is the book? What did you do with it?" So there I was caught in a big lie. My face turned red and I didn't know what to say. "Answer me! Where did you find the book? Where is it now?"

"O *Madre*," I said. "Please don't investigate me any more. Punish me with bread and water for a week, but don't ask me anything more. There wasn't any book. I just said what came into my head. I don't know how the Blessed Virgin was born."

Oh, what a shaking I got! And I got bread and water for a week besides. But bread and water was not much punishment at Canaletto. Nobody got much more. We were not made soft by too much eating, like the children in America now. So then *Superiora* told us how Maria was born. And I never forgot: Once when Sant' Anna was already an old woman she was weeping and praying God because she had no children. God heard her and He sent an angel to her husband. The angel came to Giocchin' and said, "Giocchin', embrace your wife." Giocchin' was a saint and he thought it kind of funny for an angel to tell him to do such a thing, but he did it anyway. He put his arms around Sant' Anna and he kissed her. And from that kiss Maria was born. The Blessed Virgin was not born from sin like other babies!

When *Superiora* was gone the girls all started asking questions. How could a baby come from a kiss? And what was the sin between the husband and the wife that *Superiora* talked about? What did the man do to the woman when he married her? What did other babies come from and how were they born? Nobody knew.

"Only the husband can tell a girl those things. A girl is not allowed to know until she is married."

"No, she is not even allowed to ask! It is so bad you get punished if you ask!"

Me, I had never known before that the husband did anything to the wife except sleep in the bed with her. So now I had something new to think about.

"Better you don't get married," said one girl.

"Not better for me," said Beata. "I love the young men. I don't care what he does to me, I want to get married and have a husband."

At Canaletto I was always getting punished when I was innocent, but other times, when I deserved it, I didn't get caught. One of those times I didn't get caught was when I showed all the girls how to get some water. It was on one of those hot, hot Sundays in summer. After mass in the morning we all changed to our red-and-white dresses and took our big buckets and climbed the mountain to pick blueberries. Sister Maria liked to have the blueberries to make jam for winter. So when the blueberries were ripe we went every Sunday. The sisters had a basket of food and drink for their lunch, but each girl, we had only a piece of black bread. And we got *so* thirsty up there in the hot sun. We ate the blueberries, but they were not wet enough. We were all crying for water. Our tongues were hanging out. And we were even asking Sister Teresa to let us go home before our big pails were full — we were so thirsty. And so at last it came time to go and we started running down the side of the mountain. That mountain was steep. Once we had started to run we couldn't stop. So we ran all the way down till we came to the road to the *istituto*. Then we had to wait for the sisters. And we were so hot and so thirsty we couldn't even talk. When the sisters came up to us *Superiora* said to Sister Teresa and Sister Paola, "You go on ahead and shut off all the water. If the girls drink tonight when they are so hot they will get sick." So the sisters did it. And there we had to go to bed without one drop of water. Sister Teresa came up and said the prayers, but nobody could answer. We were all dying from thirst. And so she went downstairs. But nobody could go to sleep.

And I was laying there thinking about all the cool blue water out there in Lago Maggiore and about the little streams of water in the washroom that turned into icicles in the winter. And suddenly I remembered how the sisters climbed up the ladder to fill the boxes above. I jumped out of bed, took my tin cup, and sneaked out to the washroom. The ladder was there like always. I went up and reached into the box. And sure enough, the box was full of nice clean water. But if it had been dirty, I would have drunk it anyway. I dipped my cup in and drank and drank. I drank till I wanted no more. Then I went back to bed. But I couldn't go to sleep thinking how thirsty the other girls were. If I told them, some would be sure to tattle, and *Superiora* would kill me! But after a while I couldn't stand it any longer and I told Beata. So then Beata and her partner went. Then two others. Two by two every girl in the *istituto* went and climbed the ladder and drank. The next morning when we came into the dining room there were two big pitchers of water on each long table. We all looked to each other and smiled. Nobody told, because everybody had drunk.

Another time I did a good thing and didn't get caught. (When I was a girl I was more good than I am now. Then I was always wanting to help the others. Now I'm always telling the other people to help me. I'm not good like I used to be.) That poor girl, Filomina, after she got the terrible punishment — she had to wear the dirty sheet to the mill — she didn't go to bed at all. She sat up on the bench at the side of our room for many, many nights. But then she couldn't stand it anymore not to sleep so she went to bed at night again, and again she wet the bed. She was sick and couldn't help it, I guess. So then the punishment *Superiora* gave her! She said Filomina would have to stay all night alone up in the bell tower. After dinner that night we went out on the step in the court like always, but we didn't tell stories. We just sat there waiting. We didn't believe it that *Superiora* would make that poor girl do such a thing! But sure enough, as soon as it got dark, here came *Superiora* and took Filomina and made her go. She had no candle — nothing. But what could she do? What could she say? She had to do it, that was all.

[99

Then all of us other girls had to go up to bed. Sister Teresa came and said the prayers, then she went. We didn't dare talk, but we were all thinking of that poor Filomina up there in the bell tower. She could die from the scare up there all alone! The other girls in our little room — after a while I could hear it — they went to sleep. But me, I couldn't! Slow, slow, I got out of bed and went down the passage to the stairway. Everything was quiet downstairs. The sisters were all asleep too. So then I went on down through the chapel. There was a little light in the chapel from the lamp on the altar. But when I came into the passage to the tower everything was black. Quiet, quiet I closed the door behind me. My heart was bumping and knocking on my ears. "Oh, Madonna, help me! Don't let the sisters catch me!" At the bottom of that bell tower there were some steps, but near the top there was just the ladder and you had to hold on with your hands and your feet. When I came on the ladder I started to call Filomina in a whisper. "Filomina! It's just me! It's Rosa! I'm coming to stay with you!" I was afraid if I came up without her knowing who it was she might get the scare and fall down and break her neck.

"Oh no, Rosa!" she said. "If the sisters find out they will kill you!" But I came up anyway and sat down beside her on those two or three loose boards that made a floor. She was shivering and shaking from scare and I was shivering and shaking too. The rats made a lot of noise and the wind came through the cracks and hollered at us. We didn't dare go to sleep — we might fall off. So we sat there holding on and staring into the dark at things we couldn't see. But anyway it was not so bad for two as for one all alone. And when the *alba* — that first false light before morning — came I sneaked down. And I was back in my bed when Sister Teresa came up with her *Viva Gesu* to wake us up. Beata heard me when I came back in our little room and I told her, but she didn't tell. And the sisters never knew.

11

SOME girls from Milan said that in the city they had gaslights in the silk mills. With those gaslights you had to work as long in the winter as in the summer. But in the villages we still went to work with the daylight, and with the daylight we stopped. So in winter we had more time in the evening, and we did other things. After learning the songs for *Superiora*'s birthday, we started learning parts for a play. Every year before Christmas the sisters of the *istituto* made a drama or an opera. For three or four months everyone was busy getting ready. And on the night of the play people came from all over to see it — from all the cities around Lago Maggiore. They came from Pallanza and Luino and Stresa and Arona and Canaletto, and from all over. They didn't buy tickets, but when the play was over they threw money on the stage and the sisters used the money for something needed for us girls.

Oh, that first year I could hardly wait for the older girls to learn their parts so I could see how it was going to be! Me, I just had one little part. I was one of those little black devils with red eyes in the play *Girolamo*. I didn't have much to learn, but Sister Vincenza said I must think of things to do to make the people laugh. There was one special room in the *istituto* just for those entertainments, with an outside door to go in and seats for the people and a big stage and everything. And there was all the scenery and all the costumes. One theater in Paris was giving the sisters all the things they didn't want anymore — the clothes of soldiers and kings and queens — and the sisters made them like new. There were the wigs and the moustaches and the canes and coats for the men's parts, but the girls who took those parts were not allowed to wear the pants. They were looking exactly like men on top, but instead of pants they were wearing skirts. *Superiora* wouldn't allow it that any girls from the *istituto* wear the pants of a man.

On the first night of the play I was on the stage behind the curtain waiting to be dressed. The big room in front was full of people. They had come early to get the seats, but then they were getting noisy and wanted the play to start. They were clapping and calling for it to start. It made me shiver inside to think all those people were going to see our play. I went to the end of the curtain and peeked through a crack at their faces. And I got so excited I couldn't stand still. Pretty soon the people started stamping their feet, and *Superiora* got nervous and came up through the little door at the side to see how much longer it would be before all the girls were ready. "The audience is getting too restless!" she said to Sister Teresa and Sister Vincenza.

Sister Teresa and Sister Vincenza were working as fast as they could but only about half of the girls were ready.

"What are we going to do!" said *Superiora*. "We've got to do something! Is there some girl who can go out on the stage and entertain them by singing or something?"

"Tell Rosa to go," said Sister Vincenza. "Rosa Cortesi."

"What should I tell her to do?" said *Superiora*.

"Don't tell her anything," said Sister Vincenza. "Just tell her to go out and entertain them. She will know what to do."

But *Superiora* was kind of afraid. Me, I was the youngest girl in the *istituto* and I guess she didn't know what I would do if I went out there. But when she came back near the curtain, she could hear it that the people were acting worse than before. So she pulled back the curtain enough for me to get past and she told me to go. My heart started bumping and knocking. How could I go out there alone in front of all those people? And what could I do to entertain them and make them content? No, I couldn't go out there! But there was *Superiora* holding the curtain. "Go!" she ordered. And the first thing I knew I was out there in front of the curtain. My feet were carrying me along, but I held my head down, afraid to look up. When the people saw me coming out there in the everyday dress of the *istituto* and my face red with shame, they stopped stamping for the play and started laughing and calling jokes at me. I stood there listening to them a little. And suddenly as I listened I wanted to talk back and make them laugh more. I looked up and made a long face. Then I remembered Carlo, the mailman, and how he could talk without words. So I talked like him, with my face and my hands and my shoulders and my head, to tell them that I had nothing to say — that I didn't know what to do. And they clapped and yelled more. And right then the song of the stupid peasant and his donkey popped into my head. I would sing that song, just like I used to sing it and act it with Beppo in the court of the old *palazzo*. First I was the stupid peasant walking with bent knees and heavy feet behind my donkey. Then I was angry and swearing and waving my whip. Then I was singing to him. And the people, they went crazy for that song. They slapped their knees and laughed till the tears ran down their cheeks. And when I had finished, their coins came showering down on the stage all around me. I had to duck and run off to the wing.

"*Bravo! Bravo! Bravissimo!*" they shouted. Then they were calling for more. They wouldn't keep still — they wanted more.

If they liked the song of the donkey so much they would like the song of the peasant's ox and the landlord's horse. Without waiting for *Superiora* to tell me I ran back out. It was fun to make them laugh. I would make them laugh still more.

After the second act of the play *Superiora* came back again and she said that one rich man from Switzerland had offered to buy wool to make shawls for all of the girls in the *istituto* if I would sing the song of the peasant's donkey again. And she was helping take off my hood with the devil's horns and unpinning my tail. I couldn't believe it — that all the girls could have new shawls for that one song! My black coverall suit and red eyes made me feel more than ever like the stupid peasant. And when I had finished the singing and acting I ran off the stage laughing inside for I knew without being told that I had done it better than before.

So after that night it was always my job to go up on the stage and do anything that came into my head to make the people laugh. And pretty soon everyone knew me and would laugh when they saw me coming — before I opened my mouth. I couldn't understand myself how I could make the people laugh when I didn't laugh myself. I had always said that I wanted to be like that Carlotta in the court of the silk mill, and now I was. I had a new job in life — the job of entertaining the people. Sometimes when the girls asked me to tell a story I thought it would be nice to tell one of those religious stories that Mamma Lena used to tell, to make them cry and to make them more religious. But they didn't like those stories so much. The next time they asked they would say they wanted a funny one to make them laugh. I had started out doing funny ones and so I had to do funny ones all the time.

As soon as the plays were over we started to get ready for Christmas. Every night for about a month before, we found one or two chestnuts by our place for supper beside our black bread and water. But we didn't eat them. We carried them up to the dormitory and put them in a little box under our beds to save for Christmas. Then we started learning the beautiful songs. We learned "Gloria in Excelsis Deo," all in Latin. Then we learned "Dolce Bambino," the song Maria sang to the Baby Jesus not yet born, telling Him to come and not delay. That song was so beautiful it made tears in my eyes. And it made me think that I would like to be a sister and give my life to that Baby. Then there was a lullaby, "Mio Redentore," telling the little Redeemer to sleep and don't cry. And as we learned the songs we knitted as fast as we could so our new black shawls would be ready for Christmas.

When Christmas Eve finally came nobody went to bed. And the priest came from Canaletto. At midnight he was going to sing the high mass and we were going to sing it with him. Sometime before midnight we all went into the chapel and started singing our Christmas songs. There were so many candles that the light flickered on the faces of all the girls under their gray headkerchiefs and on the faces of the sisters under their big hats. The last song we sang before midnight

[104

was that "Dolce Bambino" — we each one was Maria singing to the unborn Jesus to come down from heaven and not delay. We sang softer and softer, and then just at the end, when we were all holding our breath and the clock was striking midnight, Sister Giuseppina pulled the cord of the curtain. And there was the Madonna, all in a bright light, bending over the Baby in the crib. It was so wonderful it filled everyone's heart with love. Yes, I too would be a sister of San Vincenzo and give joy like this to other poor girls!

After mass we all went into the dining room and found a lighted candle at our place. Then the sisters came in with big trays and gave each girl a shining tin glass of boiling wine and an orange and a fuzzy paper of candy and a biscuit cake — gifts from the boss in Milan. It was hard to believe it — hot wine with sugar in it! I held it in my mouth a long time tasting it before I let it roll down my throat. At three o'clock we went to bed. Then Christmas morning, about eight o'clock, we all got up and put on our best sailor dresses and the new black shawls and marched two by two through the snow to the church in Canaletto and heard the Christmas service. For the rest of the day there was no work and we could do just what we wanted. And there we had all those good chestnuts to eat. In the afternoon the sisters brought out the music box and we took turns turning it. First we had all the Christmas songs, then we had some dance songs and we all danced. And Sister Vincenza danced with us. Nobody scolded. Everybody was happy. Our hearts were full of love. It was wonderful! Christmas with the Sisters of San Vincenzo!

12

"OH, WHY do you keep talking about going in a convent!" Beata said. We were up in the dormitory making the beds and sweeping the floor. It was the turn of the eight girls from Beata's little room to stay home for a week from the mill to do the work in the *istituto*. The other girls were doing the work downstairs. "Why do you want to be a sister?" But I never answered because Beata had heard men's voices in the court and had run to the window to see who it was. I went too. "It's the boss from Milan and his nephew is with him! Oh, Rosa, isn't it just my bad luck that they come when it's our week to stay home! All the other girls can see them in the mill! What am I going to do? I want to look at that pretty young man!"

"Oh, Beata," I said. "You mustn't look at that young man! He's not for us! He's a millionaire!"

"I don't care about his money!" said Beata. "I love him because he's so pretty! Doesn't he look like Jesus? Oh, I love that pretty young man! Let us run down and see him, Rosa!" But she knew we couldn't go down until our work was done. "Let us hurry! Here, you take the broom and I'll pull out the beds. Hurry, Rosa! Hurry!" And so we flew around.

When our work was done we ran down to the yard. And right

there in the court was Signor Adolfo and his nephew talking to *Superiora*. And some of the other girls had gathered around to see if the boss had brought them any report from their father or their aunt, whatever they had in Milan. Beata was looking at the young man and flirting. Then she went up to the boss and said, "Did my mother and my father give you a report for me?" Then she ran back by me.

"Oh, Rosa!" she said. "I'm going to be killed! *Superiora* saw me smile at that young man and she heard what I said to the boss. I'm going to be killed for sure! But I don't care!"

And all week Beata was talking about that young man and how pretty he was. On Friday I had the job to clean the chapel. And just when I took my rag to dust around the altar, the wind opened the door to the *gabinetto* — the little room off the chapel that the sisters had for themselves. And in there I saw the boss from Milan again and his nephew. Why in the world was he in the *gabinetto*? No man but the priest had ever been in that room! And there on the sofa I saw a beautiful dress — white silk with shining spangles — and a wreath of white flowers. But before I could hear anything Sister Giuseppina came and closed the door. Other days when I cleaned the chapel she always watched me, but this day she didn't — she stayed in the *gabinetto*. After a while she came out and said, "Rosa, are you almost done? Go upstairs and tell Sister Teresa to put on Beata her sailor dress. *Superiora* is going to take Beata to town."

On the stairs I met Beata coming down with her broom, so I told her about the boss and his nephew in the *gabinetto* and what I had seen. "And Beata," I said. "*Superiora* wants you. She's going to take you to town. But I can't tell you — I have to tell Sister Teresa."

So Beata followed me upstairs. And when I told Sister Teresa, all Sister Teresa said was, "Do you want to go, Beata?"

"Do I want to go!" said Beata. "*Mamma Mia*! I never went before! I'm crazy to go!"

So I went back to my work but I stayed up near the door to the *gabinetto* so I could peek and listen. And after a while I saw Beata, all cleaned and washed, coming into the *gabinetto* from the other door. "Well, Beata," said *Superiora*. "Did you say a prayer to Sant' Antoni last night?"

"Sure I did," said Beata, and she was smiling at the young man. "I never forget."

"Don't you know that Sant' Antoni is not the protector of the matrimony? He's the protector of fire and of animals and of many other things, but not of the matrimony."

"Oh, I hope I made no mistake!" said Beata.

"No, I don't think you did," said *Superiora*. "For, sure enough, Sant' Antoni was the protector of your matrimony. You're going to have the matrimony right away tomorrow. See, Beata, you are going to marry this beautiful young man."

Beata didn't know what to do. She just stood there looking at the pretty young man and didn't know what to do. But when he smiled at her, right there before the eyes of the sisters and the boss she ran over and threw her arms around his neck and kissed him. That poor young man turned red and red and was ashamed to look up. Then Beata began to cry. "It's not true!" she said. "It's not true! Me a poor girl and an orphan! How can it be true!"

The uncle, Signor Adolfo, he pulled Beata on his knee like she was a little girl to stop her crying. "Never mind that you are an orphan, Beata," he said. "The sisters were your mother and your father. And now me and Angelo will take care of you. It's true — you're going to be married in the church in Canaletto tomorrow."

"Oh, *Madre!*" said Beata. "If it's true let me run and tell the girls! I'm going to run and tell all the girls!"

But *Superiora* said no. She said Beata could not talk to the girls anymore. And she was going to stay in the infirmary with Sister Giuseppina until her matrimony in the morning.

Think of that big secret I had to keep all night! If I should tell the girls that secret they *couldn't* keep still! I had to sleep with it, that was all. I had to let them think Beata was sick. I didn't dare tell! But why had Sister Giuseppina stayed in the infirmary with Beata? Was she telling her the secrets of marriage? And how could Sister Giuseppina know what the man did to the woman when he married her?

It was already light the next morning when Sister Teresa came up with her *Viva Gesu* to wake us up. And after breakfast *Superiora* said, "Girls, you're not going to work today. You all go up and put on your best dresses. We're going to the church in Canaletto to see Beata's wedding."

"Beata's wedding!" "Beata's wedding!" "Who is Beata marrying?" "The boss's nephew!" "Impossible — the boss's nephew!" "The *boss's nephew?*" And I could tell by the way the girls said "the boss's nephew" that some of them were glad for Beata and some were jealous and some were unhappy that they were going to lose Beata. Me, I wasn't jealous — I was too young to think about marriage, but some of the girls were old.

So we were all in the church and here came in Beata like an angel from heaven in the beautiful white dress and veil. But after the matrimony she went out another door so we couldn't see her again close by. Then we all marched two by two down to the dock and there on Lago Maggiore was a beautiful boat decorated with white lilies and gold. And Beata came in a carriage and threw a kiss to us girls, but she was not allowed to speak to us. And she went up with all those high people on the boat and sailed away.

The girls all went home and cried. At supper no one could eat. So then *Superiora* came out and tried to make a joke. She held up a big sheet and said, "Come on, girls. I'm going to wipe all the tears." Then she said, "Listen, girls. I'm going to tell you the story about Beata. She was an orphan. She was left by the gate of the *istituto* when she was a baby just born."

"We know it," said the girls. "We know it."

"And around the baby's neck was a string and on the card it said, 'Please, *Superiora*, take care of this orphan baby.' So we sisters took the baby and gave her the name Beata, because sure she was blessed by God to be left in such a home. And she grew up to be a beautiful girl. Well then the boss from Milan had a nephew that he loved like a son and he wanted to give him a really good girl. He wanted a pure girl that had never been out to know things and a girl with the strong religion. So we told him about Beata and how all these years we taught her only holy things. The boss thought she was just the one, so he brought his nephew to see if he liked her. And when that beautiful rich young man saw Beata he loved her right away. And now he married her."

All of us girls were brokenhearted to lose Beata. She was so jolly and so lively and the only one in the *istituto* not afraid of the sisters. Even the men and boys that she used to laugh with in the *filatoio* were brokenhearted. We all missed her talking and her laughing. And the girls in our little room said, "Never again will we say a prayer to San Antoni! Look what he did! He took away our Beata!"

After one year I saw Beata again. When my time at the *istituto* was done I came into Milan to go home. I had the address of Beata from Sister Vincenza, so I asked the man on the wagon to take me there. It was like a palace where Beata lived. Two men dressed like soldiers let me pass the gate. And after I had passed through all the other servants I saw her. But she was not our Beata. She was a sad lady dressed up in black. She said she had lost her first baby — a little girl. She was kind to me — she had the servants give me something to eat — but she was not our Beata. Then her husband, the boss's nephew, came in and tried to make a little joke. He said, "Beata doesn't love me now like when she was a girl in the *istituto*." But Beata didn't smile. She didn't even look at him. I was even ashamed to be there and see them like that. I was wishing I hadn't come. And I was glad when the man from the wagon sent the word it was time to go. The jolly, lively Beata I had loved so much was gone.

Maybe she's alive now, Beata. I'd like to see some of those girls from the *istituto*. Sure, they must some be alive, like me.

13

ONE day that kind girl, Annina, who stood next to me in the *filatoio* said to me, "Rosa, will you put my new spool on? I can't. I can't lift it."

I didn't know why she couldn't put it on this time — she had always done it before — but I took it and lifted it up. And just as I had it on the machine, Annina fell down to the floor. Her face looked terrible — like paper. Then blood started coming out her mouth. The *assistenta* — that woman who always walked behind us — came to see what had happened. She looked at Annina's face, then she ran and called the men in the machine room. Two men came back with her and they picked up Annina and carried her away. Nobody said a word, but I could see it — I knew that Annina was dead.

That night when we came back to the *istituto* we were all waiting for *Superiora* to tell us something. But she didn't tell us anything. None of the sisters ever mentioned Annina again. There was no funeral — nothing. It was as if that poor girl had never been. So then I had a new partner to march with me, but I could not forget that kind Annina and how she had let me eat her food when she was too sick. And at night when the other girls were asleep I would say a prayer for her soul — to help her through the fire of purgatory.

Soon after Annina died, Sister Teresa came to the *filatoio* one day and told me she was taking me to the *filanda* to learn the real silkmaking. I was excited and happy. Only the older girls of the *istituto* and women from Canaletto knew how to unwind the silk from the cocoons. It was hard. Not everyone could learn. And I almost knew how already from turning the wheel all those years in Bugiarno. When I was turning the wheel for the silkmaker I had to watch all the time what she was doing. But only the tips of your own fingers could tell when the silk is too thin or too thick. And I had never before had to put my hands in the near-boiling water. Oh, how that water burned! At first I kept pulling my hands out before I had caught a single head. I couldn't stand it! But with the boss from the mill and Sister Teresa both standing watching and scolding I had to keep putting my hands back in until I had caught the heads from four cocoons. If you don't catch the heads quick enough the cocoons start unwinding themselves in the water and spoil the silk. So when I had enough heads to make the right thickness I could start to reel. But here in Canaletto we didn't have a little girl to turn the wheel for us. We had something new — a foot pedal. With the foot pedal you could turn the reel yourself as fast as you wanted it to go. I learned fast how to brush off the fuzz on the cocoons and get the heads. But every day my hands got more sore. You can't make the silk without getting the sore hands. The worst is between the fingers where the skin opens in big cuts. Every night Sister Teresa would put something from a bottle on all the silkmakers' hands, then she would give us a rock of camphor to rub on. Our hands all turned yellow but that didn't stop the burning.

At first the *assistenta* was watching and telling me when the thread was getting thin and needed a new head. But soon I could tell by myself and I was proud. Then one day the boss, Battista, stopped to watch and Sister Teresa came over too and inspected the silk on the reel. "Rosa is young," said Sister Teresa, "and has only been in the *filanda* this short time, but already she can make silk. She is a real silkmaker. She is quick and has the true sense in her fingers."

"*Bravo*, Rosa! *Bravo!*" said Battista. And I was so happy I wanted to do better and better and be the best one of all.

More than two years I had been away from Bugiarno but I had

not heard one word from Mamma Lena or anyone. Mamma Lena could read but she couldn't write — she didn't know how to write a letter.
So then one day in the summer I was sitting there in the *filanda* sweating bullets with my hands in the boiling water and I heard voices near me. I didn't pay any attention because I was trying to catch the head of a new cocoon and I had to watch what I was doing. There was always so much steam in that room from all the basins that you couldn't see anyway until someone was right beside you. But then I heard my name and looked up. It was Mamma Lena! She was standing there with Sister Teresa. I could hardly believe it. I smiled at her, but then I had to quick look back at the cocoons in my basin.

"How long has she been making silk like this?" said Mamma Lena, inspecting the thread on my reel.

"Several months," said Sister Teresa. "She's a good worker and she learned fast. What we teach the girls in the *istituto*, we teach them to do right — to do perfect."

"It's good silk," said Mamma Lena and I could tell by the way she said it how surprised she was and I was happy.

That afternoon I was let out of school so I could talk with Mamma Lena. We sat on the stone bench at the end of the court at the *istituto*. First she gave me some little things she had brought in her satchel — two pairs of knitted stockings and a piece of hard salami. Think of me, a poor girl, having that good piece of meat like the rich! There was enough to give each girl in our little room a taste. When I had smelled its good smell many times I wrapped it up again in the white cloth and waited for Mamma Lena to tell me why she had come. She said she would have come before, but that Papa Lur had been sick. When he was first sick she had asked the boss in Milan to let me come home, but the boss wouldn't allow it until my three years were up. Then Mamma Lena told me why she had come — what had happened.

One day Papa Lur had gone to the fountain and when he came back he couldn't talk. He tried to talk but he couldn't say the words. The doctor said it was paralysis and he stuck a knife through the back of Papa Lur's neck and put a silver ribbon through the hole. Then every morning he came and pulled the ribbon back and forth to make the blood come. And so he made that first paralysis go away. But then it came again. Three times it came, and the last time it came Papa Lur was paralyzed through and through. He couldn't do anything for himself. Mamma Lena had to take care of him entirely. He didn't know anyone and he couldn't talk and he couldn't move. One man came every day and helped move him. Once Zia Teresa had said, "Oh, Lena, it would be a blessing if God took him. He's more dead than alive. It would be a blessing if he died." That made Mamma Lena so angry that she wouldn't speak to Zia Teresa for three months. She had loved Papa Lur so much that she never wanted him to die. But he had died anyway. And think what a sorrow she had! And when she told me this Mamma Lena started to cry.

Papa Lur dead! Papa Lur gone forever, like Pina and like my kind partner Annina! I couldn't believe it — that I would never see Papa Lur again! And suddenly I was so full of loneliness that I busted out crying too. The best friend I had in the world had deserted me. He had gone away and left me alone. I would never see him again until I died too. (But even then, when I was brokenhearted entirely, I was not wishing to die. I wanted to live. I like to live.) So then Mamma Lena was telling me where he was buried — near Bunga's grave, where the two hollyhocks always grew. She had put up a white cross with a little roof over to mark the place. And it looked nice standing there with the tall grass and weeds all around blowing in the wind. And she was paying the priest to say masses for his soul.

"So now I am all alone," said Mamma Lena. "But I have asked the boss in Milan to let you come home as soon as your three years are finished."

It would be nice to see Caterina and Toni and Zia Teresa and Don Domenic, but without Papa Lur there to save me from Mamma Lena I didn't want to go home. "I have the wish of going in a convent," I said. "I want to be a Sister of San Vincenzo."

"*You*! You want to be a nun!" said Mamma Lena, and she stopped crying to look at me.

"Yes," I said.

"Have you asked the Mother Superior?"

"No," I said. "You ask her."

And Mamma Lena didn't know what to say. So she started telling me again how when she was a young girl she had the intention of going in a convent too, but she had married Giulur so she could take care of Bunga. "Probably the Madonna put it in your mind," she said. "You were born on the Day of the Madonna. You're a daughter of the Madonna. If the Blessed Virgin wants you to be a sister, I can't tell you no. I can't keep you from going."

So then Mamma Lena took me in and asked *Superiora*. *Superiora* said, "To be a Sister of Vincenzo the girl has to be white as snow. She has to be as white as our hats. I'm sorry, but your girl has the father *ignoto* — unknown. You don't know if her father was a butcher or a thief or what. And your girl has not the vocation. She can be some other kind. We can send her to some other convent. But not to the convent of the Sisters of San Vincenzo."

(Poor me, I didn't know who I was so I couldn't be a Sister of San Vincenzo!)

"Do you want to be some other kind?" asked Mamma Lena. But I only shook my head. If I couldn't be a Sister of Saint Vincent I didn't want to be any at all.

When my three years were finished no one told me anything, but Sister Teresa came into the *filanda* just before noon one day and told me to put away my brushbroom and come with her. And she took me back to the *istituto*. And there waiting outside was the man with the wagon that had brought the baskets. So then she told me. She said I must go up and wash and put on my sailor dress and leather shoes because I was leaving. I was leaving right away on the wagon to Milan. And I must hurry so the girls wouldn't see me. It was almost time for the lunch bell.

"Oh, Sister," I said. "If I am leaving let me say good-bye to the girls!"

"No!" she said. "The girls must not see you — they must not know you are leaving. It makes the others discontent when some girl goes home."

And she went with me to the dormitory to help me hurry and roll the clothes I had come in in a bundle. But Sister Vincenza was waiting in the dining room when I came down and she kissed me. Then she gave me the address of Beata in Milan so I could see her if I had time.

[115

The bell started ringing for lunch, but I couldn't even have anything to eat. I had to run and climb on that wagon. That Canaletto was terrible! When the mother sends for you, you beat it, that's all. In five minutes you are gone. And the other girls never know. But I never forgot how Sister Vincenza took my face in her hands and kissed me!

When I came in Milan the man on the wagon took me to the address where Beata lived, but I was wishing I had not gone. I had such a disappointment, like I already told about.

So then it was evening when I came to Bugiarno and got off the *tramvai* in the square. And there were about a hundred people waiting to see me and looking at me like I was something wonderful. When Zia Teresa kissed me she told me to look up in the church tower. And there a lot of young men were looking down to see me. In three years I had grown into a young lady and I had on that nice dress from the *istituto* and real leather shoes. And I was not homely. (Maybe I was not so much, but everybody used to say I was awful pretty — nice white teeth and big eyes and curly hair. And I must have been a little pretty anyway, because all the young men were crazy for me.) So all the people from the square followed me home to the *osteria*. Then the guards from the court and a lot of other young men came too. They all wanted to look at me and hear about my three years in the "sisters' convent." Mamma Lena must have made about a hundred lire selling drinks that night.

And I had to keep thinking and thinking what else I could tell them about the *istituto*. I told how we always marched two by two, and how all the girls in the dormitory came awake after Sister Teresa left us asleep every night, and how the butter ran away on Filomina's stomach when we sneaked the sisters' food across the border. Then I told about Christmas and about the plays and about my funny songs. And when I could think of nothing else and they still wanted more I began to entertain them with some of those songs. And they were laughing and shouting and making me do them over and over. Only one man at the far side of the second table didn't laugh. Instead of listening to the songs he was watching me. He was not young — he was old — about thirty or forty years old, and he was dressed not so poor as the men who worked on the farms or in the mills. Who he could be I didn't know, but I knew I didn't like him. And when he called for more whiskey Mamma Lena said, "Yes, Santino. Yes." And she was hurrying to obey him.

That night after all the people were gone and I was helping wash the dishes, Mamma Lena told me she had another sad news to tell me. Not long after the death of Papa Lur — just after she had come to see me at Canaletto — Don Domenic had got sick. The doctor said it was the mad hunger disease and sent him to the hospital in Milan. In the hospital he got meat and milk and soon he was like well and came home. But who of the poor can eat meat or have milk every day? In a little while that terrible sickness came back and in his madness Don Domenic went down to the river one night and drowned himself. So now we had a new priest — a young priest from another village, Father Bruschetti. And then, when I was still thinking about Don Domenic and how much I loved him and of his kind old mother, Maria, Mamma Lena told me about my cousin Luigi. Luigi was the last son left to Zia Teresa. He was a few years older than me but he always liked me and used to play with me when I was little. When there was no work for him in Bugiarno he had gone with a gang of young men and boys to work in France. But in France he had got too sick with the consumption to work and so had come home to die. "Tomorrow," said Mamma Lena, "I have arranged it already, you are going to start work in the silk mill of Signor Alberto. But after work at night you can go there and see Luigi."

The next morning when Signor Alberto saw how good I could make the silk he gave me the first place in the row. But I had never had a little girl to turn my reel before and this one didn't know how. The silk kept breaking and I had to splice it. So when Signor Alberto tested my first reel he came out from the testing room red with anger. "If your girl doesn't know how to turn you've got to punish her! You've got to teach her! Go home! And you too!" he said to the little girl.

I was disappointed because it was just noon and I had wanted to stay in the court of the mill to hear all the news from the women and girls. But the boss had told me to go, so I had to go, that was all. "Well," Mamma Lena said. "Go by Gina in the other mill, in the *filanda* of Signor Rossi. Gina will give you a place there. A good silkmaker is always welcome." And so I ran to the other mill. And Gina and Signor Rossi were surprised and happy when they saw how I could make silk and they gave me a place and a little girl to turn and so I sat down and started to reel. But before I had been working an hour, here came running in that other boss, Signor Alberto. He came in like a lion and he took me by the ear. "This girl is mine!" he said to Signor Rossi. "And you can't have her! You can't steal my silkmakers!" And still holding me by the ear he led me all the way back to his mill. He said he had only sent me home to lose one half day's pay as a punishment and what did I mean — running to the other mill! Me, I wanted to tell him that I thought he had sent me home to stay, but I was afraid. The poor were not allowed to talk to the rich. I was laughing to myself, though, how I had run to the other mill. And never again did I get one complaint about my silk when it was tested. He knew I was a good silkmaker and he didn't want me to run away. (After living in America I was not afraid to talk to the rich. That time I went back from America I went to the mill and I talked to Gina and to Signor Rossi and I would have talked to Signor Alberto too if I had seen him. And because I came from America they didn't dare punch me in the face. They answered me nice.)

That night after my supper Mamma Lena told me to get washed and to put on my dress from the *istituto* and then to go there to Zia Teresa's court to see Luigi. I was glad that I was going to see that nice boy again and I ran all the way. Zia Teresa was in her court and took me inside. Luigi was not in bed — he was lying on the bench by the window and he had on his nice clothes from France — a nice sash and some velvet pants. But he was awful sick, though, you could see it, and he was coughing when he tried to breathe. I went up and smiled, but he didn't know me at first. In four or five years I had changed more than he had. So then Zia Teresa told him it was me. He got up on his elbow and looked in my face, but instead of speaking he fell back on the bench and turned his head to the wall and started crying. "Take her away!" he cried. "Take her away! Why do you make me look at that beautiful young girl when you know I am going to die!" So Zia Teresa told me I had better go. And I was almost crying myself when I got home—to think that Luigi didn't want to see me. But then Mamma Lena told me. She said it was not my fault. She said that when I was a little girl she had promised me to Zia Teresa as a wife for Luigi, and now Luigi had to die and couldn't have me. He was sorry he couldn't have me, that was all. And me, I was sorry too. I would have liked Luigi for a husband. And I was sorry he had to die. I came home one month and my cousin Luigi died in the next month. And every night after I was in my bed I was saying prayers for all those good friends who had died.

It was in the court of the mill at noon that I had to get all the news of the last three years. I was asking what happened to this one, and what happened to this one, and the women and girls were telling me. "And Ugo," I asked. "Does Ugo still make magic in the square?" I remembered Beppo taking me to see that man when I was a little girl. He used to make the men die laughing—the things he did.

Once the men were all standing around laughing at Ugo and a poor farmer came up with a load of hay on his back. Ugo said, "Hey you! What are you doing with that big snake on your back?" And when the poor man saw the snake he dropped his hay and ran. Ugo said, "Just what I wanted!" And he took the hay home to feed his own cow. But when Mamma Lena found out that I had been watching the magic she almost broke the stick on me. She said making magic was a mortal sin. (But I don't think that man was so bad. He was just full of mischief.)

The women and girls all laughed when I asked about Ugo. They said, "Oh, that man was so bad that the city got sick and tired of putting him to jail and letting him out again, so they bought him the ticket and sent him to America."

Then the women all started telling about one poor man who had come back from America and had won in the court against his landlord. "Those poor men from the village who go to America, they get smart," the women said. "They're not so afraid anymore." That poor man had come back and planted his field and when the grain was threshed and dried he had put it in the sacks and taken it to the landlord. All the good barley and nearly everything else the poor man raised on his field had to go to the landlord for rent. There was very little left.

So the landlord looked at the grain and he said, "No, I don't want it that way. Take it back and dry it two more days on the threshing floor."

And the poor man talked back. He said, "It was three days on the threshing floor. Three days is enough. Do you want it, or don't you want it?"

And the landlord said no. So the poor man took the grain to the mill and had it ground, then he took it home to his family. So then the landlord went to court to have the poor man punished, and everyone in Bugiarno thought the poor man would be hung. But in the end the judge said the poor man was right — there was all the proof. The grain had been on the threshing floor three days and was nice and dry. And the landlord lost!

"That's what America does for the poor!" the women said. And I began wishing that I could go to America too.

Another thing had happened while I was away. The son of Signor Rossi, the owner of the other silk mill, had married the daughter of the Japanese silk merchant. Those children used to play together when they were young so when they grew up they fell in love and now they were married. And for his daughter's *dote* — for her dowry — the Japanese merchant said he would give the son of Signor Rossi a silk factory in Japan. But the son said he didn't want a Japanese silk factory. He said the Japanese didn't know how to make silk like the Italians. So the father said he would build a factory just like the Italian and that he would pay for six of the best silkmakers in Bugiarno to go there and teach the Japanese women how to make silk in the Italian way. And so those girls had gone there and their mothers were getting three lire a day for all the time they were gone. And nothing could happen to them, because that terrible strict boss, Pietro, had gone with them. When those girls came home they told me that they were like prisoners with that Pietro. He pulled the shades on the train to the boat so they couldn't see where they were going. And in Japan they were locked up in the same building with the mill — they couldn't even go outside to take in some fresh air. In the mill they were dressed up nice in white embroidered aprons and stood behind the Japanese women and showed them with their hands how to reel the silk. And the Japanese women learned good how to make the silk, but they couldn't learn to sit down on the stools. They were used to sitting on the floor with their legs folded under, so they kept folding them under on the stools too. The Italian girls would take their feet and put them down on the bars, but as soon as they weren't looking, the Japanese had their legs under them again. They *couldn't* learn to sit down! Me, I never could sit on my legs like that — I get the cramps.

And right after I came home from Canaletto I heard about the plays the new priest was making in the hall behind Signora Delida's hotel. When I heard about the plays I couldn't wait to see them. And because they were for the church Mamma Lena gave me a few *centesimi* and let me go with Zia Teresa. Oh, those plays were good! I was wishing that I could be in them. But only the higher up young men and girls took the parts. None of the poor were in them. Carlo, our mailman, he was the best actor of all. He made everyone die laughing. But when he went up on the stage he didn't say the part he had learned from the book — he said anything that came into his head. And Father Bruschetti was scolding him because when he was talking like that the other actors didn't know how to do their parts. That young priest was wonderful the way he taught the young men and girls and made the scenery and everything. But the priests in the other villages didn't like it that everyone was coming to Bugiarno to see the plays of Father Bruschetti. So they complained to the *arciprete*, or someone. They said it was not right — it was a sin — for a priest to go up on the stage and show the young girls how to act. They complained so much that the *arciprete* had to send Father Bruschetti away. So then we got Father Pietro who was so old that he couldn't hear our confessions. He couldn't hear anything we said to him. Oh, I was sorry when Father Bruschetti went away! And later I was more sorry still that we had a priest who couldn't hear!

When there was no more news in the court at noon I started entertaining the women and girls with the funny songs and funny stories, just like at Canaletto. I was making everyone laugh. So then the young men in the *osteria* heard about it and wanted me to entertain them too. But Mamma Lena said no. And I was just as glad because that Santino was always there watching me. Mamma Lena said that man was the head of a gang that was working in the irrigation ditches. He had been working many years in France and had two thousand lire saved up in the bank. That man was always talking nice to Mamma Lena, but he never said anything to me. He knew that I didn't like him.

14

CATERINA was big — almost a young lady! — when I came back from Canaletto. And she was crazy for the boys. Evenings and Sundays when I had to help Mamma Lena in the *osteria* Caterina would come and help too, so she could talk to the guards and other young men. Me, I didn't dare talk to them — Mamma Lena would kill me. But Mamma Lena didn't say anything to Caterina. Of course, sometimes when Mamma Lena couldn't see, I would smile at the young men too — I couldn't help it the way they were talking to me. And I had begun to like the boys myself. I was not yet fourteen but I was big for my age. And soon I discovered that many young men coming Sunday afternoons to see Mamma Lena were coming to ask if they could marry me — if she would promise me to them for a wife. I could tell those young men the way they stood there, and if Mamma Lena wasn't looking I would smile. It made me happy that they liked me. "But you're too young," Mamma Lena would say to them all. "You have to go for your military service and Rosa can't wait for you."

Even Pompeo came. I was hoping Mamma Lena would say yes to Pompeo. Pompeo was a grand artist. When he was a little boy going off to the hills as a shepherd he was drawing pictures on the rocks with charcoal. When he got bigger he painted pictures in the courts and the people would bring lanterns and flowers to decorate and the priest would come and bless them. His pictures were so beautiful that one priest from another place got the money from someplace and sent him to school in Milan to be the real artist. He was not finished yet, but summers he came home to work in the fields. He still talked slow like a shepherd, and he was so kind everybody liked him. Mamma Lena liked him too. But she said no — he was too young — I couldn't wait for him.

I couldn't believe it when Signor Cosimo came to ask for me. He was not one of the poor. His father, a rich man in another village, had sent him to the drugstore in Bugiarno to learn that business. I knew he liked me, because one day when I went there to get some medicine to put on my sore hands he had come and put it on for me himself. And he was so gentle. But I never thought that a high man like that would ask to marry me! He was twenty years old already and didn't have to go for military service because his father had paid a poor boy to go three extra years in his place. I was sure Mamma Lena would say yes to him. But she didn't. I could see by the way he turned and went out the door. So I ran to her and asked why she had said no to him too.

"I want to marry Signor Cosimo!" I said. "Then I will not be so poor!"

"The mother knows best," said Mamma Lena. "You can't trust a man from another village. And a rich man like that — what does he want with a poor girl like you? Probably he would make you his slave."

One Sunday afternoon Caterina came and teased, "Oh, Rosa, there's going to be a dance on the threshing floor, with a man to play the concertina. Tell Mamma Lena we are going to Sunday school and vespers and let us go!" That cement floor they used for threshing was a wonderful place to dance. I used to go there with Beppo when I was a little girl. No one could play the concertina like Beppo. It would be nice just to hear the music. I hurried and washed all the dishes without Mamma Lena's telling me, then I put on my sailor dress and leather shoes and took a little shawl for my head. I still didn't know if I was going to church or going to the dance, but Mamma Lena thought I was going to church and didn't say anything. On the way to the square Caterina teased some more. "All the nice young men will be there! The other girls can go, why can't we? We won't dance — we'll just watch. Come on, Rosa!" To go to the dance when Mamma Lena thought I was going to the church — no, I couldn't! But then I did — I started running down the road to the threshing floor, with Caterina following.

When we came to the gate of that court we could see all the young men in there and a lot of girls too. The floor was swept clean and there were seats along the side. Caterina was jumping with happiness, but I felt ashamed as we went in and sat down near the gate. I kept thinking about what the sisters would say. And Mamma Lena! Caterina began flirting with the young men and pretty soon one came over and asked her to dance. So then I was sitting there alone listening to the concertina and thinking of Beppo and suddenly a young man was standing before me. I knew him from some place, but I couldn't think who he was.

"Rosa," he said, and he was smiling at me, "don't you remember me? We were in the first communion together, and you hit me with a snowball." Oh, of course! It was Remo! But he was a young man now. I felt excited that he was talking to me. He was different entirely from the other boys. His talk was more gentle and he looked so pretty with his little sideburns and nice gray eyes and white teeth.

"Sure I remember you," I said.

"But I think you've been away. I haven't seen you for a long time. Where have you been, Rosa?"

"I've been at Canaletto — at the sisters' convent."

"Oh, but you're not going to be a nun, are you, Rosa?"

"No," I said. "I just went there to get some education and to work in the mill."

"Oh, that's good!" he said. And the way he said it I had to smile. "Can you dance? Will you dance with me?"

"I don't know how to dance with a man," I said. "I only know to dance with a girl."

"All right," he said. "If you can dance with a girl, you can dance with me." And he took my hand and pulled me out on the floor.

The man with the concertina was playing one of those lively tunes I loved best. And so we started to dance. The music got faster and faster and we were like whirling through air. Oh, Remo was a wonderful dancer! With him you didn't have to think at all where you were going — you just went, that was all.

"Oh, Rosa!" he said when the music stopped for a little, and we were both laughing and trying to catch our breath. "I have found my partner at last! I'm never going to dance with anyone else but you!"

"I like to dance with you too," I said.

Dancing with Remo made me tingle all over, like once in Milan when bugles announced the king. I didn't even notice what the other people were doing — I didn't know it when everyone had stopped dancing but us and were just watching and clapping. I didn't hear the ringing of the *benedizione*. Caterina had to come and tell me that we would be caught if we didn't go home.

The next noon I was eating my lunch with the other girls at the mill and I heard someone calling my name. And there, just inside the gate, was Bianca, the cousin of Remo, who worked in the *filanda* of Signor Rossi. Everyone said that Bianca was in love with Remo herself. Maybe Bianca didn't like it that I had danced with Remo on the threshing floor.

"Rosa!" she said, as I came up to her, and she was all out of breath from running. "Remo wants me to tell you. He said yesterday he danced with you and he fell in love with you and he wants to marry you. He is going to ask your mother. But he wants to know if you like him too. Do you like him too, Rosa? And he wants to know if he can come to the mill nights after work and walk home with you?"

My heart started fluttering so and my face got so red that I had to look down at the bread in my hands. "Yes, Bianca," I said "I like him too."

The next night when I came out of the mill, sure enough, there was Remo waiting for me. The women and girls all knew about my dancing with him and that he had fallen in love. "Run along, Rosa," they laughed. "We won't tell Mamma Lena." So I went up to him and smiled, and he smiled back.

It was just growing dark as we crossed the square and walked down the narrow road to the old *palazzo*. Remo was older than me — four or five years older — but he was talking to me with as much respect as if I was a woman already. We didn't know very much what we were saying because our eyes were talking something else. "I'm a *carrettiere*," he said. "I have a horse and wagon and am my own boss. I carry things for stores and for rich people back and forth from Milan." Then he told me things I already knew — that his mother was a widow and sold fruit in the square and that when his father died he had gone to work like the poor. "Next year," he said, "I will be nineteen. If I draw a low number I will go right away for my military service. Then in three years I will come back and marry you." And he was asking about the *istituto* and what I had learned from the sisters. And we were both laughing and laughing — not because there was anything to laugh at, but because we were happy. When we came to my gate I told him he must leave, but he said no — how could he leave when he had just found me? He was going to come in too, but he would wait a few minutes so Mamma Lena would not know we had come together. I was afraid to look up from my soup when he came in. He sat down at the end of the other table and ordered wine. And he kept ordering wine all evening. And Mamma Lena was glad because she was making more money. She never even thought that he came with me.

So after that he came in every night after we had walked home together from the mill. And soon he became a friend with Mamma Lena and came one Sunday afternoon to ask if she would promise me to him.

"But you still have to go for your military service," said Mamma Lena. "Three years is a long time to wait. Rosa is big for her age and too pretty. It's better if she's married and safe."

"In three years Rosa will still be young — only sixteen or seventeen years," Remo said.

"And Rosa is stubborn and willful," said Mamma Lena. "She needs someone older to control her. You love her too much — you would let her have her own way."

"I am the man," said Remo. "She would do what I said."

I had to smile. Of course I would do what Remo said. I would do anything he wanted. "Oh, Madonna, don't let Mamma Lena say no!" I was praying.

"Well I don't know," said Mamma Lena. "Maybe, but I don't promise, Remo. I must wait and see."

And now that Remo was so well acquainted in the *osteria* he got bolder. He would come in and sit right across from me when I was eating my supper and when no one could see he would push his feet way over to mine. So then I would slip my feet from my wooden soles and put them on his and the leather of his shoes was so thin that I could feel the warmth of his body. At such times it was like the electric going through us and we couldn't look up or speak. But that loving with our feet was the only loving we could do.

One Saturday night when I came from the mill Remo said, "Oh, Rosa, there's going to be a dance in the hall tonight and I bought the tickets already. We're going to go."

"But Remo!" I said. "You know Mamma Lena won't let me go!"

"Don't tell Mamma Lena. Wait till Mamma Lena is asleep, then come. The dance will last long into the night."

"How can I come without Mamma Lena's catching me? Her bed is right next to the door."

"Didn't you say the window is over your bed? I'm going to tell *Signore* to put a ladder to your window after Mamma Lena goes to bed. Then when she's asleep, you come." And all evening in the *osteria* his eyes kept pleading.

He left early and I ran upstairs. I knelt on my bed and unlatched the window and pushed it open, then shut it again. It creaked just in the beginning. If I left it a little open — so — no one could hear it. Quickly I got my sailor dress and leather shoes from my chest, rolled them in a bundle, and put them under my pillow. Then stepping out of my wooden soles I crawled into bed and lay there trembling and holding my breath. I had made a big sin when I went to the threshing floor and danced when Mamma Lena thought I was in church, but to go down a ladder in the night and go to a dance hall, that would be terrible! No, I mustn't even think of such a thing! Why had Remo asked me! But maybe I *could* do it without Mamma Lena catching me? And how disappointed Remo would be if I didn't come. He had bought the tickets already and would lose all that money. No one in the world could dance like Remo! I could dance with him the rest of my life and never get tired. Why was it wrong? Why wouldn't Mamma Lena let me dance with a boy? Mamma Lena was too strict! I hated Mamma Lena with her scowling eyes and stiff joints! Why couldn't Mamma Lena be round and jolly like Zia Teresa! Oh, no, Madonna, don't listen to me — I didn't mean it! I love Mamma Lena, and You wanted me to stay with her so I will get the strong religion and be saved for heaven. And she is right — there *is* a devil inside me that makes me do the things I shouldn't.

Mamma Lena was coming up the steps outside. I listened as the door opened and closed. Then I knew she was taking off her skirt and wooden soles and climbing into bed in the dark. For a long time everything was quiet. Then I heard a thud against my window sill. Maybe Mamma Lena had heard it too. I lifted my head. But no, I could tell by her breathing, Mamma Lena was asleep. Slowly I sat up and pushed the window. And sure enough, there was the ladder. And there at the bottom was *Signore* motioning for me to come. I must not keep him waiting. Quickly I threw him the bundle, then I started to climb out myself, but the cornstalks in my mattress made such a noise that I stopped halfway. Mamma Lena moved, but she didn't wake up. So then I tried again and this time I didn't stop until I was out on the ladder and closing the window behind me. At the foot of the ladder *Signore* gave me my clothes and I ran into the toolroom and put them on. Then he opened the gate. "*Grazie, Signore! Grazie!*" I whispered as I went out. And there was Remo waiting for me. And oh, he was happy! I didn't need any light to tell me that. He took my sore hand and we started to run. We ran till we came to the square. Then we let go our hands and walked across to the inn and back through the court to the dance hall.

I didn't see any other of the very poor in there, and I was glad, for there would be no one to tell Mamma Lena. But several boys knew Remo. "Remo! *Benvenuto! Benvenuto!*" they shouted. "Welcome!" "Now we'll see some good dancing!"

There was a real orchestra in there. For a few minutes while we were getting our breath from running we stood and listened to the music and watched the other dancers. Then Remo led me out onto the floor and we were off. Me and the music and Remo! I forgot everything else in the world. Sometime, in the middle of the dancing, the manager announced a prize for the last couple on the floor. But we paid no attention to him. We just kept dancing, with our whole heart entirely. The other couples kept dropping out and dropping out. And pretty soon we were the last ones. But still we didn't stop. "*Bravo!*" the others were calling. "*Bravo! Bravo!*" And I was praying the Madonna never to let it end. But at last the music got so fast we could no more get our breath. We couldn't keep up! Panting we came to a stop, but we had to hold on to each other to keep from hitting the spinning floor. Then here came up the manager holding out a beautiful silk shawl with red roses around the edge and long fringe.

"Well, what am I going to do?" he said. "I must tear it in two and give half to each one?"

"No," laughed Remo. "Give it to her. She's going to be mine anyway. I'm going to marry my partner — my Rosa." So there I had to take that beautiful thing and I didn't know what to do with it. I couldn't let Mamma Lena see it. I'd have to give it to Zia Teresa to keep for me.

It was dark on the road to the old *palazzo* and there was no one around. When we came to the gate Remo drew me to him and held me in his arms. (He did not kiss me. A man was not allowed to kiss a girl until she was his wife.) For a little I just stood there feeling the nearness of his body, and I was happy. Then all at once I began to shiver. I didn't know for what but I was ashamed and I was afraid. I couldn't stand it! Suddenly I slipped out of his arms, pushed open the gate, and closed it quickly behind me. Then I put my ear to the crack and stood there shaking and listening.

"*Addio*, Rosa," he whispered, but I did not answer and I did not move. "*Addio*, Rosa." And after a little I heard his footsteps down the road and knew that he was gone.

I left my best clothes and the prize shawl under the bench in the toolroom and climbed back up the ladder and into bed without Mamma Lena waking up. But I couldn't go to sleep. I had fooled Mamma Lena but I couldn't fool the Madonna. The Madonna knew everything. She even knew what I was thinking. I took out my rosary and tried to pray. "*Ave Maria. Ave Maria. Gratia plena.*" But I was thinking of Remo and how Remo could dance better than anyone else in the world. Why was Remo a boy and me a girl? Why hadn't God made us all alike? "*Ora pro nobis peccatoribus, nunc et in hora mortis nostrae.*" And then I began to pray the Madonna not to let me die before Saturday night so I could go to confession and have God's forgiveness. I would confess everything — even how I had stood in Remo's arms. "*Ave Maria, gratia plena* . . . Oh, Madonna, don't let me die before Saturday night!"

Another time I deceived Mamma Lena and didn't get caught — not at the time.

Ever since I was a little girl I had heard the story of the Madonna of the Black Water. Once many years ago a poor wagoner was going through the woods near San Martino and the wheels of his wagon went down in the mud and the wagon wouldn't come out. That poor man and his horse, they were pulling and struggling and doing this and doing that but the wagon wouldn't come out. They stayed there for about an hour and the poor man didn't know what to do. And there beside the road was a little shrine with a Madonna in. "Oh, Madonna," said the man. "What am I going to do? You've got to help me!" And just as he said that, the horse gave a hard pull, and the wagon came out of the hole. So when the people heard of the wonderful miracle that little statue made, they began calling Her the "Madonna of the Black Water" and they made a church around Her right there in the middle of the woods. And every year they made a big *festa* to honor Her. Papa Lur had promised to take me there, but he never did. I had never seen that little Madonna, and this summer — the summer I danced with Remo — all the girls I knew were going to that *festa* and I wanted to go too. But when I asked Mamma Lena, she said no.

"You think I don't know how it is?" she said. "I was a young girl myself once and I know how it is. The girls and the boys all walk in the woods together! No, you can not go!"

All week the girls talked of nothing else. "You've got to go, Rosa!" they said. "Forget Mamma Lena! She's too strict!"

Sunday morning after mass they were ready to start. "Oh, Rosa, all the boys are going! If you can't come for all day, come for the afternoon anyway! We told Remo you will be there, so now he's coming too."

I couldn't remember making up my mind, but when I got home I knew I was going. I hurried and changed my dress and helped serve the men in the *osteria*. Then I washed the dishes and did everything to please Mamma Lena. And when the rush was over I ran up and put on my sailor dress again and grabbed a little shawl for my head.

"I am going to Sunday school and vespers," I said to Mamma Lena when I came down, but I was afraid to look in her face. And I could tell by the way she nodded that she was glad not to be teased any more about the *festa*.

At the cemetery I stopped long enough to take off my shoes and fasten up my skirt so I could go faster across the fields and through the river. But I was so afraid I'd come late for the procession that I didn't stop again until I could hear all the people and see the booths and the colored banners.

"Rosa! Rosa!" the other girls and boys all shouted when they saw me. And sure enough, there was Remo in a little round hat and nice sash.

"That's good you came, Rosa!" he said. "Now we'll have a wonderful time." And he took out a clean handkerchief and wiped the sweat and dust from my face.

There were crowds of people laughing and talking and gambling at the booths in front of the church. There was one of those peepshows too. But the boys and girls from Bugiarno were going to a little place to eat back in the woods.

"The boys arranged it already," the girls said. "We're going to have a good meal."

When I heard that — that they were going back into the woods just as Mamma Lena had said, I didn't know what to do. "Come on, Rosa! Come on! We're going to have the *minestra* and wine and everything! The boys have paid already. Remo paid for you."

Why had I come! Why hadn't I listened to Mamma Lena! It was a long, dark building like a stable, and men from the city were making the soup and pouring the wine. You could never trust men from the city. Maybe they would put something in our wine to make us drunk.

Oh, Madonna, help me! And so we started to sit down, the girls all together and the boys all together, when here came the explosion of the fireworks.

"Mamma Mia!" the boys shouted. "The procession is starting!" And everybody jumped up and ran. And right there I saw my chance. No one was watching me — everyone was running to the church. I hid behind some trees and waited until they were gone. Then I started running the other way through the woods. I started running as fast as I could go, back to Bugiarno. "Look how the Madonna helped me," I thought. "Right when I was praying Her, She sent those fireworks — She gave me my chance!"

It was a long way through those woods and once it started to get dark and I got the scare — I thought it was night already. But then the sun came out again — it was just playing tricks on me, hiding behind the clouds. And so I came across the river again and there I could see the church tower. Oh, how beautiful it looked! But I didn't stop running. I didn't stop till I came to the cemetery. Then I put on my shoes and let down my skirt. And as I came down the little road to the square, between the trees, the *benedizione* started ringing. I was just in time! Vespers was just over! The Madonna of the Black Water had made another miracle. Mamma Lena would never know.

Mamma Lena was so busy she didn't even look up when I came home. But about nine o'clock at night, here coming into the *osteria* were all the boys who had been at the *festa* — ten or fifteen boys. They had come to find out what had happened to me. I put my finger on my mouth and rolled my eyes toward Mamma Lena. They understood and sat down and ordered wine, but they were all whispering and motioning to ask me what had happened — where I had gone. They knew how strict Mamma Lena was and they didn't want to make trouble, but *Mamma Mia*, what stupid actors! Mamma Lena was too busy — she didn't notice. But Santino at the end of the second table was listening and watching. He was like the Devil, waiting for me and reading my guilt. I could feel my face red and I was grinding inside trying to make those boys go home.

The next noon I learned from the other girls how they had come home after dark and all got the beatings from their mothers. Even

Caterina. But thanks to the Madonna of the Black Water I had not been caught. And at the end of the day there was Remo waiting for me like always. "Oh, Rosa," he said and he was smiling into my eyes. "You did right to run home. You are really a good girl. I love you even more than before." And I was happy and thanking that little statue Madonna.

Winter was coming. The days grew shorter and the evenings grew longer and Remo grew more gentle and more loving. Every night he was waiting when I came from the mill. And sometimes when it was awful cold and storming so no one could see, he would take off his coat and put it on me. He was afraid I would catch cold with nothing but a shawl and my dress soaking wet from the steam. Oh, it was nice to be a young girl when you were in love! I could forget the hard work and sore hands when I thought about Remo and how we would both be sitting in the stable in the evening listening to the same stories and songs. Of course he had to stay down in the straw with the animals and other men and I had stay up with the women, but we were together anyway.

Christmas was nice too. The poor people never gave any presents — how could they? — but the people started getting ready sometime before anyway. They brought pine branches and piled them in a mountain before the church. The old women said that the fir tree could burn green like that because Saint Joseph had blessed it. They said that the night Jesus was born it was so cold Saint Joseph didn't know what to do. The Blessed Virgin and the Baby Jesus would freeze. He couldn't find any wood so he was striking two stones together to burn some straw and a little fir tree that was standing there caught fire and burned the whole night and kept the Virgin and the Baby warm. And Saint Joseph was so happy that he blessed that little tree. And ever after, that kind of tree can burn green and the old people called it the "Tree of Saint Joseph." Maybe that's just a story, but it's true that no other tree can burn green.

Christmas Eve night Mamma Lena kept a little fire in the fireplace and everybody dressed in their best clothes and waited for midnight. And us girls and boys were allowed to talk together and have a good time and nobody scolded. Everyone's heart was full of love. Then a little before midnight we all went to the square. Me, I walked with Remo, and Caterina went with Emanuele, one of the guards. Toni walked with us too because he was too young to go with a girl. It was so cold in the square we all had to keep moving, but we were reverent anyway. Then just as the bell tolled midnight the priest came out with three candles on a long handle and lighted the branches. In silence the people watched and when the fire had burned to the ground we all went in for the Christmas mass. After church everyone was happy — Jesus was born. And everyone went home to drink the white wine and eat cakes. Me and Caterina and Zia Teresa helped Mamma Lena serve all the people who came to the *osteria*. Then we sat down too and ate. And when some of the old women asked, I started singing the beautiful Christmas songs from Canaletto. Without standing up I sang. And Remo sitting there across was looking at me like I was really the Blessed Virgin singing to the Baby Jesus.

In no time at all it was the first of February. On the second of February I would be fourteen (or maybe it was only thirteen) years old. That night as we walked home Remo gave me a present. He said it was for my birthday. Imagine a poor girl like me getting a birthday present! I had never had one in my life before, and this was a beautiful present — little jet earrings with a band of gold around them. Oh, I was happy. Then came the season of carnival, just before Lent, and for the first time I was allowed to dance with the masqueraders when they came into the stables. The poor must not know who those rich young men were — it was a crime to guess — but I guessed them all anyway. I knew right away when six came in with a bugle and a concertina that the tall one was Signor Cosimo. And sure enough he came and danced all three dances with me. And when the masks left and threw nuts and sweets in the girls' laps I picked mine up and found a ring. It was a gold snake with its head in its mouth and a diamond eye. It was the ring Signor Cosimo wore on his little finger. But the next noon when I ran to the drugstore to give it back to him, he said, "No, Rosa, that mask was not me. The ring is not mine. You'll have to keep it." And I could tell that he really loved me — that he was not fooling. But I was glad Mamma Lena had said no. I would rather marry Remo than the richest man in the world.

Then came Litany Week in the month of May and every morning before daylight we went in a procession to the fields while the priest blessed the ground. Way in the back of the line we couldn't hear what the people in front were singing, so we were all singing to a different saint, but it sounded nice anyway. I was walking with Remo, and Caterina was walking with Emanuele and Toni. In the Litany Week you made the plenary indulgence: if you died in this time you would go straight to heaven. "Yes," I thought, "probably the old people would, but not us young ones!" We were reverent in the Communion afterwards, but in the procession we had more a good time than anything else. We would have to stay in purgatory a little while anyway. One morning as we walked to the fields Remo brought me another present. He brought me a beautiful little prayer book with a velvet cover and gold letters. I told him I would keep it as long as I lived. (And I did too. I have it yet.) Yes, it was good to be a young girl in the springtime in Bugiarno. There were more men than girls and I was not one of the homely ones. And every night after work Remo was waiting for me.

But then one night I came out of the mill and Remo was not there. For three days nobody knew where Remo was or what had happened. But then on the fourth day Bianca came running with news at lunchtime. Some men had found his wagon broken down on the road to Milan. One of the wheels had come off. "His wagon was packed full of china," Bianca sobbed. "And most of the china got broken! His mother thinks and my father thinks too that he ran away to not go to jail! That china belonged to a count!"

Two weeks went by and still there was no word from Remo. Maybe he was gone forever. Maybe I would never see him again. Maybe he had no place to sleep and nothing to eat. Maybe he was already in jail. The sick, tight feeling inside of me hurt more than my sore hands as I caught the heads of the cocoons and twisted the thread through the eye on the basin. But then one noon Bianca brought me a letter. She said it had come inside one to her father, Remo's uncle. I stood there trembling, looking at my name, and waiting for Bianca to go. But Bianca was waiting for me to read it. So I broke the seal and opened

[136

the paper. And there it was just like hearing Remo talk to me. He called me his *cara sposa*, his dear wife-to-be. He was in France and had found work, but he could never pay back for the china of a count. He could not come home and was in despair because he could not see me, his dance partner, his wife-to-be. But he would save all his money so sometime he could send for me.

"My father and Remo's mother are giving all the money they have for a lawyer," said Bianca. "Maybe a lawyer can save Remo in the court so he can come home without going to jail."

When Bianca was gone I read the letter again, then I put it inside my chemise next to my skin. And that night as soon as I got home I wrote a letter back. Remo was still alive and still loved me!

15

A FEW weeks after Remo disappeared a stranger came to Bugiarno one Sunday looking for silkmakers for his new mill in Germignaga. He was going in all the courts talking to the mothers. He said he would give one *lira* and sixty *centesimi* a day. For that much money everybody was signing up, even some of the older women that didn't have husbands and children. So when he came in our court Mariana came and asked Mamma Lena if she would let me go. If I could go, Caterina could go too.

"It's twice as much as we get for them here," said Mariana.

"Yes," said Mamma Lena. "And if they are locked up, as this man says, they will be safer than here. Here they are always talking and smiling with the young men in the *osteria*."

"I have sixty girls already," said the man. "If I get one hundred I will hire a wagon to come once a week and bring the baskets of food from the mothers."

So Mamma Lena said yes. (Oh, when Signor Rossi and Signor Alberto learned how that man from Germignaga had taken nearly all their silkmakers, they were like wild! They almost had to close their mills.)

We all came on a wagon to Germignaga and the boss took us to a

[138

big stone building about two miles out in the woods near Lago Maggiore. That was where we were going to live. There were a few farm girls living there already. At first the boss had all farm girls but they always left when there was work in the fields, so he liked better to have us girls from the village. "In the morning the farm girls will show you the way to the mill," said the boss. Then he had the man on the wagon unload our baskets, and he went.

The woman who took care of the building, the *portinaia*, showed us where to leave our baskets in a big room downstairs that had a fireplace for cooking. Then she took us upstairs to let us choose our beds. The whole upstairs was one room with rows of double beds made of planks. Me and Caterina chose a big bed by the window where we could look out and see the beautiful mountains and the lake. It was just like around Canaletto here — beautiful and beautiful — but there were no sisters to make us do this and do this, and no Mamma Lena. At night the *portinaia* locked the door, but she didn't watch what we did. She had a little room downstairs and she stayed down there with her husband. We could do what we pleased.

The first morning when we came into the mill in Germignaga, the boss was there with his book and started calling the names.

"Cortesi, Rosa!" — he called me the first one.

"*Presente!*" I said.

"Come on," he said. "You're number one. You take the first place." So I had to go up and take the first place in the row making silk. And there he had those nice big yellow cocoons that almost unwound themselves in the water.

That boss was young and I could tell by the way he looked in my eyes and smiled that he liked me best of all. But he was good to all the girls. What his name was we never knew, and we didn't know if he's married — nothing. (Not like now in America! The American girls know everything about their boss — entirely everything!) He used to come in with his book after they tested the silk in the proving room, but he always passed me by. He never found one little fault with my silk. He would just smile at me and go on to the next one.

"Oh, yes," the girls said. "The boss is in love with Rosa!"

But one woman, "the Redhead," said, "Rosa's mother sends him the wine, that's why he likes her and never finds fault with her silk!" How could Mamma Lena send him the wine? She didn't even know him! The Redhead was jealous because the boss smiled at me and was always scolding her and making her lose some pay when he tested her silk.

"Don't listen to her!" Caterina would say. "She's jealous, that's all. She doesn't know how to make silk and the boss knows it too. That's why he's all the time scolding." Everyone said that the Redhead's husband joined one of those gangs and went away to America just to get away from her scolding. And probably it was true, because he never sent back for her. But I knew she was angry with me because I was always telling stories and entertaining the girls at night when she wanted to sleep. Every night we were keeping the lamp burning and knitting and telling stories until three or four o'clock morning.

"*Sangue della Madonna!*" she would scream, jumping up from her bed. "How can anyone work without sleep! Keep still, do you hear! Keep still! *Per l'amore di Dio*, you are driving me mad!"

At first when the Redhead yelled like that I would stop in the middle of a story. But the girls wouldn't keep still anyway and they teased so much that I learned to pay no attention and kept on telling the story. So the Redhead blamed me for everything. Every time the boss scolded her for her silk she said it was my fault because I wouldn't let her sleep. And then she was angry with all us girls because we were laughing and talking back to some young men who were making the railroad along the road to the mill. And one day when the foreman of all those men came and asked the *portinaia* what my name was and where I lived because he wanted to ask my mother if he could marry me, the Redhead screamed with laughter. "I suppose you believed him!" she said. But I didn't answer. It wouldn't have been the first time a high man had asked to marry me.

Saturday noon, that was the best time of all. The boss let us stop work so the farm girls would have the time to walk to their homes for Sunday. And the girls from Bugiarno, we would run down the road and wait for Ernesto, the man who brought all our baskets from home on his wagon. By Saturday everybody's food was gone. And I got better than the others — sometimes a little bag of rice in with the potatoes and black bread, or a cabbage, or even a piece of cheese, and a few *centesimi* wrapped in a cloth. Mamma Lena was good to me!

We each had our own pan and were supposed to cook for ourselves in that fireplace downstairs. But with only fifteen chains, some of us were waiting until midnight to get our supper. So I got an idea and told Caterina. We carried our potatoes to work and put them in the dirty water with the worms and cocoons. So at night when we emptied our basins there were our potatoes all cooked and ready to eat. And when they were peeled you couldn't taste the stink of the water at all. They were good. So then everybody cooked their potatoes at the mill and the boss never knew it. For breakfast we carried a piece of black bread to work and stopped for about half an hour at nine o'clock to eat it. Then at noon the boss had one man in the court make a big kettle of soup and we stood all in line like soldiers to get it. And there was a lady there to mark our names down so the boss could take it off from our wages. But it cost very little and that way the boss knew that we had one good meal a day anyway. Yes, that boss was good to us. One day he even spoke to me. The day I came to work with my face all blood. Some nights when we only got one hour or two hours' sleep — we were staying up until three or four o'clock and walking to work at five — we were walking with our eyes shut, asleep. So I was walking asleep like that and I fell over a pile of stones in the road and cut my face. When the boss saw me come in he said, "Why, Rosa, what happened?" But me I was ashamed to answer — a high man like that talking to a poor girl like me!

Only one Sunday Caterina and me walked to the town Luino to go to mass. After then, because Caterina wasn't going, I didn't go either. Caterina didn't care what anybody said and if she didn't want to go to church she didn't go. She didn't have the strong religion like me, and she didn't like the priests very much. So because she was cool to the priests and to religion, I let mine go a little too. Instead of going to mass we would go down to the lake and wash our clothes and our hair and when no one was looking we would take off our clothes and wash ourselves. It was all nice woods around. "Caterina *Matta*," the others were calling Caterina — "Crazy Caterina." But I liked her so much because she was so lively and so jolly, and I was all the time with her. (She's in America too, now, but she lives in Joliet.)

One week about nine of us girls went on a pilgrimage to the Madonna del Monte at Varese. That's the Madonna that came to life for the stupid, Gionin, in Bugiarno. So I wanted to go there to that *festa* too. We left about two o'clock Saturday afternoon to walk to that mountain, but when we came to the foot of the mountain a terrible storm came. It was night but we saw a little light in one house so we went there and asked the man if we could stay in his stable. The stable was not used anymore so he said yes and opened the big door and we went in and put up the two-by-four to lock the door after us. So we were in there in the dark on the straw and here came some drunken men, a couple of drunks, and tried to get in. We started crying and screaming from the scare. For about one hour we were hollering and crying and those men were punching the door. But then they got tired and went away. So we came out and started walking again in the rain and about four o'clock we came up the mountain to the Church of the Madonna del Monte — just in time to hear the first mass. And we were starved and so tired and so scared. (If we were nine American girls we would have opened that door and broke the necks to those men, but we girls in Italy, we were scared. We had a terrible scare!) So then we bought some figs and bread and sat down by the church and ate breakfast. And we stayed for the procession and walked all around the mountain to those little chapels. But we couldn't stay for the fireworks. We took off our shoes and our stockings and walked all night back. Think how free and happy we were — us girls in Germignaga! We never had it like that in our life before. But think how tired we were too. We came home four o'clock morning and at five o'clock we were in the mill and had to work all day with our eyes falling shut. When the boss saw us come in he said, "Where are the girls who went to the Madonna del Monte? Did you all come back all right?"

Here one day, a few weeks after I first came in Germignaga, the boss gave me a letter. It was a letter from Remo. But how I got that letter I don't know yet. It was addressed "Rosa Cortesi, at the silk mill, on Lago Como." I had written to him just before I left Bugiarno and told him I was going someplace else to work and I thought it was on Lago Como. But I guess all those bosses in the silk mills know each other and ask if anyone has a girl by that name. Remo said in his letter that he was still in France, but his mother and his uncle had got the lawyer and the lawyer was going to court about the china. If only that china had not belonged to a count! What chance did a poor man have in the court against a count? Then he told me again how much he loved me and that some day he would send for me, if he couldn't come home to get me. I wrote a letter right back so he would know I'm in Germignaga. But I guess I didn't know how to address it, because he never got it.

So then after a couple of months I got another letter. This time Ernesto brought it when he came with our baskets from Bugiarno. Remo had come home. He had been so happy when he got the letter from his uncle telling him that he had won in the court. The judge had asked who had packed the china, and when he found out that the count had packed it himself, he said it was the count's own fault that it broke and he could get not one *centesimo*. But as soon as Remo had come home he had drawn the low number in the draft and so had to go off again for his military service. He had gone to Mamma Lena to ask her again if she would promise me to him — if she would let me wait until he came back from the military. And at first Mamma Lena didn't know what to say. But that Santino was there and listening, like always. And Santino said it would be a pity if we couldn't dance together anymore — if we couldn't win any more prize shawls. So then Remo had to tell about everything — Mamma Lena made him. And when Mamma Lena learned how we had deceived her she said no. "Never!" she said. "You helped Rosa deceive me, and you deceived me yourself! I will never let you marry Rosa!" So now Remo was in despair and asked what we could do. And when I read the letter, I was in despair too. And it was all the fault of that man Santino! How I hated him! I would hate him forever! And I began to wonder what Mamma Lena would do when I got home — to punish me for going down the ladder and to the dance hall. Probably Santino had told her about the *festa* too! I'd like to stay in Germignaga forever and never go home anymore.

[143

"Come on, Rosa! Don't pay any attention to her!" Caterina called. It was Sunday afternoon and all of us young girls had run ahead of the women to go to the *festa* in Germignaga. The Redhead was calling names at us and telling us we had to wait for the women to go with us. But since Caterina and the other girls kept on running I did too. When we came to the square a lot of boys started following us around and laughing and talking and we smiled back and were having a good time. So then we started to watch a fortune-teller. Fortune-tellers always came to Bugiarno when we had the *festa*, but Mamma Lena would never let me watch them. Fortune-telling and magic were terrible sins. It was a sin just to watch them. But there was no Mamma Lena to stop me here, so I listened with the others. And that old woman with her red cheeks and big earrings and all her bracelets and rings was wonderful. She looked in the people's hands and could see letters and long journeys and weddings and money and tears. In the young men's hands she could see beautiful girls, and in the girl's hands she could see young men. Probably she could tell me about Remo. I wanted to know about me and Remo more than anything else in the world! Could we ever get married? I pulled out my handkerchief that had my *centesimi* tied up in the corner. When I had untied it I gave one *centesimo* to Caterina and took one for myself. Then slowly I tied the knot again and put the handkerchief back inside my chemise. Even if it *was* a sin I had to know what was going to happen to me and Remo.

I was trembling when I sat down on the box in front of the old woman and stretched out my sore hands. And I trembled still more when she took them in hers and started examining my palms. "You are a beautiful girl and a good girl." That was not what I wanted to hear! I wanted to hear about Remo! "Here I see a long life. And here two long journeys." And sure enough, I could see them too! "And here's happiness. You will have happiness in the end. But first there is trouble — much trouble. And here is a beautiful young man. In the end you are going to marry this beautiful young man. In the end you are going to marry the young man you love." That was just what I had wanted to know — just what I wanted to hear! But how did that fortune-teller know about Remo and about the trouble we were in?

"*Grazie, signora!*" I said. "*Grazie molte!*" And not even the threats of the Redhead to tell Mamma Lena could spoil my joy.

The next week Gina, a farm girl, invited me and Caterina to go home with her Saturday noon and stay until Sunday night. There was going to be a dance on the threshing floor and the boys wanted more girls. The Redhead said she would tell our mothers if we went without an older woman.

"Maybe we should ask *her*?" I said to Caterina.

"Oh, to the Devil with her!" said Caterina. "She's only jealous because Gina didn't ask her too. Why should we let her go and spoil our fun? The farm girls go home alone every week. Why shouldn't we go too? Our mothers are not here to say no." And so on Saturday noon we started off alone for the country while the Redhead stood in the road behind yelling and scolding. Caterina and Gina just laughed, but me — I was trembling inside wondering what Mamma Lena would do if she knew. And so we walked that five miles with Gina to the farm. When we got there her mother told us to come in and sit down with the others and she gave us potatoes and milk and some sausage they made themselves. And at night we all three slept on Gina's straw mattress. The next afternoon we danced with all the farm girls and boys. But we didn't make any hit. We just danced, that was all, then came walking back five miles to Germignaga and two more miles to the house where we lived. And when we came upstairs in the middle of the night — the *portinaia* got up and unlocked the door for us — there was the Redhead standing in the doorway trying to keep us out and calling us bad names for staying out all one night and most of another and dancing with the boys.

"Just wait till your mothers know!" she said. But me, I was more afraid what Mamma Lena would do if she knew I had gone to the fortune-teller. Fortune-telling is a terrible sin!

More and more the Redhead was getting the scolding and losing some of her pay when her silk was tested. And then one Friday the boss told her to leave — that she didn't know how to make silk — and she could go back to Bugiarno with Ernesto the next day when he came with the wagon. Oh, that woman was mad! "Fifteen years I've been reeling the silk," she said, "and he tells me I don't know how! But to the young girls he just smiles! And it's all your fault!" she said to me. "How can anyone make silk without sleep! *Sangue della Madonna!* But I'll get even with you!" And so Ida, the Redhead, left. She went back to Bugiarno on the wagon with Ernesto. And we were all happy that we don't have to listen to her anymore.

But the next week on Saturday afternoon when we ran down the road to meet Ernesto there was no basket for me. Instead Ernesto brought a little package and the message from Mamma Lena that I must come home that same day on the wagon with him. When the girls heard that some of them were even crying, and I was crying too. And when I ran back to tell the boss, he said, "Couldn't you stay just another two months until the farm girls are through in the fields, Rosa?" Sure, I was more sorry than him that I had to leave, but when Mamma Lena said something I had to do it, that was all. But why had Mamma Lena sent for me? Why did I have to go home when the other girls could stay? But inside of me I knew — the Redhead had snitched to Mamma Lena, just like she said she would do.

So I was on that wagon with Ernesto and we were going a long time when we came to a little town and he stopped at an *osteria* to get some supper. I climbed out too and stood beside the horses to eat the black bread Mamma Lena had sent me. The near horse turned his head and looked — he wanted some too. I broke off a little piece and let him pick it up from my hand. It was funny the way he blew through his nose and dropped spit on my hand. So then I gave the other horse a piece. But I was too hungry to give the horses any more. I finished eating and climbed back into the wagon. It grew dark but still Ernesto didn't come back, so I laid down on the seat and went to sleep. About midnight I heard him coming. He had been drinking too much, I could tell. And as the wagon rattled off across the square he started singing — so happy that he didn't care if he woke up the whole town. But then he grew quiet again and we came into the dark woods and he got drunk — funny. He jumped up and grabbed me in his two arms. Oh, I had such a scare! I pushed him away and jumped out of the wagon and I was walking along behind in the black night. I didn't know what to do, alone in the dark woods with that drunk man, so I started praying the Madonna. When Ernesto heard me he stopped the horses

[146

and told me to get in — that he wouldn't bother me anymore. So I climbed in the back with the empty baskets. And right away the Madonna made that man go to sleep — I could hear him snoring. The horses took us home themselves. Oh, I was happy when the light of the morning came and I could see the tower of Bugiarno. As soon as we came into the square I jumped out and ran all the way home.

I was still shivering and shaking and half crying from the scare when I came into the court. The guards had eaten and gone. Mamma Lena was alone in the *osteria*. She stopped scrubbing the table and looked up as I came in. "You say you're so strict because you have to protect me!" I said, and I was looking right into her pale, scowling eyes. "And then you make me come home all night alone on a wagon with a drunk man!" And I told her all that had happened.

"Well, Ernesto was drunk and didn't know what he was doing," she said at last. "Better you don't say anything more about it to make a long story. And you did right to pray the Madonna." And taking the bundle from my hand she went and laid it on the table.

"But why did you make me come home?" I asked. "Why did you make me come home from Germignaga? I wanted to stay!"

Mamma Lena opened the bundle and started examining the clothes — afraid I had brought home some bugs.

"Why did I have to come home?" I said again, and I was crying and angry.

"I couldn't let you stay there," she said. "Not after I knew what you were doing. You are going to be married. You have to be married to be safe."

"Remo?" I asked, holding up my breath and waiting for her answer.

"No," she said. "You and Remo deceived me. And you cannot wait for him. You are going to marry Santino."

Santino! Was Mamma Lena trying to make a joke? I went around the end of the table so I could look in her face. Her lips were tighter than ever and her scowl was deeper.

"Santino is generous. He gave the money and I bought you a nice wedding dress," she said. "I bought it from a rich lady who was selling everything she had to get her husband out of jail. And Santino has the

[147

gold ready too. And besides the earrings and the ring he bought you a nice breast pin to wear on your dress."

At first I was like punched in the stomach — I couldn't breathe! Then my breath came so fast that I couldn't hold it back. "No!" I shouted. "No! No! You can't make me marry Santino! You can't! I hate him! I hate him! I HATE HIM!"

Mamma Lena got stiffer but she didn't speak.

"I won't marry Santino! I won't!"

Minutes passed but still Mamma Lena didn't speak. She just stood there with her lips tight, breathing hard. The bell started tolling for mass. With a jerk Mamma Lena pulled off her gunnysack apron and went back and hung it up on a nail by the fireplace. "Wash yourself and change your clothes," she said as she passed me on the way to the door. "You'll be late for church."

I heard Mamma Lena stamping off upstairs. Then I heard her come down again and knew she was standing in the door looking in at my back. But still I didn't move to obey. At last, without a word, she went off across the court and out the gate. I was alone in the *osteria*. Alone in the world! What could I do? If Remo knew, Remo would help me. But how could I get word to Remo in time? Then I thought of Bianca. Bianca would do anything for Remo. I would run to Bianca and ask her to let me hide in her house until she got the word to Remo. Then Remo would come and save me. And I turned and went across the court so fast that the chickens got a scare and flew out of my way.

16

NO ONE was home at Bianca's but Bianca's father, Zio Ferdinando. All the women and girls were in church. When Zio Ferdinando heard my story he was so angry that he said he would go himself to get the word to Remo. "But there's nothing Remo can do, Rosa," he said. "There's nothing anyone can do against the will of that Mamma Lena!"

When Bianca and her mother, Zia Chiara, came home, Zia Chiara made me come out from under the bed to eat and Bianca stayed by the door to watch out for Mamma Lena. Zia Chiara gave me a big bowlful of rice soup, then she washed the dust and tears from my face and let me go back under the bed.

It was night when I woke up and heard voices at the other end of the room under the lamp. I heard Bianca's voice and Zia Chiara's and Zio Ferdinando's. And . . . yes, it *was*! Remo had come! And he had come in time! He had come before Mamma Lena could find me! I wriggled out from under the bed and brushed down my skirt and waited for him to see me.

"Rosa! Rosa!" he said and came running across to where I stood.

I was too happy to speak. It was just as I had hoped. He had come in time and would save me from Santino. As he took my hands I looked into his eyes and smiled.

"Remo must be back in the barracks before morning," said Zio Ferdinando, coming across the room to hang up his hat. "And the last *tramvai* has gone. He will have to walk."

Zia Chiara wiped her eyes on her apron and told Bianca to run and tell Remo's mother that he was here. Bianca had been standing there looking at us, but she went out when her mother told her. Then Zio Ferdinando went back to the table and sat down.

"I got the permission and I came as soon as I heard," said Remo, looking into my eyes. "But I have to run right away back. Rosa, I love you. I love you. I will never love anyone else but you! Don't marry Santino! Promise me that you will not marry Santino!"

"How can I *not* marry him if I stay here?" I asked. "Let us run away, Remo. I will run away with you tonight and we will get married before Mamma Lena can catch me and make me marry Santino!"

"But I can't, Rosa! I can't do that! I can't run away from the army! They would catch me wherever I went and give me a terrible punishment and put me in jail!"

"But even if they do put you in jail, you would have to come out *sometime*, no?" I asked.

"No, we can't run away, Rosa! We can't do that. A man can't run away from the army! And you are too young. You are too young to get married without the parent! And what would happen to you alone in a strange city?"

"I would say I am sixteen — that I am eighteen. And I can work in the silk. There are silk mills in the city. There are even silk mills in France. I am not afraid. And if you go to jail I will wait for you. I would wait for you forever!"

"No, Rosa, you are too young," said Remo. "Mamma Lena would tell the police to find you and bring you back and then it would be worse for you than now. And I can't run away from the army. But don't marry Santino! Don't let Mamma Lena give you to Santino! You must wait for me!"

"My love is stronger than your love!" I said. "I'm not afraid of the punishment. I have the courage — I would go anywhere with you!"

"You are too young — you don't understand, Rosa. It's impossible

[150

to run away. I can't run away from the army. But you must wait. Don't marry Santino!"

Oh, I was brokenhearted entirely! I was in despair! I was even thinking that Remo was false because he didn't have the courage to run away. Even if they killed us I wouldn't be afraid — I would run away with Remo. Remo didn't know what to do. He just kept saying, "Wait for me, Rosa! Wait for me! Don't marry Santino! Don't let Mamma Lena give you to Santino!" How could I wait? How could I not marry that man if I didn't run away? If Remo didn't love me enough to run away and take the punishment I didn't care about anything anymore.

Bianca came back with Remo's mother. Remo's mother came running across and took him in her arms. Then she hugged me too and kissed my forehead. "*Poveri figliuolini!*" she kept saying, and brushed tears from her eyes. "Poor children! Poor children!" But then she went back to the table and sat down with Zia Chiara and Zio Ferdinando. Bianca stayed by the door, watching out for Mamma Lena. I went and sat down on the chest at the foot of the bed, so Remo did too.

"As long as I live I will never love anyone else but you, Rosa," he said, but when he reached for my hand I pulled it away. What was the use of talking? Remo had failed me when I needed him most.

For a long time no one in the room said anything. Bianca got tired of standing and sat down on the bench by the door. At last Zio Ferdinando spoke. "Remo," he said. "Better you come and eat. You will have to be starting to get back before morning. You must not be late. And as I said before, there is nothing you can do. There is nothing anyone can do."

"I can't eat," said Remo.

A pain like a knife was cutting inside me, but I couldn't even cry to let it out. Remo was going away again and he wasn't taking me! He was leaving me behind — leaving me to Mamma Lena and Santino.

The clock in the church tower started striking midnight. Again Remo reached for my hand and this time I didn't even bother to pull it away. What difference did it make? As he squeezed it sobs caught in his throat and shook his body, but I didn't care. I felt no sympathy.

[151

"*Addio*, Rosa!" he said. "*Addio!*"

But I didn't answer. And I didn't even turn my head to watch him as he ran across the room and out the door.

The next day Mamma Lena came and found me and dragged me home. And oh, how she beat me! For three days she was beating me and would give me nothing to eat. But it was not the beatings or the starving that made me stop saying no. It was the fear of God. By defying Mamma Lena I was offending God and the Madonna. For a child to disobey a parent is a terrible sin. God and the Madonna would punish you for such a sin. If I died while defying Mamma Lena I would go straight to hell and there would be no chance for me ever. What could I do? In the end I would have to marry Santino anyway. Better I stopped saying no before Mamma Lena killed me.

So after I stopped saying no Mamma Lena was all right again. She gave me to eat and showed me all the things she had in the two wooden chests for my *dote*, my dowry — all the linen chemises and the twenty-five white knitted stockings for summer and twenty-five black knitted stockings for winter, and the yellow silk bedspread. (Every poor girl in Bugiarno always had that yellow silk bedspread to get married. It took years to spin the silk and weave that beautiful yellow silk spread. It was made from the silk veils the bad worms left on the ceilings instead of making cocoons.) Then she hemmed up the rich lady's dress to fit me. It was a brown silk dress with brown brocade roses. "Santino is generous," Mamma Lena said. "And he has money saved up in the bank. You and your children will never have to go hungry." Me and my children. How was it possible that I should have children? If I did have children I did not want them to go hungry. But I did not want them to have Santino for a father, either! Oh, Madonna, make something happen so I don't have to marry Santino!

"He has paid for a nice dinner and for a concertina to play for dancing and has bought a whole basketful of *confetti* candy to throw in the procession. I could not let you marry one of those boys who like you so much. They would let you have your own way. You need someone to control you. You need an older man to make you meek and save you for heaven in the end."

Getting ready for a wedding was like getting ready for a worm camp. Instead of going to the mill I had to help Mamma Lena whitewash the walls and clean the floors and shine the pans and kettles and change the cornstalks in the mattresses. Mamma Lena was going to sleep in my narrow bed by the window and me and Santino would have the big bed by the door.

"If you were married to one of those boys who live in Bugiarno you would have to go and live with his family, and his mother would take care of your babies. But with Santino for a husband you can stay here with me and I will take care of the babies," said Mamma Lena.

Daytimes Santino was off working on the irrigation ditches, but evenings, when he came in the *osteria* I could see him looking at me and I tried to keep out of his way. At times, when I couldn't get away from his eyes, I would give him an angry look to tell him how much I hated him. Maybe then he would change his mind. But he didn't — he only smiled. What could I do? How could I get away? Without thinking I did whatever Mamma Lena told me. I took a candle and sat on the steps of the wine cellar and filled bottles and bottles with wine — wine for my wedding. I carried Mamma Lena's dough to the baker's and kneaded it into loaves, then waited on the bench with the old women while the baker baked it in the oven. "Never mind, Rosa, that you have to marry a man you don't like," the old women said. "He is not so poor. You will not be hungry." Those women knew what it was that the man did to the woman when he married her, but I was not allowed to ask them. And none of the girls knew. Whatever it was that Santino was going to do to me after the marriage, I wanted to know it before. But how could I find out?

Sunday came and for the third and last time the priest read the banns in church — my name and Santino's. As soon as mass was over I came out from the church and ran home without waiting for anyone. And there in our court was Pompeo. He was up on a ladder finishing the picture Mamma Lena had asked him to make on the wall to celebrate my wedding. He had made all the angels and was painting a little lamb. He stopped as I stood there watching and told me how sorry he was that I had to marry that man I didn't like, and there were tears in his eyes. And all at once it came in my mind that maybe Pompeo knew what I wanted to know. If he knew probably he would tell me. "Pompeo," I said, "do you know — can you tell me — what the man does to the girl when he has the matrimony with her?" And I was even asking if it was going to hurt. Think how I was talking to that good boy! But I didn't know it was bad and I wanted to know. Pompeo got to be one of the greatest artists, but in that time he was a very, very friend with me.

"Yes, Rosa," he said. "I know, but a man can't tell a girl that. I'm sorry. Only the husband is allowed to tell the girl that after the matrimony."

The night before the wedding day I was on my knees in the confessional. "Bless me, Father, for I have sinned." If only Don Domenic were there behind the grill instead of the old priest we had now! If Don Domenic had lived he would have helped me! I must make a good confession. I had stopped defying Mamma Lena but I was still praying that something would happen so I wouldn't have to marry Santino. Maybe just praying against the will of Mamma Lena was a sin? I asked Father Pietro, but there was no answer. He was too deaf — he couldn't hear me. "O my God I am heartily sorry for having offended Thee and I detest all my sins because I dread the loss of heaven and the pains of hell . . ."

And before I could finish Father Pietro started giving me the absolution. "May our Lord Jesus Christ absolve thee from thy sins in the name of the Father and of the Son and of the Holy Ghost. Amen."

So then the time came. I was in church waiting to be married with Santino. The priest was there in front and he was asking me the question. But I couldn't answer. I *couldn't*! I couldn't say yes! I was just there, that was all. I couldn't say anything. But Father Pietro didn't know I didn't answer and he didn't make me. He married me with Santino anyway. But the people all knew. When the people came home to Mamma Lena's for the wedding dinner all the women were saying, "Rosa didn't say yes!"

"Why didn't you say yes, Rosa?"

[154

"You're not married when you don't say yes!"

"Rosa didn't say yes!"

I can't stand it to tell about that marriage and about Santino! I have to leave them out of my story, that's all. I can't tell about them!

The next day I was back at work in the silk mill of Signor Rossi and bringing my wages to Mamma Lena like before.

17

ONE night a few months after the marriage when I came from my work Santino said we were going to the dance hall. I was tired and kind of sick. "Why do you want to go when you don't know to dance?" I asked him. He didn't like it that I asked him why and he didn't answer. Mamma Lena was brushing crumbs from the table to the chickens. She was listening but she said nothing either. So I knew I would have to go. I ate the black bread and cabbage soup that Mamma Lena gave me for my supper, then I washed, put on my sailor dress and leather shoes, and we went.

Santino didn't try dancing himself — he knew he couldn't. But he told me to dance with his friends — a lot of men that were there. He wanted to show them how I could dance. I didn't know those men, but I did like he said — I tried to dance with them. But those men didn't know how at all. It was impossible to dance with them! So I sat down at the side and Santino and his friends sat at the table drinking.

After a little while Pio, the son of the *portinaia* at the mill, came in. I knew Pio when he was a little boy. He was an old friend to me and he was a wonderful dancer. So when Pio asked me to dance with him I was glad. And we danced the whole evening. Then because I was feeling so sick and tired I went home by myself and went to bed.

When Santino came home he was drunk and so mad that I had danced with Pio that he said he would kill me. He pulled me out of the bed and threw me on the floor.

Other nights when Santino was drunk and beating me Mamma Lena had sat up in her bed and watched, but she had said nothing. This night — I guess she could see it that he wanted to kill me for sure — she jumped up and came over and stopped him. She pulled him away so he couldn't reach to kick me. When she did that he started fighting with her. He should have known better than to try to fight Mamma Lena! Mamma Lena was so mad she didn't care what she did. She wasn't afraid of hurting him or anything. And in the end she put him out the door and he went rolling down the steps. "And don't ever come back to this house!" she yelled after him. "Don't ever come back! I never want to see you again!"

Before he married me that man was always talking sweet to Mamma Lena to make her like him. But after the marriage she could see it herself — how bad he was. He was all the time drunk and beating me, and she didn't like him herself.

A few weeks after the fight — Santino was not living in Mamma Lena's — one of those agents from the big bosses in America came to Bugiarno to get men for some iron mines in Missouri. The company paid for the tickets, but the men had to work for about a year to pay them back, and they had to work another year before they could send for their wives and families. So this time when that agent came Santino and some of his friends joined the gang and went off to America. He didn't even come back to the *osteria* to get his clothes.

When I heard that Santino was gone, oh, I was happy! I was thinking that probably I would never see that man again. America was a long way off.

Mamma Lena was better to me now and gave me more to eat. And I kept getting bigger and bigger. And then one day I felt kicking inside of me and I knew it was a baby. How that baby got in there I couldn't understand. But the thing that worried me most was how it was going to get out! A baby couldn't make a hole and come out like the moth in a cocoon. Probably the doctor would have to cut me. I didn't want to ask Mamma Lena, but what was I going to do? That baby was kicking to get out — I would have to ask someone. So I told her.

"Well," said Mamma Lena. "You'll have to pray the Madonna. If you pray the Madonna with all your heart maybe the Madonna will make a miracle for you and let the baby come out without the doctor cutting you."

And so I started to pray for that miracle. I prayed to the little statue Madonna over the chicken coop and I prayed to the big Madonna in the church. And every night I gave myself more Ave Marias to say, so that when I woke up in the morning I would find the baby there in the bed beside me. But it never was. It was still inside and kicking.

At last there came a day when I had to leave my work and go home. After that I didn't know what happened. I was three days without my senses. Mamma Lena got two doctors — she got the village doctor, then she got the doctor she had to pay. But both doctors said the same. They said the baby could not be born — that they would have to take it in pieces. And they were even scolding her. They said, "How can a girl make new bones when her own bones are not finished growing? The girl is too young!" Mamma Lena was in despair. She wanted that baby. So she told the doctors to go and she ran to the church and prayed to the big Madonna. She told the Madonna that if She would let that baby be born alive she would give Her that beautiful shawl that Remo and me won in the dance. (As soon as Mamma Lena had found out about the prize shawl she had made Zia Teresa bring it to her. And she would not speak to Zia Teresa for about three weeks because she said Zia Teresa had helped me deceive her.)

And right then when she was praying, my baby was born — a nice little boy. She came home and she could hear it crying. Think what a miracle! Two doctors said that baby couldn't be born! For a long time she didn't know whether I was going to live or not, but she was so happy to have that baby that she was thanking the Madonna. She took the shawl to the priest the next day. And that shawl made so much money in the raffle that the Madonna got all new paint and a new sky and new stars behind Her.

In the fever that followed the birth of my baby I lost my hair and my voice. Little by little my hair came back, and my voice to speak came back too, but I could never sing like before. And as soon as I could walk again I went back to my work in the mill. They had a special room in the mill just for nursing the babies. So Mamma Lena would bring the baby to me and I would stop work and go in there and nurse him. And I nursed him at lunchtime too.

Not long after the baby was born Mamma Lena got five little coral horns one day from another lady and tied them on a string around his neck. She said she didn't want anyone to witch that baby with the evil eye and make him sick. I told her I didn't believe in those things. I said, "Only God and the Madonna make you sick and make you well. How can people make you sick!" She didn't scold. She said it was good that I believed only in God and the Madonna. But she kept those horns around the baby's neck anyway. How could anyone witch that baby with the evil eye when the Madonna made a miracle to let him be born? I guess Mamma Lena remembered Braco and she didn't want to take any chance.

There used to be a lot of men, and women too, in the villages of Lombardy that the people called witches — *maliardi*. The people thought those men and women had the evil eye. In this country too some of the old people believe in the evil eye. When my Visella got the heart trouble and died some of the women were saying it was the evil eye. I said no. I said God wanted her, that was all. But that Braco, I remember him myself. He was all the time singing. But then one day someone witched him and he couldn't talk and he couldn't sing. He was *muto*. Three years he couldn't talk and he couldn't sing. After three years a man appeared and said, "Braco, you're going to sing and you're going to talk again." And when Braco tried, he could! He could sing and he could talk! As quick as he could Braco grabbed a big knife and started after that man to catch him. Braco ran all through the town trying to catch that *maliardo* to kill him. But he never saw him again. That man disappeared entirely. No one knew where he came from or where he went. (Nobody can witch me, though. I'm too strong in believing in God and the Madonna.)

So I was around fifteen years old and I had to be like an old woman. I was not allowed to walk with the young people when they went to the square on Christmas Eve or dance with the masks when they came to the stables in the time of the carnival. I couldn't even sit with the other young girls at lunchtime at the mill. But as I got strong again I began imitating funny people and telling stories again to make the women and girls all laugh. And nighttimes and Sundays I had my baby, my Francesco, to give me joy and make me laugh. And now that I was married Mamma Lena no longer scolded or beat me like before.

"But you did wrong to make that beautiful young girl marry a man like Santino!" Zia Teresa would say.

"Yes, I made a mistake," Mamma Lena would say. "But it was not my fault. I didn't know before how bad he was. And now Rosa is married and has her baby and I don't have to worry anymore."

My Francesco had learned to walk and was learning to talk when here, coming into the *osteria* one Sunday, were some of those men who had gone to America with Santino. I stopped playing with my baby and went and called Mamma Lena from the wine cellar.

"Those men in the iron mines in Missouri need women to do the cooking and washing," said one of the men. "Three men have sent back for their wives, and two for some girls to marry. Santino says for you to send Rosa. He sent the money and the ticket." And the man pulled them from an inside pocket and laid them on the table. Then all four sat down and ordered wine and polenta. Mamma Lena took the ticket and the money and put them in the pocket of her underskirt, and without a word started serving them.

When the men were ready to leave the one who had brought the message spoke again. "In two weeks another gang of men from the villages is leaving for the iron mines in Missouri. Your daughter and the other wives and girls can go with them." But still Mamma Lena didn't tell him if I was going or not going.

After they were gone I helped her clear the table and wash the dishes. Then I took Francesco in my arms and waited for her to speak. She took her rag and started to wipe the table, but instead of wiping it she sat down on the bench beside it.

"Yes, Rosa," she said. "You must go. However bad that man is, he is your husband — he has the right to command you. It would be a sin against God not to obey. You must go. But not Francesco. He didn't ask for Francesco and I would be too lonesome without him."

Me, I was even wanting to sin against God and the Madonna before I would leave my baby and go off to Santino in America! But Mamma Lena said I must go. There was nothing I could do.

Mamma Lena was good to me though. She thought I would be not so lonesome — not so homesick in America — if I had the oil like the poor always had in Bugiarno. So she made me three bottles full and sealed it up so it looked like wine. That oil is made from the seed of the mustard plant — mustard or turnip? — I don't know what it's called in English. You eat the part underground but it's not pinchy like radishes. Only the rich people in the cities in Italy can have the olive oil. We poor people used that oil that the women made themselves.

And so I had to leave Mamma Lena and my baby and go off with that gang of men and one or two women to America.

18

THE day came when we had to go and everyone was in the square saying good-bye. I had my Francesco in my arms. I was kissing his lips and kissing his cheeks and kissing his eyes. Maybe I would never see him again! It wasn't fair! He was *my* baby! Why should Mamma Lena keep him? But then Pep was calling and Mamma Lena took Francesco away and Zia Teresa was helping me onto the bus and handing up the bundles.

"But Rosa, don't be so sad!" It was the other Rosa and Zia Maria in the station in Milan, kissing me good-bye and patting my shoulder. "It is wonderful to go to America even if you don't want to go to Santino. You will get smart in America. And in America you will not be so poor."

Then Paris and we were being crowded into a train for Havre. We were so crowded we couldn't move, but my *paesani* were just laughing. "Who cares?" they laughed. "On our way to America! On our way to be millionaires!"

Day after day in Havre we were leaving the lodging house and standing down on the docks waiting for a ship to take us. But always the ship was full before it came our turn. "O Madonna!" I prayed. "Don't ever let there be room! Don't ever let there be room!"

But here, on the sixth day we came on. We were almost the last ones. There was just one young French girl after us. She was with her mother and her sister, but when the mother and sister tried to follow, that *marinaro* at the gate said, "No more! Come on the next boat!" And that poor family was screaming and crying. But the *marinaro* wouldn't let the girl off and wouldn't let the mother and sister on. He said, "You'll meet in New York. Meet in New York."

All us poor people had to go down through a hole to the bottom of the ship. There was a big dark room down there with rows of wooden shelves all around where we were going to sleep — the Italian, the German, the Polish, the Swede, the French — every kind. And in that time the third class on the boat was not like now. The girls and women and the men had to sleep all together in the same room. The men and girls had to sleep even in the same bed with only those little half-boards up between to keep us from rolling together. But I was lucky. I had two girls sleeping next to me. When the dinner bell rang we were all standing in line holding the tin plates we had to buy in Havre, waiting for soup and bread.

"Oh, I'm so scared!" Emilia kept saying and she kept looking at the little picture she carried in her blouse. "I'm so scared!"

"Don't be scared, Emilia," I told her. "That young man looks nice in his picture."

"But I don't know him," she said. "I was only seven years old when he went away."

"Look at *me*," said the comical Francesca with her crooked teeth. "I'm going to marry a man I've never seen in my life. And he's not *Lombardo* — he's *Toscano*. But I'm not afraid."

Of course Francesca was not afraid. "Crazy Francesca" they called her at the silk mill. She was so happy she was going to America and going to get married that she didn't care who the man was.

On the fourth day a terrible storm came. The sky grew black and the ocean came over the deck. Sailors started running everywhere, fastening this and fastening that and giving orders. Us poor people had to go below and that little door to the deck was fastened down. We had no light and no air and everyone got sick where we were. We were like rats trapped in a hole, holding onto the posts and onto the iron frames to keep from rolling around. Why had I worried about Santino? We were never going to come to America after all! We were going to the bottom of the sea!

But after three days the ship stopped rolling. That door to the deck was opened and some sailors came down and carried out two who had died and others too sick to walk. Me and all my *paesani* climbed out without help and stood in line at the wash-house, breathing fresh air and filling our basins with water. Then we were out on the narrow deck washing ourselves and our clothes — some of us women and girls standing like a wall around the others so the men couldn't see us.

Another time there was fog — so much fog that we couldn't see the masts and we couldn't see the ocean. The engine stopped and the sails were tied down and a horn that shook the whole boat started blowing. All day and all night that horn was blowing. No one could sleep so no one went to bed. One man had a concertina and the ones who knew how to dance were dancing to entertain the others. Me, I was the best one. There was no one there to scold me and tell me what to do so I danced with all my *paesani* who knew how. Then I even danced with some of the Polish and the French. We were like floating on a cloud in the middle of nowhere and when I was dancing I forgot for a little while that I was the wife of Santino going to him in America. But on the third day the fog left, the sails came out, the engine started, and the ship was going again.

Sometimes when I was walking on the steerage deck with Giorgio — the little boy of one woman from Bugiarno who was all-the-way seasick — I would look back and see the rich people sitting on the higher decks with nice awnings to protect them from the cinders and the sun, and I would listen to their strange languages and their laughing. The rich always knew where they were going and what they were going to do. The rich didn't have to be afraid like us poor.

Then one day we could see land! Me and my *paesani* stood and watched the hills and the land come nearer. Other poor people, dressed in their best clothes and loaded down with bundles, crowded around. *America*! The country where everyone could find work! Where wages were so high no one had to go hungry! Where all men were free and equal and where even the poor could own land! But now we were so near it seemed too much to believe. Everyone stood silent — like in prayer. Big sea gulls landed on the deck and screamed and flew away.

Then we were entering the harbor. The land came so near we could almost reach out and touch it. "Look!" said one of the *paesani*. "Green grass and green trees and white sand — just like in the old country!" The others all laughed — loud, not regular laughs — so that Pep wouldn't know that they too had expected things to be different. When we came through that narrow place and into the real harbor everyone was holding their breath. Me too. There were boats going everywhere — all sizes and all kinds. There were smoke chimneys smoking and white sails and flags waving and new paint shining. Some boats had bands playing on their decks and all of them were tooting their horns to us and leaving white trails in the water behind them.

"There!" said Pep, raising his hand in a greeting. "There it is! *New York!*"

The tall buildings crowding down to the water looked like the cardboard scenery we had in our plays at the *istituto*.

"Oh I'm so scared!" said Emilia again. "How can I know that man I am going to marry? And what if he doesn't meet me?"

Us other women and girls were going to meet our husbands, or the men to marry, in the iron mine in Missouri. Only the man to marry Emilia lived in New York and was meeting her here. He didn't work in the mines. He played a trumpet and had his own band.

"Look," said Pep. "Brooklyn Bridge! Just opened this year with fireworks and everything."

"And there's Castle Garden."

"Castle Garden! Which? Which is Castle Garden?"

Castle Garden! Castle Garden was the gate to the new land. Everyone wanted to see. But the ship was being pulled off to one side — away from the strange round building.

"Don't get scared," said Pep. "We go just to the pier up the river. Then a government boat brings us back."

Doctors had come on the ship and ordered us inside to examine our eyes and our vaccinations. One old man who couldn't talk and two girls with sore eyes were being sent back to the old country. "O

[165

Madonna, make them send me back too!" I prayed. "Don't make me go to Santino!"

About two hours later me and my *paesani* were back at Castle Garden on a government boat, bumping the dock and following Pep across a boardwalk and leaving our bundles with some officers. I wanted to hold onto my bottles of oil — they might get broken — but the officers made me leave those too. Then one by one we went through a narrow door into Castle Garden. The inside was a big, dark room full of dust, with fingers of light coming down from the ceiling. That room was already crowded with poor people from earlier boats sitting on benches and on railings and on the floor. And to one side were a few old tables where food was being sold. Down the center between two railings high-up men were sitting on stools at high desks. And we had to walk in line between those two railings and pass them.

"What is your name? Where do you come from? Where are you going?"

Those men knew all the languages and could tell just by looking what country we come from.

After Pep, it was my turn.

"Cristoforo, Rosa. From Lombardy. To the iron mine in Missouri."

Emilia was holding me by the skirt, so I stayed a little behind to help her. "Gruffiano, Emilia. From San Paola. What *signore*? You don't know San Paola?"

"She's from Lombardy too," I said. "But she's going to stay in New York."

"And do you know the man I am going to marry, *signore*?" asked Emilia. "See, here's his picture. He has to meet me in Castle Garden. But how can I know him? He plays the *tromba* and owns his own band."

"Get your baggage and come back. Wait by the visitors' door — there at the left. Your name will be called. All right. Move on!"

There were two other desks — one for railroad tickets and one for American money — but we *Lombardi* had ours already so we went back for our bundles. But I couldn't find my straw-covered bottles. Everybody was trying to help me find them. Then an inspector man came. "What's all the commotion?" he asked. "Oh, so those bottles belonged to her? Well ask her," he said to the interpreter. "Ask her what that stuff was? Was it poison?"

When Pep told him he said, "Well tell her her bottles are in the bottom of the ocean! Tell her that's what she gets for bringing such nasty stuff into America! It made us all sick!"

My *paesani* looked at their feet or at the ground and hurried back into the building. Then they busted out laughing. That was a good one! That was really a good one! And even I had to laugh. I was brokenhearted to lose my good oil but it was funny anyway — how Mamma Lena's nice wine bottles had fooled those men in gold braid.

We *Lombardi* put down our bundles and sat on the floor near the visitors' door. At last after all the new immigrants had been checked, an officer at the door started calling the names. "Gruffiano, Emilia" was the first one.

"*Presente*! *Presente*!" shouted Pep jumping to his feet and waving his hands. But Emilia was so scared I had to pull her up and drag her along after him.

At the door the officer called the name again and let us pass. Then here came up a young man. He was dressed — O Madonna! — like the president of the United States! White gloves and a cane and a diamond pin in his tie. Emilia tried to run away but Pep pulled her back. "*Non è vero*! *Non è vero*! It's not true!" she kept saying.

"But it *is* true!" the young man laughed. "Look at me, Emilia! Don't you remember Carlo who used to play the *tromba* in San Paola when you were a little girl?" And he pulled her out from behind us and took her in his arms and kissed her. (In America a man can kiss the girl he is going to marry!) "But I never thought you would come like this," he said, holding her off a little and looking at her headkerchief and full skirt. "I'm afraid to look. Did you come in the wooden soles too?"

"No," said Emilia, speaking to him for the first time. "My mother bought me real shoes to come to America!" And she was lifting her feet to show him.

"She looks just the same as when she was seven years old," the young man said to Pep, and he was happy and laughing. "But I'm going to take her up Broad Street and buy her some American clothes before I take her home."

I was glad for Emilia that she was going to marry that nice young man, but why couldn't something like this ever happen to me?

Other visitors were called. Some families separated at Havre found each other again and were happy. But that nice young French girl, she was there all alone — nobody could find her mother and her sister. I don't think they ever found each other again.

When the gate was opened men wearing badges came running in, going to the different people. One dressed-up man with a cane and waxed mustache came to us. "*Buon giorno, paesani*! *Benvenuto*! Welcome to America! Welcome to the new country!" He was speaking Italian and English too and putting out his hand to shake hands with Pep. We other *paesani* looked on in wonder. A high man like that shaking hands with the poor! This was America for sure!

"I heard your talk and knew you were my *paesani*. I came to help you. You have the railroad tickets and the American money?"

"*Si, signore*," said Pep and we all showed our tickets and our money.

Then Pep asked about the women's chests that had come on an earlier ship. "Leave it to me," said our new friend. "Leave it to me, your *paesano*, Bartini. I will find them and send them to Union. And in three days when your train goes I will put you on myself so you won't go wrong."

"Three days! But no, *signore*! We want to go today."

"My dear man," laughed Bartini, "you're lucky I found you. There's no train to Missouri for three days. But don't worry! Bartini will take care of everything. You can come and eat and sleep in my hotel, comfortable and nice, and in three days I will take you and put you on the right train."

And in three days he did put us on the train but he took all our money first, about thirteen dollars each one. He left us not even a crust of bread for our journey. And we didn't even guess that he was fooling us.

The American people on the train were sorry when they saw we had nothing to eat and they were trying to give us some of their food. But Pep said no. He was too proud to take it. Me, I would have taken it quick enough. But I couldn't after Pep said no — even with that little Giorgio crying with his face in my lap. Those American people were dressed up nice — the ladies had hats and everything — but they were riding the same class with us poor — all equal and free together.

"Look, Giorgio," I said, to make him forget his pains. "Horses and cows just like in *Italia*. But here there are no shepherds to watch every blade of grass they eat. Here they can go all around and eat what they want."

At last we were in the station in St. Louis changing trains for Union. We were sick for food but everyone was awake now — everyone excited. Domiana could scarcely wait to see her husband, Masino. And Francesca — "Crazy Francesca" — was trying to find out from Pep what kind of a man was waiting to marry her. All the *paesani* were laughing, but not me. Me, I was hiding my rosary in my hand and kissing the cross and trembling inside. "O Madonna," I prayed, "You've got to help me! That man is my husband — I must do what he wants, to not offend God and offend You! But You've got to help me!"

Then the conductor was calling, "Union! Union!" And everybody was picking up bundles and pushing to the windows. There was a little wooden station ahead and beside it were all our *paesani* from the iron mine with two wagons with horses to meet us.

"Look, Rosa, the one with white teeth and black mustache, he's my cousin, Gionin. I think the young man beside him is the one I'm going to marry!"

"He looks nice, Francesca," I said.

I thought maybe Santino didn't come, or maybe I'd forgotten what he looked like. But then I saw him — a little back from the others — just as I remembered him.

Pep, a bundle on his back, was getting off first — laughing and excited — proud that he had brought us new *paesani* all the way from the old country.

"*Benvenuto*, Pep! *Benvenuto, paesani! Benvenuto*! But *Gesu Maria*! Why those three days doing nothing in New York?"

"Bartini said there were no trains for three days."

"No trains for three days! There come two trains every day to Missouri. Wait till we can get our hands on Bartini! But forget it now. Now we are all together. Just a little ride through the woods and you are in your new home. And in camp there is plenty to eat. Can a girl as beautiful as Rosa help cook it?"

It was like a *festa*. Everybody in their best clothes and everybody talking and laughing.

Francesca's cousin Gionin was introducing Francesca to the man she was going to marry, but they didn't know what to say. They just stood there getting red and red. Masino, the husband of Domiana, was laughing and crying at the same time, hugging Domiana, then taking Giorgio in his arms and kissing him. Without looking I could see Santino still back at one side eying me with his half-closed eyes. He did not come to me and I did not go to him. Instead I stood there talking and laughing with the *paesani* who had come to meet us — mostly young men I had known in Bugiarno. Twelve of them were going to eat in my house. I was to cook for them. "But I don't know how to cook!"

"*Per l'amore di Dio*, don't worry about that. We will teach you!"

"Watch close the way we are going, Rosa." It was Gionin, the cousin of Francesca. He was sitting next to me on the wagon. "You will be walking back here every two or three days to get groceries and ask for mail." He was not *Lombardo* like the others — he and his friend were *Toscani*. I had to listen careful to understand his words. But his talk sounded nice and so respectful. "Here in America they have the courthouse and the jail on the square, in place of a church."

The old *paesani* were all asking questions at once of the new ones. They wanted to know about this one and that one and all that had happened in Bugiarno since they went away. Only Santino said nothing. I could see him out of the corner of my eye sitting up near the driver watching me. But somehow I was not so afraid with Gionin beside me. And Gionin was one of the twelve going to eat in my house.

After two or three miles the wagons came out from the woods and there, below, was the iron mine and the camp. Down there there were no trees and no grass — just some shacks made of boards and some railroad tracks. The sun was going down behind the hills and a few miners with picks and sledgehammers were coming out from a tunnel. Other men down in an open place were wheeling away their tools in wheelbarrows. The new *paesani* grew silent — as if they had expected something else — as if they were no longer sure they were going to be millionaires. And me, looking up to see which shack Gionin was pointing to, met the eyes of Santino.

19

I HAD never seen houses like these before — nothing but boards. The one where we stopped was larger than the others and had two doors to go in. Me and Santino were going to live in the side we were going in, and Domiana and Masino in the other. There was one large room with a long table and benches and a big cook stove and some shelves with pans and things. Then behind was a little room with an iron-frame bed and straw mattress. Gionin and some of the other men carried in my two chests. Then they came back and put food on the table.

Bread! White bread! Enough for a whole village! And butter to go on it! I ate until I no longer had any pains in my stomach. Then I went back by the stove to watch Gionin. He had built a fire and was making coffee. Never in my life had I made coffee and I would have to learn if I was going to cook for these men in America.

"But it's easy, Rosa," Gionin said, and his eyes smiled into mine. "Just make the water boil and grind the coffee and put it in like this. And always we have plenty of sugar and cream to go in. The German women on the farms taught me that."

When the coffee was on the table Gionin sat down with the others and started telling Francesca the plans he had made for her. Until she and Orlando were married on Sunday she was going to stay with an old Sicilian woman, Angelina, who was like a mother to all the young girls in camp. But after Sunday she and Orlando would live in a shack by themselves and she would do the cooking for another bunch of men. She was going to be married in a little village four miles down the tracks. But before then, on Saturday night, she must go to confession. Enrico, the boss of the iron mine, would go with her and interpret.

"*Santa Maria*! I have to tell my sins to a man not a priest? Better I don't get married!" Francesca was so comical she made everyone die laughing.

Gionin was laughing too and teasing Orlando about choosing a wife with sins so black that only a priest could hear them. But then he explained. He told how Enrico went in the priest's house with the girls and stood one side of the priest and the girl the other. Then the girl put her hand in the priest's hand and the priest asked the questions in English and Enrico said them in Italian. If the girl *did* make the sin — she did not go to mass on Sunday, or she stole something worth more than a penny — she must squeeze the priest's hand. Enrico couldn't see if she did or didn't. And in the end the priest gave her the penance and that was all.

"God is a dog," muttered Santino. "I'd burn in hell before I'd squeeze the hand of one of those black crows!"

"Listen to Santino!" laughed Pep. "Every Saturday night he's pinching the backside of his fat Annie or of some of those other bad women over Freddy's saloon. But he wouldn't squeeze the hand of a man — even to keep out of hell."

"Man, bah! I spit on all those black crows that wear dresses!"

As soon as I could I went into the bedroom and opened up my chests. I had never expected to see them again. And there inside I found the featherbed and sheets Mamma Lena and Zia Teresa had put in. And I found the little Madonna and the crucifix Don Domenic had blessed. I kissed the bleeding feet of Jesus and said a little prayer. With that crucifix over my bed I would not feel so alone — so afraid. God would help me to be meek. I went into the other room to find a nail and Gionin came back and nailed the crucifix up for me. "Tomorrow, Rosa," he said, "I'll make you a shelf for the little Madonna."

[173

Summer was not yet over but it grew dark early. That little boy, Giorgio, had fallen asleep with his head on the table. So now Domiana went off to her side of the house to open her chests and make her bed. Then some of the men left too. Gionin and Orlando went off to take Francesca to Angelina's. So me, I lighted the lamp in the bedroom and made the bed. Then I sat down on one of my chests and took out my rosary. "*Ave Maria, Mater Dei, ora pro nobis. . . .*"

When everyone else had gone Santino blew out the lamp in the big room and came looking for me. Just inside the door he stopped. It was the crucifix over the bed that stopped him. He started cursing: "God is a dog! God is a pig! Can't a man sleep with his own wife without God watching him from the wall? Take it down, I tell you! Take it down!"

A wife doesn't have to obey her husband when he wants her to do something against God or the Madonna. I held my rosary tighter, waiting for him to come after me and watching for him to tear the crucifix down himself. But he didn't do either. He stood for a while just staring at it. Then without moving his eyes he backed away to the lamp and blew out the light. He was afraid — I could tell by the way he acted — afraid to have Jesus on the cross looking down at him. (But I have to leave that man out of this story. The things he did to me are too bad to tell! I leave him out, that's all!)

The next morning I was up early making a fire in the stove and bringing water from the spring. When Gionin came to show me how to make breakfast he was surprised. He said he was the one chosen to collect the money and buy the food for the men who were going to eat in my house. He said the men wanted me to do the cooking and make their beds and clean their shacks and once every week wash their clothes.

"But I don't know how to cook," I told him.

"Don't worry, Rosa. Angelina will teach you everything — even how to make the spaghetti and ravioli like the people in South Italy. But this morning, Rosa, you take the big sack from the woodshed and go back up that path between the hills to the first farmhouse. That farmer's wife knows you are coming and she will give you some chickens."

[174

"But how can I talk when I don't know English?"

"No use to know English for Mrs. Quigley. The farmers around here speak only German. You just make her understand, that's all. When she starts to give you the rooster, you don't take it."

For breakfast there was white bread again and butter and coffee with cream and sugar and sausages and eggs besides! *Mamma mia!* Did all the poor people in America eat like kings?

When the men had eaten I watched them go off to the sheds for their picks and drills. Most stayed in the open mine, but Santino and a few others went half up the hill and into the tunnel. For a while I couldn't see Gionin, but then I saw him down by the tracks marking empty cars and writing in a notebook. Gionin was more educated than my *paesani*. I was lucky to have him in my house. I liked the way his white teeth were shining under his black mustache when he smiled, and the way his eyes grew kind when he looked into mine. It's funny how you can tell by a man's eyes when he likes you.

For my own breakfast I ate all that I wanted. Then I cleared the table and was washing the dishes when there came a crash that made my ears deaf and shook the whole house. Holy Mary, Mother of God! When I looked out all I could see was a cloud of dust and dirt. Then here came running Domiana with Giorgio. We thought all the men — all the miners — were dead. But when the dust and dirt cleared away we could see the men standing back and watching. It was something they did on purpose. Something that would come again.

Because Angelina was too old to walk four miles down the tracks, I went with Francesca and Enrico on Saturday night and waited outside the priest's house while Francesca made her confession. It was dark when we started home and Enrico walked ahead with his lantern. We had reached the marshy place — almost back at the camp — when suddenly I saw a little flame at one side of the tracks. I stopped and looked. That little flame wasn't burning anything — it was just dancing over the ground.

"Hail Mary Mother of God pray for us now and in the hour of our death!" I said. "Enrico! Enrico! Look! The *fiammetta!*"

Francesca grabbed hold of me and started shaking.

"Sure, it's the *fiammetta*," said Enrico, "but what of it? The *fiammetta* doesn't hurt anything. It's only some gas that comes out of the ground when it's warm and damp. Those people who think it's the evil spirit are foolish — stupid. Come, I'll show you." And there he took his lantern and went after the little flame and put his hand where it was and touched all the places where it had been. And sure enough it didn't hurt him at all. So then me and Francesca tried, and nothing happened to us either.

"I'm going to get those other *Lombardi* and show them too," said Enrico. "If I don't, they will be afraid to pass this place on their way to the lower quarry."

Enrico's real name was Henry but because he could talk in Italian the men all called him Enrico. He was high-educated and was the boss of the mine, but he talked to us poor like we were equal and taught us the things we must know. That was how it was in America. What a pity that all the people of Bugiarno couldn't come to America and learn not to be afraid. They almost died when they saw the *fiammetta* in their fields. In the daytime the priest would come with his holy water and bless all the ground where it had been, but then he would run away. He was afraid too. And the ground where it had been — no one wanted to work there anymore.

"How do you say it in English?" I asked Enrico.

"Will-o'-the-wisp," he said. "But here in America the people know what it is and are not afraid."

As the weeks went by I grew friendly with other Americans too — with old Mr. Miller and his daughter, Miss Mabel, in the store at Union. They were the boss of the store and of the post office, but they were treating me like I was as good as them. "Here's Rosa!" they would say when they saw me come in. "Hello, Rosa! Come in!" And when they saw how much I wanted to speak English they were helping me. And as it grew cold with the winter they made me come in to dry my feet and get warm. And they gave me coffee.

But those saloons in Union were bad. I didn't even want to walk past. Freddy's saloon was the worst. Some of those bad women who lived upstairs were always standing in the window looking out over the half curtain. And Annie, the friend of Santino, always thumbed her nose at me and made faces. She didn't know that I was more happy when he stayed with her than when he came home. Probably she didn't like it that Santino left most of his pay in the pocket of my underskirt so she and his other friends in Freddy's saloon couldn't get it when he was drunk.

Santino had started getting whiskey from some American men who brought it to the camp. More and more he would come home drunk and start beating me. Probably he would like it better if I was not so meek — if I fought with him. But I didn't want to offend God and the Madonna. Gionin couldn't stand it. He would put his head in his hands. Or he would get up and go out. Gionin really loved me — that I knew. And that made me feel not so lonesome. But Gionin couldn't do anything — Santino was my husband.

20

DOMIANA was bigger than me. Her baby was coming first. "And what are we going to do way off here in the mining camp with no doctor, no midwife — no one — to help us?" asked Domiana. "My husband, he's all the time drunk now. He gets the whiskey from those American men and he's all the time drunk. Masino is kind — he's not cruel like Santino — but how can he help me when he's drunk?" Then she told me I must listen and if I hear her knocking on the wall in the night I must come.

"It's no good for me to come, Domiana," I said. "I don't know how babies are born. I was three days without my senses when I had my Francesco."

"Never mind if you don't know, Rosa. You come and I will tell you what to do. You come and help me then I'll help you when yours comes."

I almost died when my first baby was born and I had two doctors and Mamma Lena and Zia Teresa besides. What was I going to do this time? And how was I going to help Domiana? Domiana said that the husband planted a seed in his wife and it was from that seed that babies grew. I never knew before where the babies came from but it sounded probably true. But even a seed couldn't grow into something alive unless God and the Madonna made it.

And sure enough, one night in the middle of the night there came the knocking on the wall. I sat up and saw a light coming through the cracks in the wall. The knocking came again. "Hail Mary Mother of God pray for us now and in the hour of our death!" I prayed as I climbed out of bed, put a skirt over my chemise, and went out my door and into Domiana's. The lamp was smoking but I could see Masino drunk on the floor. And there on the bed by Domiana was the new baby already born, but it was attached to Domiana with a funny twisted cord. It was kicking its arms and legs and crying with all its might. I was afraid to go in — afraid to go near.

"Don't be scared, Rosa!" Domiana called. "Bring the scissors and string from the table."

I went in and picked up the scissors and string and took them to her.

"Tie the string around the cord near the baby's stomach. Then take the scissors and cut off the cord."

"Oh no, Domiana! I can't! I'm afraid. I will kill you!"

When I didn't do what Domiana said she began crying and praying. So then I started to pray too. And suddenly the Madonna gave me courage. Even if it killed Domiana I must do what she said.

Domiana didn't die — she didn't even feel it when I cut the cord. The Madonna is wise. The Madonna knew all about such things. So then I brought warm water from the reservoir and bathed the baby's skin like Domiana told me and bound him up in the clothes Domiana had ready and laid him on the bed beside her. And there the first light of the morning was coming in through the window.

"*Grazie*, Rosa! *Grazie*! I can take care of the rest myself. But before you go wake up that drunk husband of mine."

So I went there and pushed Masino with my foot. "Wake up, you old drunk!" I said. "Wake up! You ought to be ashamed — lying there drunk and your wife having a new baby all alone! You're the father of another nice little boy!"

That poor man — he was not like Santino — he loved his wife and his babies. But he was all the time drunk.

"Get up and build a fire in the stove and make coffee. Then you can stay awake and help your wife and that new baby."

[179

So after I helped her that night Domiana told me, "Now if I'm here, Rosa, when your baby comes I'm going to help you. But if I have to leave, you know what to do anyhow. You do like I showed you."

And sure enough, right after Domiana had her baby, the iron mine in Union started laying off men and Masino was one of the first to go. And because some of the other men were going to a new iron mine in Michigan, Masino was going there too. Domiana had to go with him. So poor me, I was going to be there all by myself! I was so scared I didn't know what I was going to do when the worst came! I almost died when my first baby was born with two doctors — two professors. This time I thought I would die for sure — all alone by myself. But what could I do?

So it was Monday morning and I was trying to do my washing. I always washed the men's clothes Monday morning. But when I tried to hang them up I couldn't. I couldn't. When I first felt those terrible pains I thought I was near the end, so I prepared the string and the scissors ready on the table. Then I got so sick I thought I had come to the end of my life! I went in and grabbed hold of the table and I couldn't let go. I stayed there holding onto that table. "O Madonna, pray God to forgive my sins. But don't let me die anyway! Don't let me or my baby die!"

"Rosa! Rosa!"

Who was calling? Where was I? What had happened? I opened my eyes and slowly I remembered. I was on the floor in my house. My baby had been born. I had tied the cord and cut it, the way Domiana showed me, but then everything had turned black. The baby was lying there with no cover — nothing. But it must be alive. I heard it cry.

"Rosa! Rosa!"

Then I knew from the voice and from the way she said "Rosa" that it was the German farmer lady from on the hill — Mis' Quigley. Probably Mis' Quigley had guessed something had happened when she didn't see the clothes on the line. I wanted to speak to her but before I could lift my head Mis' Quigley had run away. What could I do? I tried to sit up but I fell back. My poor baby was lying naked on the boards! Everything turned black again.

The next thing I knew old Angelina was leaning over me talking in Italian. Mis' Quigley hadn't deserted me after all — God bless her! She had only run off to get Angelina.

"*Santa Maria*, Rosa! You cut the cord and tied it yourself? Why didn't you send your husband to tell me when you felt the pains? Oh, the poor baby!" And Angelina was picking up the baby and wrapping it gently in her apron. "But he's too little! He was born too soon! What did you do, Rosa? You carried the heavy tubs of water and made your baby come too soon? You're all right yourself, Rosa? You'll be all right if I fix the baby first and then come back to you?"

Angelina bathed the baby and banded him up nice, then she helped me get clean and back onto the bed beside him. But then Angelina had to run to her cooking. "When your husband comes," she said, "tell him to fix you a bowl of warm water with the bread and butter in. That's what the women like best when they have the baby just born."

I lay listening. When I heard the hammering of the picks stop I knew the men would be coming to eat and there was nothing prepared. What could I do? I tried, but I couldn't get up. Santino came in first — the others had gone off to their own shacks to get washed. He stood still in the other room for a minute or two. Then he came to the door and looked in. I knew he was angry because there was nothing prepared. I trembled and put my arm around the baby. But he didn't come in. He just stood there looking at the baby as if he was afraid.

I was hungry and so thirsty. Maybe if I had something to eat I could get up. I remembered what Angelina had told me so I asked Santino if he will bring me a bowl of warm water from the reservoir with bread and butter in it.

He didn't answer at first. Then he started swearing and told me if I wanted something to eat to get up and get it myself.

Gionin and some of the others had come in and were standing near the door. How glad Gionin would be to get me whatever I wanted! But I knew he couldn't with Santino there watching. Instead he and one or two others made the meal themselves. Then he went early away and sent his cousin Francesca back and Francesca gave me something to eat.

The next morning, as soon as Santino and the others who worked in the tunnel had gone, Gionin came in himself with a big bowl of warm milk and bread and butter. He smiled down into my eyes, then lifted the corner of the blanket. And as he stood there looking his own face puckered and grew red — just like the baby's.

"He was born too young," I told him. "I don't know if he can live. If he dies before he's baptized he can never go to heaven. Gionin, you and Francesca be the godparents and take him to the priest and have him baptized before he can die."

"Yes, Rosa, I will be glad. Right away tonight after work."

On the second morning I was up doing the work as always. My baby was still weak — I didn't know whether he would live or die — but thanks to Gionin he had been baptized. And he had the name Domenico after Don Domenic. For sure the spirit of Don Domenic would help him if he died.

Gionin was watching the baby as much as I was. All the men who ate in my house, except Santino, were watching and hoping he could live. But Gionin most of all. Gionin was loving that baby more than a father. He even made him a cradle out of boards and when it was finished he brought a big pillow and put the baby in and the baby went right to sleep. Santino watched with the others. He said nothing but I could tell that he didn't like it that Gionin was loving that baby so much.

"But Rosa," said Miss Mabel the first time I went to the store with the baby. "Why didn't you tell me? I thought you looked kind of fat — but those full skirts and chemises! I never even guessed! What did you do, Rosa, with no doctor and no one to help you?"

I could not understand all that Miss Mabel said but I could understand that Miss Mabel was surprised — and sorry too — that she had not known so she could help. Sure, I had wanted to tell Miss Mabel but I had been ashamed. In the old country a woman not married is not supposed to know about such things.

"Oh, how sweet, Rosa! How nice! Let me hold him!"

As the baby grew stronger his crying grew louder. His crying angered Santino. He would shout at him to keep still. Then angered still more that the baby did not obey would go to the cradle and slap him. One evening the baby was crying harder than ever. I held him as long as I could but then had to put him down while I cleared the table and washed the dishes. The men sat on, playing cards. Now and then Santino swore and shouted at the baby to shut up. He was losing at the game and he was angry. Finally he slammed the money he owed on the table and swearing, he lifted his leg over the bench. I saw his eyes on the cradle. Dropping the dish I was drying I made a dash for the baby, grabbing him up just in time — just before Santino could reach him — and ran to the corner.

Since he couldn't get at the baby Santino struck out at me. He struck me several blows on my head, then he struck my back. The men at the table sat silent, watching. They still did not move or speak when Santino finally turned and faced them. Maddened by their disapproving silence Santino stalked across the room, snatched his hat from the nail, and went out.

I came from the corner and watched. He was going off up the road to Union — going to spend the night with Annie. I turned back to the room. Most of the men still sat at the table. But Gionin had risen and was going toward the stove. What was he doing — taking the big bread knife from the rack? Suddenly I dropped the baby in the cradle and ran to Gionin.

"No, Gionin! No!" I said, grabbing his arm and reaching for the knife.

"Let me go!" said Gionin, trying to shake me off. "Let me go! I am going to kill that man for you, Rosa! I am going to kill him!"

"No, Gionin, no! You mustn't even say such a thing! It's a sin just to think it! God lets him live — we've got to take it, that's all. Do you want to sit in jail the rest of your life? They could even put you on the rope! No, Gionin! No!" And I burst out crying.

"If I can kill that man for you first, Rosa, I will gladly sit in jail the rest of my life!"

"No, Gionin, no! To kill a man is a terrible sin! God will make you burn in hell forever and ever!"

Finally Gionin let me take the knife and went and sat down at the

[183

table, burying his head in his hands. I stood looking at him for a little, then putting the knife back in the rack I went and picked up the crying baby. I walked back and forth for a while then I sat down on the bench at the end of the room and gave the baby my breast.

The men at the table collected their cards and one by one got up and took their hats and went out.

The baby fell asleep and I put him back in the cradle. Then I turned down the light in the lamp and sat down at the table across from Gionin.

Gionin ran his fingers through his thick black hair several times before he looked up. "*Gesu Maria Giuseppe*, Rosa! I can't stand it to see anymore! I can't stand it! If I stay here and see anymore there is going to be trouble, that's all! Something is going to happen!"

"Then better you leave, Gionin. Better you go somewhere else to eat, so you don't see. Go to Francesca's."

For a long time Gionin did not answer. When at last he spoke, I could hardly hear him. It was like he spoke only to himself. "Yes," he said. "Yes. If you don't want me to fight with that man, Rosa, it's better that I go." And holding his hands out to show there was nothing he could do he got up, took his hat, and went out.

And so Gionin went from my house. But every Sunday morning I was with him when we walked the tracks to go to church. I walked with the women and he walked with the men, but we were together anyway. And we were listening together when the priest sang the beautiful Latin words of the mass.

21

ONE day when I went in to the little store and post office in Union they told me there was a letter for me. It was from Mamma Lena. Mamma Lena didn't write it — she couldn't write — but she had somebody write it for her. In the letter she said that she was getting old and sick and that I must come back and get Francesco. She said she had all my wages from America and a little besides to pay for the trip.

Oh, I was happy when I thought I could get back my Francesco! But would Santino let me go? I had to wait till he came home from the mine at night to ask him.

"Yes!" he said. "Just what I want! I don't trust the men that go back. You go there and get all my money from the bank. I am going to buy a business of my own and get rich." But he didn't tell me what the business was.

All the men and the girls in the camp were excited when they heard I was going back to Bugiarno. And one old man, Lorenzo, he asked to go with me. Lorenzo was sick with the consumption and the doctor said it would be nice if he could go home to die.

Enrico, the boss of the mine, found out how and when we could go and he bought the tickets and wrote it all down. Then came the Sunday to go and Gionin and all my *paesani* went on the wagon to

Union to say good-bye at the train. Miss Mabel and Mr. Miller were there too. But not Santino. Santino, like always on Sunday, was at Freddy's saloon with Annie and those other women.

"You be careful of my little godchild, Rosa," said Gionin as he lifted Domenico up to me on the train. "Don't let anything happen to him. And bring him soon back."

Gionin talked only of Domenico but I knew from the way his eyes were looking into mine that he was thinking of me too.

When the trainman called, "All aboard!" Lorenzo rushed in to the window and stood there waving back with tears running down his old cheeks. When the train went around a bend we could no more see our *paesani* but Lorenzo still stood there.

I put Domenico on the seat, then pulled the hat pins out of my hat and took it off.

"A hat is no good for a poor woman with a baby and satchels and bundles," I said, holding the hat up for Lorenzo to see. I had to say something to make him forget his sad parting. "I never had a hat before, but I thought it would be nice to be wearing a hat when I come back from America. Then that rascal Cicco, Nick's little dog, found it on the table and chewed up all the feathers."

"You look beautiful in a hat, Rosa," said Lorenzo. He wiped his nose and cheeks with the back of his hand and sat down across from me. "You will look nice coming home in a hat."

I stuffed the hat into one of my bundles and put on my headkerchief. No need to bother with the hat till I got off the *tramvai* in Bugiarno.

But would we ever get to Bugiarno? I had learned more English in two or three years than anyone else in camp. But would anyone but Miss Mabel and Mr. Miller and Enrico understand me? And would I understand their answers? If we got on the wrong train in St. Louis we would go to the other end of America. But Enrico had been good. He had taught me the things I must say.

I was shaking and shivering when we came out in the station in St. Louis, but I just smiled at Lorenzo and marched up to the man at the gate: "Please will you tell me where to get the train to New York?"

"The train to New York? In one hour it goes." The officer held up one finger and took out his watch and showed me. Then he motioned to one of the long seats. "You sit down and wait there and I will tell you when it is time."

"Thank you, *signore*. Thank you."

Think of that! I had talked English to a strange man and he had understood me. Lorenzo was looking at me like I was something wonderful. So then I started watching the clock and counting the minutes. But that minute hand moved so slow that I thought the clock must be wrong. So I went back to the man by the gate — I wasn't afraid at all. In America the poor can talk to anyone and ask what they want to know.

"Yes, yes," the man said. "I didn't forget you. It's still early. But if you are nervous you can go and stand over there by the gate and wait. That train outside is the train to New York."

So me and Domenico and Lorenzo were the first ones to go through. And before we climbed on I asked again, "Is this the train to New York?"

"Yes," said the trainman. "Yes. This is where you go." And he even took us in and showed us the seats to sit on.

So there was no mistake. We were going right. There was nothing more to worry about until we came to the end of the line. And we didn't have to worry about where in New York we must stay overnight for Enrico had it written down on a paper so all those men from the lodging houses couldn't cheat us.

In the lodging house Lorenzo slept in the big room for men and me and Domenico in the smaller room for women. And the next morning we were ready and down in the waiting room hours before it was time for the man from the lodging house to take us to the pier. So we got there all right. And, thanks to the Madonna, on this ship all the women in the third class went in one room and all the men in another. And because I had some extra money in the pocket of my underskirt I gave some to the *marinaro* and made him understand it is for water every day to drink and to keep the baby clean. We were only allowed some water to drink with our meals. Most of the other women were French nuns and they were all the time playing with Domenico. They loved Domenico. (But coming back, on this trip too, all the men and the women had to sleep in the same room and even in the same beds.)

Italia! We were in Italy again! I could talk to everyone! And I wasn't afraid now that I came from America. "Will you please help me with my little boy?" I said to the trainman as we changed trains in Turin. I didn't really need help but I wanted to ask for something.

"*Ma si, signora,*" said the trainman politely, taking Domenico while I climbed up with my bundles.

"*Grazie, signore. Grazie molte!*"

Lorenzo had climbed on first and was looking out the window. His old hat was pulled down over his eyes, but I could tell by the stiff way he sat on the board seat how excited he was. And I was excited too. Now we were so near, it was hard to wait to see my Francesco. And Mamma Lena. And Zia Teresa. And Toni. And Remo? Would I see Remo? He had been so brokenhearted when I was married to Santino that he had signed for another three years in the *militario*. Maybe he would not know that I was in Bugiarno — or could not come if he did.

Nearly all the poor people in Bugiarno were there waiting in the square when we got off the *tramvai* Sunday morning. Some of those young men that used to like me even went up on top of the church tower to see me get off the *tramvai*. Two of the old women who came to help me with my bundles reached out and touched my skirt and kissed my hand. They had known me ever since I was a little girl saying the Latin prayers for them in their courts. But now because I came from America and was wearing a hat and new shoes they thought I was something wonderful.

Then I saw Mamma Lena and Zia Teresa at one side with a little boy between them. That little boy must be my Francesco! I ran and threw my arms around him and kissed him. But he pushed me away.

"Give him time, Rosa," said Zia Teresa. "He was only a baby when you went away. You will have to get acquainted all over again."

But by the time we passed through the gate to the old *palazzo* I had Francesco's hand in mine and was swinging it back and forth, and he was half smiling at me. Sure it wouldn't take us long to get acquainted, me and my Francesco!

The big dark *osteria* smelled just as it always had — the same smell of men and of sour wine and of cabbage soup and of the chickens in the coop. A few of the guards who lived on the court had already come in and were sitting at the tables waiting for their noonday soup.

I took off my hat and hung it careful on a nail, but I didn't put on an apron. Today I had the job to entertain the people and I wanted to look nice. Zia Teresa and some of the other women who had come in would gladly help Mamma Lena.

All afternoon and far into the night the tables in the *osteria* were full. Even those young men from the church tower came in the evening and ordered wine so they could look at me and listen. The women sat on benches along the sides of the room and kept making me tell the same thing over and over. *Mamma mia*, but that was hard to believe — poor people in America eating meat every day! Tell about that again, Rosa. And about the streets of New York — show them how the people are always running and how they have to jump to get out of the way of the carriages and horses. And about those streetcars running right over the heads of the people! No wonder the horses get frightened! And about the ships. And tell how that Bartini got all your money, Rosa. And the mustard oil. Tell about your nice bottles of mustard oil. I myself liked to tell about that mustard oil. The men would laugh until they almost fell off the benches and slap each other on the back — to think of those high American men in all their gold braid trying to drink my mustard oil.

"And is it true, Rosa, that the *fiammetta* comes in America too?"

"Yes," I said. "There too I saw the *fiammetta*. But in America the people are not afraid like here. In America the high people teach the poor people and tell them not to be so scared." Then I told how Enrico had taken his lantern that night and made us poor Italians go there to the edge of the swamp where the little flame was and touch it, to show us that it wouldn't hurt anyone and how he had said that it was only some gas that comes out of the earth and not evil spirits at all.

"But if the *fiammetta* is not the evil spirit why does it come most in the cemetery?" said one old woman.

I didn't know, but I said, "I guess there's more grease in the cemetery and that's why."

I could see those people didn't believe me — that they would go right on almost dying from the scare when the *fiammetta* appeared in their fields.

"And Enrico says there is no such thing as people witching you with the evil eye," I told them. "He says it's foolish to be so scared of the *malocchio*. Nobody can make you sick just by looking at you." But even when I spoke the word *malocchio*, some of the old women crossed themselves in fear.

The first day the savings bank was open I went there with the papers to get the money for Santino. What Santino wanted with all that money I didn't know. There was nothing to buy in the mining camp in Missouri. But he had told me to get it and so I was getting it. There were many people already in line at the window. And all the time more men kept coming and the women had to wait and let the men go first. I stood there waiting and waiting and I got tired. There were some nice chairs there on the other side of a little railing — chairs for the high people. But why should the high people have chairs and not the poor? The more I thought about those chairs, the more I wanted to go in there and sit down. Those chairs were doing nothing — why shouldn't I sit on one? So finally I did it; I pushed open the little gate and went in and sat down.

"Oh, Rosa!" gasped the other poor women in the line. "Come back! Come back! You'll get arrested. They'll put you in jail!"

"Well the chairs are here and nobody is sitting on them," I said. "You come too and sit down."

Soon the janitor came.

"*Che impertinenza!*" he said. "Who gave you the permission to sit down?"

"Myself," I said and I smiled at him because I was no longer afraid. "The chairs belong to the bank, isn't that so! And the people who have money in the bank have the right to use them, no?"

"You think you're smart because you come from America!"

[190

"Yes," I said. "In America the poor people do get smart. We are not so stupid anymore."

And there the janitor could do nothing — he gave up and went away.

At last all the men had finished their business and only the women were left. So I got up and took my place before the window. And when it was my turn the officer smiled and bowed and didn't say anything at all about my sitting on the chair.

"If you please," I said in English. "How do you do. Thank-you. Good-bye." That Italian officer wouldn't know that the words didn't fit and I wanted to show him that I was learning to speak English.

And there he was bowing and smiling so polite and the women were all looking and looking, with their mouths hanging open.

So I gave him my papers and told him what I wanted. And he was shaking his head yes and saying, "*Si, signora. Si, si.*" And he arranged it so the bank would send the money to America for me, so I wouldn't have to carry it with me.

After all that good food I had had in America, I was no longer content with the sour-tasting black bread, or the thin onion-and-water soup, or a little polenta. I wanted to make thick soup with rice in it every day or cook the rice the way I had learned to cook it in America. "Whoever heard of such extravagance!" Mamma Lena would scold. "The people in America make pigs of themselves. They are like pigs!"

And if I turned up the lamp a little at night so I could see to clean the tables and do the knitting, Mamma Lena would scold, "You are all the time wasting! Don't waste the oil like that!"

Even when I played with Francesco and Domenico Mamma Lena would scold, "It's a sin to spoil the children like that!" Though she was always picking up Domenico and holding him.

"Rosa," she said one day when she was holding him. "When you go back to America with Francesco you can leave Domenico with me. He's younger. I can take care of him better."

"No!" I said. "No!"

Mamma Lena didn't say anything — she didn't even scold. Before I went to America I would have been afraid to say no.

[191

Saturday night I went to confession. And on Sunday I went to mass and again to vespers. Mamma Lena and some of those other women thought I was not so religious, not so good, now that I came from America. I had to show them I had just as strong religion in America as in Italy. In the mining camp there wasn't any way to go to confession, except for those girls who were getting married, but that was not my fault.

Bianca, the cousin of Remo, with her straight hair and big nose was waiting for me outside the church after vespers. I left Zia Teresa and ran to see what Bianca wanted.

"Rosa," whispered Bianca, "I sent word to Remo that you were back and he got leave and came home. He says for you to come to our house for supper tonight and he can see you there."

All week women had been asking me to come to their houses to eat so they could hear about America. But I had said no because I knew those people would have to go hungry a week after. Mamma Lena would think I said yes to Bianca because her family was not so poor. Mamma Lena would never know that Remo was there.

"Yes, Bianca," I said. "I'll go first to tell Mamma Lena, then I'll come."

Remo's mother and his uncle, Zio Ferdinando, and his aunt, Zia Chiara, had all come to the *osteria* with Bianca during the week and greeted me there. So when I came into their big room Sunday night they stood back and let Remo greet me alone.

There he was, dressed like a soldier, but looking just the same as he always had. He didn't even seem any older.

"*Benvenuto*, Rosa," he said. "Welcome!" And his eyes smiled, shy like, into mine.

"Hello, Remo," I said. But after that there seemed to be nothing to say or do.

"Well, let us eat," said Zio Ferdinando. "Let us go to the table and eat."

Bianca and her mother served the wine and the Sunday rice, the *minestra*, and we all sat down and ate. And after eating they all just sat there waiting for me to say something — waiting for me to entertain them. But what could I say? I couldn't think. It was in this room that

[192

Remo had said good-bye and run back to the army, afraid of the punishment. It was in this room that Mamma Lena had found me under the bed and dragged me home to marry Santino.

"Tell us about the mines, Rosa," said Zio Ferdinando. "Do the men work in tunnels down under the earth?"

"No, Zio Ferdinando," I said. "There is one tunnel — one big hole — but most of the men dig the iron right out of the open quarry."

I could feel Remo's eyes on me as I spoke. I should not have come. I was a married woman now and the mother of two children.

"No, Zio Ferdinando. They use hand drills and picks. . . . No, they load it on railway cars and it goes to the blast furnace near another town. . . . Yes, the single men all go together to eat. . . . Yes, I cook for twelve now. At first I had thirteen."

I wanted to tell about Gionin — about how Gionin couldn't stand it to see Santino beat me and beat the baby and that was why he had gone away. But what would Remo think if he knew about Gionin?

"Those men are good," I said. "At first I didn't know anything about cooking and I was feeding them plaster. But they didn't scold or anything. They just tried to help me."

When there was nothing more to say Zio Ferdinando asked when I was going back to America.

"I don't know," I said. "Some men are leaving next week for Missouri and my cousin Giuseppe, Zia Teresa's last son, is going with them. But Mamma Lena doesn't want me to go so soon."

At last the *lume* started flickering — the oil in that little lamp was almost gone.

"It's time I went home," I said. And as I got my shawl and chewed-up hat, Remo got his cap and coat and waited by the door.

"Better you go with them, Bianca," said Zio Ferdinando.

Bianca hesitated, looking first at Remo and then at me.

"Yes, Bianca," I said. "You come too." And I waited for her to get her shawl and headkerchief.

"Rosa," said Remo as soon as we were out in the darkness of the court. "Don't go next week! Please don't! Other men will be going to America later. Listen, Rosa. I'll tell you a secret. I think there is going to be a war. If war comes all those men in America will have to come back and fight. Santino too. Then maybe he will be killed. Maybe there will be a chance for me yet. Stay here, Rosa, and see if the war comes."

And Remo held my hand in his as we walked in silence across the square and back to the old *palazzo*.

"Addio, Remo," I said when we reached the gate to the court. Then I threw my arms around Bianca and kissed her on the cheek. "Dear, kind Bianca," I said. "I know how much you love him too!"

Then pushing open the gate I closed it quick behind me and stood there leaning against it. Mamma Lena had not gone to bed. There was still a light in the *osteria*. But I didn't want to go in just yet. I must decide what to do. Suppose the war did come and Santino got killed. Did I still want to marry Remo? I could dance all my life with Remo! But what about Gionin back there in Missouri? Gionin couldn't dance at all, but Gionin was ready to sit in jail the rest of his life to save me from Santino. He was even ready to die. Remo had been afraid — afraid of the punishment — when I wanted him to run away with me. Gionin was not pretty like Remo and he didn't care about the nice clothes. But Gionin was bigger, stronger, safer. Gionin had never even tried to touch my hand, but the gentleness that came into his fiery eyes when he looked into mine! Just the thought of Gionin made me stop shivering and feel more calm. And how Gionin loved my little Domenico! I smiled as I thought of the sympathy that strong man had for a helpless baby. And how happy he had been when he made the nice cradle. Gionin would love Francesco too. Gionin was crazy for the children.

Slow, slow, I took off my hat and walked on across the court. The *osteria* was empty except for Mamma Lena and one old drunk man who sat at the end of the second table. I went over to Mamma Lena and watched her for a while as she scrubbed the boards of the table with sand and a wet rag to make the rings of the wine glasses go away. "Mamma Lena," I said at last, "I think I will go back with those men who are going next week."

For a moment Mamma Lena let the rag rest on the table and just looked at me. Then she picked up the rag and an empty wine bottle and went on to the man at the end of the table. "Pay your bill and get out!" she said, shaking him by the shoulder.

The man looked up with sleepy eyes, then started feeling in his pockets. Finally he pulled out a little wallet, but couldn't untie the string. Mamma Lena did it for him, counted out what he owed, and gave the wallet back. Then she stood and waited as he got to his feet and staggered off across the room. When he had gone she came and sat down by the table across from me. For a long while we sat there together in silence. And when at last Mamma Lena spoke she was not like Mamma Lena at all. She was just like any other old woman who was alone and sad. "I wish you could stay a little longer with that new baby, Rosa," she said. "But you must do what you think best."

22

EARLY in the morning a few days after I returned to the mining camp in Missouri there came a queer-looking bird and it sat on the little thorn-apple tree by the outhouse. It didn't sing like other birds — it would just chirp a few timid questions and then scold with all its might. Santino went out there and looked. Then he called me.

"What kind of a bird is it?" he asked. "What kind of a bird is it?"

So I went out and I looked. That bird it wasn't like any bird I had ever seen in my life. It looked kind of like a bluejay in front but its body was all red and bare skin.

"What kind of a bird is it?" Santino asked again, and I could tell he was scared.

"I don't know," I said. "I never in my life saw a bird like that before!" And I even felt a little scared myself.

So then when the men started coming for breakfast Santino made them look too. But nobody — nobody — had ever seen a bird with naked skin like that.

Santino got angry. "God is a dog! Why does that bird just stay there and keep on talking and scolding?" And he picked up some rocks and tried to kill it, but he missed and the bird flew away.

The next morning, just the same, there it was again. And again Santino tried to kill it with rocks, but again the bird flew away.

When it came back the third day Santino was wild. "Who is going to die in this house?" he wanted to know. "That bird isn't going to make *me* die!" And he got the ax from the shed and went out and chopped the little tree down.

After that the bird didn't come anymore — there was no other tree — and Santino was content: death couldn't get *him* — *he* had chased death away.

Gionin had been in my house while I was away — that I knew, for there in the bedroom waiting for Francesco when I came back was a little bed made of boards with a straw mattress already on it. It was funny: anyone could see how that little boy looked just like his father — just like Santino — but he was afraid and wouldn't go near Santino at all. But on Sunday, when Gionin offered to carry Francesco those four miles to the church in Arcadia he was glad and didn't want Gionin to put him down at all.

"Domenico *carino*," sang crazy Francesca, stopping in the middle of the tracks to pinch Domenico's cheeks and make him grab her fingers. "When it's not nice weather, Rosa, you leave Domenico with me. I don't have such a strong religion that I have to walk four miles going and four miles coming back to go to mass in bad weather."

Yes, everybody in camp loved Domenico and my Francesco — except their father. Only Santino paid no attention — unless they cried. When they cried he went after them to slap them.

Santino was angry with me when I came back from Italy without the money. He wanted it right away and he didn't trust the bank to send it. So every day I had to put Francesco and Domenico in a little cart and walk those two or three miles to the post office in Union to ask if it had come. I didn't mind the long walk — I was even glad — because I liked so much to see Mr. Miller and Miss Mabel and to learn a little more English every day. And after some weeks, sure enough, there was the money from the bank in Bugiarno. But it came all in Italian and Santino wanted American money. So then I told the men in the camp. When I told them I would give Italian money for American, oh, they were happy and they came running to my house after work with all the savings they had. They didn't believe much in

American money — they were not used to it — and they were happy when they could change it. Enrico, the boss of the mine, told me how much to give in exchange and I did the figuring and was keeping the accounts. Santino couldn't do it himself — he had never been to school to learn reading and figuring.

Mamma mia, those men had a lot of pennies! They must have been saving them the same as me. I had tied mine in a cloth and they were in the bottom of my chest. I had been saving them for a long time. I didn't think it was a sin to save out pennies from my husband — a penny is such a little thing. God couldn't be bothered with a penny. It's only a sin to take something big like a dollar. Santino would never miss the pennies — he wouldn't know the difference. Then if I needed money sometime I would have it.

The days grew colder. Santino hardly came home at all any more. Where he went and what he did I didn't know, but I was happy he stayed away from me.

But one day about twelve o'clock night he came home and shook me to wake me up. He said, "Put on your clothes and come. I've got the wagon with horses. We're going in the woods to see a new house."

Me, I didn't know why we go in the middle of the night, but what he said I did, that was all. I put my Francesco and Domenico under a blanket in the back of the wagon and we went. We went far and we came to one house all alone in the woods. There were a lot of men in there when I went in to look. And right away one of those men came up and put both his arms around me. I punched him away. He said, "Well, why for you come here, then?"

I said, "I came with my husband. My husband brought me."

So that man could see I didn't know and he told me what kind of a place it was. I asked my husband and he said, "Yes."

But I don't ever want my children to know about that bad business my husband bought. I never told them — never! I can't even tell them now. That man, maybe he's alive yet, and rich. He can kill me if I tell about him. He's got the policemen and all those high-up politicians for his friends. He makes them the present of a pile of money, and when someone tries to make him trouble, the politicians help him along.

[198

Just think! My husband paid all the money he had for that place. And he arranged already with one other man to come in there with him, because that man could play the concertina. So then he told me, he said, "Tomorrow you're going to move in this house with the children. You're going to live here and manage the business and take in the money."

When I heard that terrible thing I started fighting with him. He said, "Well, if you don't want to do with the men yourself, all right. But you're going to manage the business anyway."

I said, "Never! Never! I belong to God and the Madonna! You can't give me to the Devil! God will help me! God is stronger than you! God is stronger than the Devil! You can't give me to the Devil!"

Oh, my husband was mad! He even started hollering at God and calling God names — terrible, terrible names. I was even looking to see if God didn't strike him dead, the terrible things he said about God!

Five hundred dollars was a lot of money in that time. And there he thought he would lose it all if I wouldn't do what he said. He was beating me and beating, but he couldn't make me go. I belong to God; he couldn't give me to the Devil! He was even beating my children. That man was like insane when I wouldn't do what he said.

Once Don Domenic told me it's a sin for a wife not to obey her husband. But when the husband wants the wife to sin against God, then it's a sin to obey him. I remembered that now, but what could I do? Me with two little children! I was praying God and praying the Madonna. When night came I left a little lamp burning on the shelf in the bedroom, but I was not sleeping. I was watching and I was listening. Santino said he was going to kill me. And I believed him.

I heard him come home. I heard him sharpening his razor. Then I heard him come slow, slow, into the room to not wake me. But I had my eyes wide open looking at him. When he saw me looking like that, with my rosary held tight in my hand, he went away again. The next night just the same he came in quiet, quiet, with that razor. But he couldn't catch me asleep. Me, I'd rather die than go to the Devil, but I didn't want to die either, and that man meant it for sure. He was only waiting till he found me asleep. I was too scared to go to sleep and I

[199

didn't know what to do. I was praying the Madonna and praying God, what I could do.

After two nights like that, I couldn't stand it. Early in the morning I went by Francesca, the cousin of Gionin. She said, "Run away, Rosa. Don't stay there and let him kill you! Ask Gionin. Gionin loves you. He will tell you what to do."

So I went by Gionin. I knew that man was good — he had the strong religion. He was one to never miss when we walked those four miles to mass on Sunday.

Gionin was not in the mine — he was outside. When I told him, he said, "Don't wait, Rosa! Run away before he can kill you. Go to Chicago to my cousins. I will send the telegram to Tomaso and tell him you come. Go before Santino comes out from the mine. You go, and so soon as I can I will come myself to Chicago and help you." Then he gave me a paper with the name of those cousins in Chicago and the street and number where they lived.

I ran home and made a little bundle of clothes for me and my children. Then I went in the bottom of my wood chest and took out all the pennies, about twenty-five dollars I had, all in pennies. I took that bag of pennies and my two children and the little bundle and I sneaked out. I caught right away that man that goes all the time with the meat wagon to Union.

The man in the station was a kind man. He told me I could go on the train from St. Louis right to Chicago, without changing trains. Then he counted all the pennies how much I needed for my ticket and he gave me the ticket and let me go.

About one o'clock night I came in the big station in Chicago. No one was there to meet me and I didn't know I could stay there in the station. I went right through and came out in the street. (It was good I didn't think I could stay in the station, because the policemen, they had the telegram already to arrest a young Italian woman with the shawl over her head and two children. I didn't know then about the police, but they couldn't catch me anyway, because I was right away out in the street.) So I was out there in the street in the night and I was talking to my Francesco and my Domenico in Italian. I said, "Oh, children, what are we going to do? Where are we going to go?" And then I was praying, "Oh God help me! I don't know where I'm going to go! Oh Madonna, You pray for me!"

I always was praying. And it is true — I don't remember one time when I asked for something with all my heart and I didn't get it from God. I pray God and the Madonna and all the time I get my prayer!

So I was standing there in the street praying and the man in a little fruit store heard me. He came out and he said, "Lady, I'm Italian too. Don't you know where you go?"

Oh, I was happy when I heard that man talking in Italian! He was talking *Toscano* like Gionin. I said, "Well I've got the name and the number for one *Toscano* man, but I don't know where to go. Do you know him? His name is here."

"Well I don't know," he said. "But I'll take you near on the streetcar. I'll take you by one other *Toscano* that has a fruit store up Milwaukee Avenue."

So we came on the streetcar near to Chicago Avenue. Then that man had to change to another streetcar to go home, but he showed me where to go. I went in the fruit store he showed me and I found another *Toscano*. So I showed him my paper with the address and asked him where to go.

He said, "Yes, I know that man. You're going to go about three blocks up this way. You walk this street till you come by one store where are the coats and the hats for men in the window. Next to that you'll see a little gate with three steps going down. You go in that gate, then you go way back behind the store and you'll find the back door to that man you want."

Me, I was kind of scared in the night like that, and I was afraid I couldn't find it. I ask that *Toscano* if I could just stay there in his store till the morning. But I guess he was afraid to have me there with two children. He said he had to close the store. So then I went. I walked those three blocks and past the store I found that little gate. I went in and way back in the dark till I found the door with a little piece of roof over, like he said. I put down my bundle and I started to knock on the door. *Bump-bump, bump-bump,* I was knocking and it sounded so loud. But nobody came.

I sat down on the step with Domenico sleeping in my arms and

Francesco holding my dress. Then it started to rain. It poured rain. About an hour we stayed there and we were getting so cold — my children were crying with the cold. I said, "Oh, I'm going to knock again," and I began to pound and pound.

Pretty soon, sure enough, I heard a noise inside — somebody was coming. They hollered through the door, "Who is it?"

I said, "Rosa, the friend of Gionin. Rosa Cristoforo."

"Oh yes, yes!" They opened the door. "Yes, sure we knew about you from Gionin. Come in. Come in. We knew you would come but we didn't know when." So then they made some coffee, because we were wet through and so cold, and they made me and my children go to bed and rest. They were very good and very kind, because they were good friends and cousins with Gionin — they came from the same town in Tuscany.

But after one or two days I didn't like to stay no more with two children and make them so much bother. So I asked them where I could go to find work and the room to stay in. They sent me by some other *Toscani* who were working in the plaster, making the statues for the cemetery and all those ornament things. There were sixteen men and they said they would give me five cents each to wash their shirts.

Those shirts, I had to take the knife and scrape before I could wash them, and then I was rubbing all the skin off my hand. But I was glad to have those sixteen shirts. I got eighty cents a week. Oh, that was good to have! Then I found one restaurant to scrub the floor.

Three days I stayed by those good *Toscana* people. Then here came Gionin.

23

GIONIN found three little rooms for me in a big wooden house by the railroad. There were about ten Norwegian families in that house and two Italian men, Toni and his old father. Toni, he was North Italian like us but he was *Genovese*. He was a nice young man — short, but he was pretty with black hair and gray eyes. He was one of those artists that put down the marble to make the *mosaico*. That old father had a hand-organ, but he was too old and sick to go very much on the street. They were in one of those three rooms when we came, so we let them stay and help pay the rent — we were all North Italian together.

Gionin, he had a little money from the mine at Union so he could pay the rent. Then he bought a little secondhand stove and some wood and coal. The table he made himself from some boards he found in the street, and he made the bed too. But no chairs. For chairs we were sitting down on those big American Family Soap boxes. Then we had to buy some blankets. But Gionin was afraid to stay there with me — he was afraid the police would come. So he was sleeping by some of those other *Toscani* and by his cousin Tomaso.

The other people from *Toscana* were not religious, but Gionin never missed one Sunday to go to church. So here it was the first Sunday in Chicago and we didn't know where there was a church. Oh my goodness! We walked and walked and walked and walked and all the time asked somebody else, but everybody kept saying, "You're going right. It's far." We went way to that church on Franklin and Illinois. Me and my children froze to death walking. But we never even thought we could take that streetcar with the horse on. I was in America ten years and I never took the streetcar. We needed those five cents to eat. Five cents was enough to make the whole supper for the family in that time. Only the rich people could take the streetcar — not us poor people.

After not long Gionin found work. The first work he had in Chicago, he was carrying the bricks and mud for the new church they were making over past Chicago Avenue. It's a Polish church now but in that time it was Irish. He used to come by me with his shoulders all sore — all open — from carrying those bricks and I was making him some cotton-cloth pads to put on his shoulders so they don't get so cut. And every noon I used to carry him a little pail with the stuff to eat.

But sure enough! One day I was home doing the washing — I was bending over my tub scrubbing and rubbing those plaster shirts and with my foot rocking the cradle because my Domenico was sick and all the time crying — and here came the policeman to take me to jail. I couldn't understand much what he said so he talked to Toni. Toni told the police I was not the kind of woman he said and I didn't run around with no man. He said, "Don't take her to jail. She's an angel from heaven the way she works and takes care for her children!"

The police could see when he looked how I was doing all that heavy washing and taking care for my sick Domenico. So he said he didn't want to arrest me — he thought it would be a mistake. But then he told Toni I had to be in the court tomorrow morning. He said if I promised to be there and didn't run away he wouldn't put me in jail. He was good, that policeman. He didn't arrest me and he gave me fifteen cents to get some kind of medicine for Domenico. He wrote it on a paper what kind of medicine I must get from the drugstore.

So the next day I was in the court with my two children. Gionin and all his friends came there with me. Toni too. There I was, a young Italian girl with a shawl over my head, and I couldn't understand nothing. When we went by the judge, there was Santino from

[204

Missouri! He was telling the judge that I was the worst kind of woman — that I ran away and was living with all the men, and this and that. He wanted the judge to punish me and put me to jail.

I can't tell you very much what happened, because the judge was talking English to all those friends of Gionin and to Toni. When he asked me the question Toni told me what it was and I answered the truth, that's all. In the end the judge told Santino to get out of town. He said if he was not gone by six o'clock the same day he would put *him* to jail instead of me. Then he said, "And don't you ever come back, either!"

Six o'clock night, when the train was supposed to leave for St. Louis, Gionin and all his friends and all his relatives in Chicago were there in the depot with stones. If Santino didn't go they were going to stone him. When Santino saw all those people taking my part he had no intention to stay. He went back to Union. He went back there and got the divorce; then he married one of those women he was living with. But I heard later from his sister-in-law that that woman wouldn't take so much like me. When he started beating her she got him put in jail. He sat in jail twenty months for one beating he gave that new wife! That man, I have to leave him out of my story, that's all.

So after Santino had the divorce Gionin and me went to the court in Chicago and got married together. The priest said he couldn't marry us in the church because I had that first husband living — only when he died we could be married in the church. Me, I was crying with tears coming down my eyes and praying God, "Oh God, why do You make it a sin for me to live with this good man Gionin? He's so good and so religious! My children will starve if he doesn't take care! Why do You make that a sin? How can that be a sin?"

Once a long time after, when Father Alberto came to America, I went by him and told him how I didn't say yes that time I was married with Santino in Bugiarno. I told him the priest was deaf but the people knew it that I didn't say yes. He said, "Well, if you can find all the people who were at your wedding and they sign their names on the paper that you didn't say yes, then I can marry you in the church."

But how am I going to find all those people? I can't, that's all!

[205

(After Gionin and me were married together about ten years and have already three children, a missionary from Italy came in our church. He preached so strong against the divorce — what a sin it is against God, and the punishment God is going to give those people, and all and all — that Gionin got the scare and he went away and left me. About three months he left me alone to take care for all those children. Nobody but me knew why he went away that time, but I knew it was all the *missionario*'s doing. So then one day he went to confession to Father Alberto and Father Alberto told him it's a sin to leave me alone like that with those children. Oh, Gionin was glad to hear that, so he could come back! He said he only left me because he didn't want to go to hell.)

My husband he was many months carrying the bricks and the mud for that new church. But then those other *Toscana* people — that little bunch of *Toscani* were all very friends together — they said to him, "Oh, you're foolish, Gionin. Why you don't get the horse and wagon and sell the bananas like us?"

So he did it — he got the horse and the wagon and he used to peddle the bananas. And when the cranberries came he sold the cranberries too.

Oh, now I remember another little thing to tell. One time Gionin bought a new horse and he came home and told me about it. He said he changed in the old one and he gave some money too for another one. He said, "Rosa, I bought a nice horse this time. But I don't know if I did right. There was another horse there for ten dollars more — it was still a nicer one. What d'you think?"

And I said, "Well, if you think it's worth ten dollars more you give it to him." But we didn't say no more about it. We went to sleep and we think no more. So in the morning my husband took the bananas and the horse and wagon and he went.

Then here came a *Toscana* man and he said, "Lady, you're the wife to Gionin?"

"Yes."

"Well Gionin, he said for you to give me the ten dollars because he wants to go by Guido and take that other horse."

And I said, "Why do *you* come for the ten dollars? Why did he send you and not come himself?"

"Well he sent me because he wanted to wait there on Franklin Street."

"Well," I said, "can't that other *Toscana* man give the horse, anyway, and trust my husband for ten dollars? If Guido won't even trust him one day, I don't have the ten dollars to give him!"

"Well," said the man, "don't get sore about it. I only do like he told me."

And I said, "Well, I don't have one dollar — not one cent. I can't give it to you."

There I had all my husband's money in my underskirt pocket, but I told him I had not one penny.

So then my husband came home at night and I asked him why he sent that man for ten dollars, instead to come himself.

He said, "Why Rosa, I didn't send nobody. I didn't go by Guido today. I didn't go."

"Oh, for the love of Mike!" I said. "That man came here and he said to give him the ten dollars. And he was a *Toscano* too." So then I told all about it.

Gionin said, "Well, God, He blessed you this time, Rosa, that you didn't give it!"

And nobody — nobody — knew where that man came from! I don't know yet who he was or how he could know about that other horse.

My husband when he was young was a beautiful man — nice teeth, nice hair, nice face, and big and strong. So all those ladies on Franklin Street, they liked him. And one woman, Dina, she loved him. And she all the time sent for him. But I don't think he did anything with her — he was just a very friend of her husband because they both sold bananas and would go together to buy them. I was brokenhearted, but I never said anything about it.

Well then one day a *Toscana* woman she came by me and said, "Oh Rosa, I saw your husband go in Dina's house and stay all night last night."

And sure, I knew he didn't come home till one o'clock. I was crying by myself and asking myself what I am going to do. So after that *Toscana* woman left me I said, "I know what I'm going to do to get happy again!"

I took my new baby in my arms — my Visella was just two or three weeks old that time — and I walked way to State and Superior Street to the Holy Name Church. I don't know if it's there anymore, but there used to be a crucifix in the front hall of that church with Jesus about nine feet tall. It made you shiver to look at Him. I kneeled down saying all the prayers and crying for about one hour. And then I was looking up at the face. When you go here that face looks at you, and when you go there it looks. Where you are makes no difference — those eyes look at you anyway.

So then I took my little baby in my arms and started home. And all at once I was happy — I didn't have that worry no more in my heart. And after I passed Franklin Street and came by the bridge on Indiana, I met Cesca, the wife of Tomaso the cousin of Gionin.

"Oh my goodness, Rosa!" she said. "Where did you go with that little baby?"

I said, "I just went on State Street."

"Oh, you went to the Boston Store?"

"No, just on State Street."

She said, "Your eyes are so red. You've been crying?"

But me, I didn't tell. I didn't say nothing.

Then she said, "Oh, Rosa, didn't you kill your husband last night?"

"Why do you say that?" I asked her.

"Oh," she said, "those three cousins they make me so much trouble! They were playing cards in my house till one o'clock night and I couldn't chase them away. They learn to gamble with those cards like the American men, and I can't chase them away."

So then when my husband came home that night he was so sleepy. I said, "Sure you're sleepy. Why not when you come home one o'clock night?"

He said, "Yes, I went by Cesca's and I was playing cards."

So then I began weeping and I told him all that I had done.

He said, "Why Rosa, I have no intentions with those other

women — they're jolly, that's all. Do you think I can put the beauty of you with that Dina and her rotten teeth?" And the tears were coming down from his eyes too. He said, "Rosa, I tell you, I'll never again walk in Dina's house! Never!" And he surely never did. And he even stopped buying bananas with Dina's husband.

Those other *Toscani* they were not religious. Only Gionin had the strong religion. And that husband of Dina was terrible. When he and Gionin took their wagons and went together to peddle bananas and they came near a church he would say, "Hey, Gionin, hurry up and move away from this bad-luck place!" He wouldn't go near the churches and he hated the priests. He'd say, "Those blackbirds in there make me sick. If they put God alive in *my* mouth I will spit Him out! I will chew God up and spit Him out!" That man was so bad I was glad when Gionin stopped peddling bananas with him. It was only because they were *Toscani* together that they were friends like that. They had only a little bunch of *Toscani* in Chicago. The other Italians around there came later and they were Sicilian.

The people from *Toscana* they're not good like the people from *Lombardia*. But they're not bad like the people from *Sicilia* — I should say not! The people from *Piemonte* are a little more bad than the people from *Lombardia*, but they come next. *Lombardia* is the last in the world to do wrong things. The Italian government made that investigation and they said so. Gionin was not like the other *Toscani* in Chicago, but they were all *paesani* — they all stuck together and helped the other.

24

PRETTY soon after the World's Fair — that Fair of 1893 — there came such a hard time. Oh, it was so poor a time! Some people had no room to sleep in, so the city was making a big wooden building to cover them up. Oh, that was a terrible, terrible poor time! There was no work; the men couldn't stay in Chicago. So Gionin he went away too. He pawned his watch and my wedding gold — all that we had he gave that pawn man to get ten dollars for the big boots and the ticket. Then he went to the sawmill in Wisconsin where they saw the trees, and he was taking care for the engine in the nighttime. But he had to go the whole month before he got the ten dollars' wage to send me. Me and my children were home there and starving.

One time I remember I had nothing to eat for three days in the house, and Domenico he came up *so* hungry. He said, "Mamma, Mis' Sibel downstairs, she's got a whole loaf of bread! I came past her door and I see it — she's got a whole loaf of bread on the table and one little piece too!"

I said, "Well, I don't know. You want to ask her for some?"

"No, Mamma," he said. "If I ask her maybe she don't give it. I'll just go in and take that little piece."

"No, no, Domenico," I said. "That's stealing — that's a sin."

That poor little boy he was crying and crying, and *so* hungry. Pretty soon he couldn't stand it anymore. He went down by that lady's door. He was there looking at the bread and waiting for Mis' Sibel to come back. That lady didn't come and didn't come, so Domenico he took that little chunk of bread and ate it up. When he saw Mis' Sibel coming up the stairs, he told her. That woman, she was the wife to the saloon man, she was rich — she had plenty to eat — she didn't care for the little chunk of old bread. When she saw how starving my little boy was she was sorry. Instead of licking him for stealing she took him in her house and gave him that whole loaf of bread to bring home.

In that time I was scrubbing the saloon — all the floors in the saloon downstairs for fifty cents. But I didn't get the fifty cents; the man he kept that for my rent. Then I had to move to the attic on the top floor. We were right under the roof in the really attic, because I could no more pay those six dollars rent we paid on the third floor: I was doing the scrubbing and giving two dollars more. He gave me the attic for the scrubbing — four dollars a month rent. Oh, sometimes I was wishing I was back in *Italia!* But sometimes not too.

In that time the city hall was giving food to the people. The people were standing in line there on Clinton Street where the rope pulled up the streetcar. We used to get for one week a piece of salt pork and some dried peas and the loaf of bread and some coffee or some tea. Sometimes we stood there half the day and when it's our turn they had no more left to give. One day I was standing there early, early in the morning, so I would come in before the food was gone. Us poor women were frozen to death; we didn't have the warm clothes, and there was such a storm with the snow and the wind! Eight o'clock, when the door opened, all the people were pushing to get in. There came the police with their clubs and they were yelling like we were animals. Then one of those police hit the woman next to me on the head with his club. I didn't see her, but I don't think she pushed. The people behind were pushing us, that's all. When I saw that, I said to myself, "Better I starve before I let that policeman hit me!" And I ran home from that line. And I never, never went there again.

Another place the people were waiting in line was the police station. Every day they gave a little pail of soup and a piece of bread for each family. I used to send my Domenico and Visella. But Visella was so little she couldn't stand it — she chewed up half the bread before she came home. We used to get a little coal sometimes from the city — like two bags in one month. We were freezing up there under the roof. When we could find nothing else to burn, Domenico and Visella used to go and find the wood blocks that came loose in the road so we had something to burn in our stove. All the roads were made of those wood blocks in that time. My Domenico, he was six or seven years old, he used to go for five cents a week by one lady and carry the coal and the wood. Every day he carried two pails of coal — big pails — from the basement to the third floor, and he chopped the wood and carried that too. So every Saturday he got one nickel. Oh, how glad he was to come home with that nickel! He gave it to me and we bought the big soup bone and had good soup. You know in that time the meat was cheap — for five cents you got a big piece; but we didn't have the nickel to buy. Now the women complain the meat is dear, but they've got the fifty cents to buy it.

Once in that poor time I was crying and praying. All the night I was praying. I said, "Oh God, if I can only have a crust of bread for these children! I have not one crumb in the house — not one thing!"

Early in the morning I went down the stairs to empty the dirty water in the basement. There in the snow I thought I saw something shine like money. I put down my pail and went there. I thought probably I mistake — it's a piece of tin — and there I was scared to pick it up. But sure enough, I took it in my hand and it was a quarter! Think of that miracle! I ran to the store without even a shawl on my head. For fifteen cents the lady gave me a whole bag of bread pieces, because they were stale, so I had ten cents for another day. I came home and I hollered, "Children, get up! Get up! I've got a big bag of bread!" Those children, they couldn't believe it — they had to see it for themselves. So then they all jumped up and we had that bread with some tea I had left from the city hall. Three children I had home that time: my Domenico, my Visella, and my Maria. And me, I was in family-way with my first Leo. I no longer had my Francesco. Just after I came in Chicago Mamma Lena sent word for Francesco to come back to Bugiarno with some men who were going. She said she had arranged already to send Francesco to school to make him a priest. And when I knew she wanted to make him a priest I couldn't say no. But he didn't make a priest. After a few years the school said it's no use. Maybe he can be an artist or something else, but not a priest.

That quarter I found when I prayed God for some bread, it was really a miracle! But you know, even when I was so poor, I never wanted to die. I used to suffer and didn't get discouraged because I thought it was supposed to be like that. I had such a strong religion — such a good faith. I thought God wanted it that way and when He wanted different it would be.

One day a beautiful lady came in my house — a beautiful dancer. She said she wanted somebody to wash her clothes and clean her house. She went by those American ladies in the house next door first — Mis' Nelson and Mis' Regan — and they told her about me. I said, "Well, lady, I can wash good, but I don't know to iron. I never did the ironing."

She said, "Oh yes, you can do it — they're all silk things." So I went there with her — far on the north side. We went on the streetcar, because it would take the whole day to walk.

She said, "Here." She gave me just a little bundle of washing — a bunch of handkerchiefs and the silk kimono and the underwear — and she said, "When you get through the washing, you can clean the house." She showed me those three rooms and what to do. Then she said, "When you finish you close the door and leave the house." She put there on the table meat and potatoes; then she gave me one dollar. When I saw those good things to eat and one dollar for such a little work I almost fainted! Then she went — she had to go back to her work in the theater.

So I continued for a long time to do that little work every week and made one dollar. Think how nice — how happy I was! But then one day she said she had to leave — she had to go away with the company. She said, "Rosa, when I come back, the first thing I'm going to find you again."

I came home so sad and so sorry. I met that Mis' Nelson and the other lady and I had tears coming down from my eyes. But I told them that she was going to find me again when she came back.

[213

So it went along and it was April, in that terrible poor year, and a lot of snow. Here came that Mis' Nelson in my house and she said, "Rosa, I got a letter from that dancing lady. She's in the same place and she wrote the letter to tell you to go right away back — today. She thought you wouldn't understand if she wrote to you. You go to that same place."

I had only one nickel in my house to make the supper for my family, but I was so glad. I took that nickel and went on the streetcar; then I had to walk a long piece too. My shoes were all broke open, with my feet cold and freezing, so I had the chill — wet and a chill. But anyway I was happy. I knocked on the door. Here came a lady I never saw before. I said, "Some ladies said I have the letter to come here and wash the clothes for Miss Miller."

She said, "Well, I don't know; I don't think she's coming back. She didn't come back yet. But you come in and get warm. I think I know what those women did to you. Those ladies, they fooled you. Today is the April Fool. But that's no way to do to a poor lady that can't understand! I don't think it's right for the American women to fool a poor lady that doesn't know how to talk English!"

She let me get warm and she gave me a cup of coffee. Then she went to her closet and found some shoes to put on me, and she gave me some stockings too. Me, I wanted to cry — I had even no money to go home. That good lady, she gave me the carfare. But how did I know in America they make the April Fool? I didn't even know what it was. And there I lost that nickel I was saving to make some supper for my children.

Toni, he had no work in the mosaic and he couldn't find no work anywhere. So then he remembered that organ his old father used to carry on the street. He said, "I don't care for me, but those poor children!" He had many meals nothing to eat himself, but he couldn't stand it when he heard my children cry for hunger. So he took that organ on his back and he went the whole day — but far away where there were rich people. I remember he had three or four songs in that organ. He used to play "Rosie O'Grady," and "After the Ball Is Over," and one song it went like this: "Boy and girl together, me and Maimie Morain" — or O'Ryan or something that sounded like that. So he used to go around and pick up a few cents with that organ.

One night he came home after all day and he said, "Here, I made fifteen cents today! Take it and we'll make a polenta!"

We ran out and for three cents we got the bag of cornmeal; then we got some liver. The liver was cheap in that time — they were throwing it to the cats and dogs. (Not like now, huh? Now it's the style to eat liver.) So I cooked that cornmeal with the liver in it and made a nice polenta. My children, when they got that good supper — oh, I wish you had seen it! They thought it was the king's wedding!

He all the time helped us in that hard time, Toni. I guess if he didn't, me and my children would be starved. He had no work, but he carried that hand-organ every day the whole day and picked up a few cents from the rich. What he had he gave to me to make the meal so everybody could eat. After the poor time, Toni got the good job again making the mosaic. Then my husband made his sister come from *Italia*, and Toni married her. But that sister was working in those places to sew the clothes — those dark places where they used to make the clothes — and she got the consumption and died. When their two children got the consumption too, Toni went insane. And he's there now, sitting in the insane house in Kankakee. He doesn't even remember that those two children died. I feel sorry for that good, kind Toni.

When Gionin came home from Wisconsin at the end of that winter he brought for three months the pay — thirty dollars he brought. You were like a millionaire if you had thirty dollars in that time! I got a nice clean cloth and wrapped that money, then I put it under the clothes in the bureau drawer. It was not yet two hours when here came in our house one of those cousins of his. That man said, "Gionin, I've got to have the money. I've got to have! Let me have some money."

My husband said, "Well, I brought just thirty dollars and my wife she needs it. She has no clothes for the children — the children are naked. And it's almost the time for the new baby to be born."

"Give it to me," he said. "Gionin, let me have it and I'll give it back right away on Saturday night."

[215

"You're sure you will give it back Saturday night?"

"Sure! Give it to me! I've got to have it!"

So my husband came to me and said, "Rosa, give me the thirty dollars back."

I said, "No! Why are you going to take it? I need it! I need it!" Then I began to cry.

"Give it to me!" he said.

So there I had to give it to him and I had not one penny left in the house. All the night I was crying, because I lose that thirty dollars. Gionin he couldn't stand it to hear me cry like that. He got up from the bed about nine o'clock and he went. (In that time we were going to bed when it was dark — six o'clock, or what time it got dark. We didn't have no oil to burn and we had no place to go.)

In the morning when I went to the house of Mis' Mill to do the cleaning, she saw that I had been crying so much, and she asked me about it. When I told her, she said, "Well don't cry, Mis' Cavalleri." And she went and found some little stockings and clothes to put on my children.

Gionin, when he saw me crying like that, he went again and again in the night by his cousin and asked him, and begged him, for the thirty dollars back again. But all the time, every night, that cousin had some sad-luck story. After a few weeks my husband got tired and he didn't even ask anymore. He knew he wouldn't get it. And I don't have it yet! But God He helped us, and that cousin of my husband, he stayed a poor man. That's the punishment he got from God. But oh, I was brokenhearted when I had that thirty dollars and lost it.

I don't know if I should tell about that fire we had when we were living over the saloon — that man he's alive yet and he's more religious than anybody now. He all the time goes to the Italian church. Sometimes he looks to me like he wants to say something — but I never speak to that man. He got so religious after his wife died. Well, that time in the poor year, he had a lot of wine in his saloon and it went bad and he wanted to get the insurance. So he chopped up some wood in the basement and made a fire. My husband woke up in the middle of the night and he heard that wood chopping, but he didn't wake up enough.

The next thing he woke up and we were all ready to burn up — all smothered with smoke. That saloon man was outside hollering, "Fire! Get out!"

There we had not even time to put a coat on. Some of that family from the second floor were on the stairs. The little girl was falling over in a faint — she said she couldn't go. And that big cat they had was already dead. Visella came down with two shoes in her hand, but that's all the clothes we saved. We came out in the snow with no clothes, and *so* cold. We had to run way down the next block, to our knees in snow, and barefoot, in the middle of the night. Tomaso, the cousin of my husband, he took us in and they made hot coffee with whiskey in, but I got sick from that cold anyway — and my baby not yet born.

When the insurance came to investigate they found out the saloon keeper had his family all moved one block away with all their things — with the clothes and the furniture and all what they had. When they saw he made the fire himself he got not one cent. Our things didn't burn, though; the firemen came and put out the fire before it could reach the attic. Only the windows broke, and they fixed them the next day so we could go back. I guess that man thought he could tell us in plenty of time after the first floor burned. But what did he think we're going to do in the attic if all the underneath burned first? Did he think we could stay up in the air with nothing under?

The night my first Leo was born my husband came home with his first pay — seven dollars for one week. We thought we would jump to the moon when he found that good job in the candy factory with seven dollars' pay for one week! The midwife was gone already when he came home with that pay. He ran out and bought the butter and some bread and made that hot water with the bread and butter in, like us Italian women always drink when we have the baby just born.

Then that boss in the candy factory said, "Why do you want to pay the rent? You and your family can come here in these nice rooms behind the factory."

Gionin thought it was nice if we could leave that attic and have the rooms to live in without paying the rent, so he said yes.

But that man, he was not good. He came after me. He said it's such a poor time he's going to buy me the clothes and all the things I want. Then he talked bad — he wanted me to be like a wife. When he came after me like that I got the scare. I told Gionin. Gionin said, "Well, we don't say anything — we will just go away. We're going to get out without the fighting."

So there my husband had that nice job in the hard times and he had to lose it. He was good, no — to go away and lose that good job to save me from the boss? Seven dollars a week in that time was something wonderful! He found three nice light rooms, but far away from those other *Toscani*. We moved to Union Street where there were all the German and Irish and Norwegian. And then Gionin had to go and go and try to find another job. He used to come home with his feet all blisters, trying to find a job.

25

THOSE new rooms we had in the big house with the Norwegian families, oh, I used to love them. They were so light and big with the high, high ceilings; I just loved them. But then one day a high-educated man came there, Dr. Taylor, and he wanted to rent the whole building to make something. So the boss came and he told all the families that we had to move. He said we could stay one month with the free rent, but after that we must be out, because there was going to be some kind of big home there.

Everybody was telling a different story: some people said it was going to be a hospital; some said it was going to be a home for girls; some said it was going to be a home for the orphan children. Nobody knew what it was. The boss didn't know — nobody knew. But they said it was going to be something good for the people. Dr. Taylor, he told the boss that something good was coming. He said it was going to be a good home to teach the poor people good things. But whatever was coming, we had to get out anyway.

Me, I was so sorry to leave that house, and I didn't know where to go. I couldn't find no more good rooms, because nobody would rent to Italians. I was staying there till the one month was gone. Then I had to go someplace. I had to go in a basement about one block away next to a factory. That factory, I don't know what it was, but they were melting all the waste from the tin — the scraps of tin they brought there and melted. They had so much fire in that factory that when the wind was one way, all the hot cinders came down on the sidewalk and the children scalded their feet — those cinders all the time burned the children's feet. I was so sorry that I had to live in that basement! I used to take my children and go back and watch those carpenters working on our old home. I thought maybe we could get our old rooms back again. But even before the carpenters got through the work, the people started to move into that building. They were all high-up people, dressed up nice. Me, I was even mad with them that they made us poor people get out. I was crying — I had no more the nice light rooms to live in.

Then one night after a while it rained hard. My poor rooms had one foot of water in. The baby's cradle was swimming around, and that basket of clothes I used to wash, it was swimming around too. We were all the night up from the scare. My husband was throwing the water out with a shovel and sweeping it out with a broom. When morning came I went by our old house and I was standing by the door crying and angry. A nice lady, a nice young girl, came out and said, "Why are you here, lady? Why are you crying?"

I said, "It's you people — on account of you people I had to get out from this home! And now come and see where I live! Last night I was drowned with the water, me and my children!"

That young lady felt so sorry. She came along and saw my house. And still my husband was shoveling the water out. She said, "Oh, I'm very sorry! Very sorry! I'm going to go right away and look for a house for you."

And she did. She went and she found a house and paid the rent and sent the wagon. She had to pay the rent ahead of time, because it was such a poor time nobody had any money. Before six o'clock in the evening I was in the new home. It was three nice little rooms in the front on the first floor of a wooden house. (They made the bridge there now for the railroad. They tore down those houses when they made the railroad.) So we were in that nice little house. And as soon as I could I collected all the little money I had and paid back the lady all the rent and the express she had to pay for me. Then I was nice and happy.

That lady — she wore a nice red blouse — she got a little work for me in the new settlement house. I started to wash the clothes for the residents and cleaned around the building and helped the cook — anything they told me. But when I first started that job — scrubbing the floors in the Commons — I was still *so* afraid of the teachers. And one day, I didn't see it, but a hole in my apron caught hold of one of those iron curls on a big lamp that was standing on the floor and that lamp fell over. I heard the crash and I looked around and when I saw that beautiful pink glass lamp shade in a million pieces on the floor I fell over in a faint. I thought I would be put in jail! I thought I would be killed! Miss May and one other teacher, they came running in to see what had happened. When they saw me there on the floor without my senses they woke me up and carried me into the kitchen and made me drink hot tea with sugar in it. "Rosa! Rosa!" they said. "Where are you hurt? Where did it hit you?" And when they learned that I had only fainted from scare because I had broken the pink glass lamp they started to laugh. "But Rosa," they said, "you did a good thing! That lamp was terrible! Somebody gave it to us, so we had to keep it. But now it's gone and we won't ever have to see it again. You did good! We're glad it's broken!"

Think of those angel women! They didn't scold me or anything. They were giving me hot tea with sugar in it and patting my shoulder and telling me they were glad. How can I *not* love America! In the old country I would have been killed for breaking a lamp like that!

So after that time of the pink glass lamp I said to myself, "Oh, I hope I do my work good so I never have to leave this place! I'm never going to leave!" And I truly never did. Forty or fifty years I've been scrubbing the floors, cleaning the rooms, doing the cooking, and telling the stories in the Commons. I grew old with that building. I love it like another home. I know every board in the floors, and I think those little boards know me too. Now I am old, I only have the little job to do the cooking when the regular cook is off. But even if they didn't pay me I would not want to stop working in the Commons. Never!

In that time us poor women, we didn't have any pleasures — no movies, no shows, no this, no that. And so many drunken men there were! Some men — those *Toscani* on Franklin Street and Gionin — on Sundays they used to play *boccie*. They'd throw the wood balls in the alley, and they'd play *cheese* too. They had that *forma*, the Italian cheese, and they'd throw that. They all went together to buy it, but the one that threw hardest, he won the cheese. But the alley was too dirty; when they had the cheese, they'd go far away where there was the clean road or some green grass.

Those swill boxes in the alley used to stay so packed full that the covers were all the time standing up. Oh my, oh mercy! It was stinking so the poor little children were holding their noses when they ran back the alley to come home. Inside those boxes the wood was all rotten and juicy. One whole box of garbage was nothing but white worms. After the wagon passed to shovel the box out — they weren't careful how it was falling — all the alley was full of white worms. The children, they didn't like those worms! They used to pick up stones and tin cans to throw at them. They couldn't stand it when they squashed them with the bare feet. That garbage was terrible, terrible! I don't know why everybody in Chicago didn't die.

Rushing-the-can like the men, that's all the pleasure the poor women had in that time. In the summer when it was so hot you couldn't stay in those buildings, the women and the boys and girls and babies were sitting down in the street and alley. All the women would bring down their chairs and sit on the sidewalk. Then somebody would say, "All the women put two cents and we'll get the beer." So everybody did and the children would run by the saloon and get the can of beer. The saloon had ice and they kept that beer ice cold. So the women, and children too, were drinking beer to get cool. Nobody but the saloon had ice in that time. That's all the pleasure we had — the cool from the beer in summer. Even when we started the club in the settlement, the women in the alley were drinking beer.

After not long, one lady from the settlement house — she was American but she could talk German too — she asked me if I wanted to go round the neighborhood with her and ask all the women to come and start the woman's club. Those women didn't know what it was, but they wanted to come anyway. Oh, I remember there was one lady — everybody knew her — she was tall, tall, about six and a half feet, with red hair. She was really a lamp post on the street. That woman, for one dime she would choke the Devil, so stingy she was for the money. And bad! Everybody was scared of that lady. She had the saloon and she was getting drunk herself, and she was swearing terrible and chasing the children. She fought with everybody. Mis' Reuter, she said to me, "We're going in the saloon and ask that lady."

"Sure not, Mis' Reuter!" I said. "If she comes in the club the other women won't — they'd be too scared."

But Mis' Reuter, I guess she went sometime when I didn't know it and asked that lady anyway, because one day here she was in the club. The other women were saying, "She's in our club? She's coming in our club? What are we going to do?"

That lady, in two or three weeks, she changed from a devil to a lamb — honest to goodness! She got good. When it was her turn she was the first one to go and wash the dishes and make the coffee. And she was talking nice to the women to make them laugh, so they would like her. She got to be the best one of all. And when she moved to California the woman's club were so sorry they gave her a big well-fare party. And some were even crying. (What was that lady? I guess she was Irish or German. I remember her name, but I won't tell it. I'll leave it to the people to find out if they want to know who she was.)

In the first beginning we always came in the club and made two circles in the room. One circle was for those ladies who could talk English and the other circle was for the ladies who talked German. Mis' Reuter talked German to the German ladies, and Miss Gray talked English to the other ladies. But I guess they both did the same preaching. They used to tell us that it's not nice to drink the beer, and we must not let the baby do this, and this. Me, I was the only Italian woman — where were they going to put me? I couldn't talk German, so I went in the English circle. So after we had about an hour, or an hour and a half of the preaching, they would pull up the circle and we'd play the games together. All together we played the games — the Norwegian, the German, the English, and me. Then we'd have some cake and coffee and the goodnight song.

One nice lady, Miss Chase, she used to teach the girls and the women to sew. Some young girls were ready to get married and they had never held a needle before. And Miss Chase, she'd teach them to make their own wedding dress. She was teaching me to sew too. She was a wonderful lady, Miss Chase, but she died after one year.

Oh, I have to tell you about the two gray hoods I made my Maria and my Visella from somebody's thrown-away underskirt. I found that old petticoat in the trash, all holes and torn, but it was wool and warm. All the other children in the sisters' school were Irish. They used to laugh at my two little girls and call them "spaghetti." When those other children laughed at those hoods, Visella used to carry hers by the string behind her. Gionin, he couldn't stand it to see those little girls crying because they had to wear those funny hoods, summer and winter — they had nothing else. So one day — he said nothing to me so I wouldn't stop him — he walked downtown to the Boston Store and he came home with two little red-and-black knit caps. He said he got them very cheap. Those little girls were just crazy with joy to have the really caps! I had stitched up those two hoods any which way so the cloth stayed on their heads. But after Miss Chase started teaching me, I made nice little dresses — well not *so* nice with all old cloth, but they were not so funny anyway.

Pretty soon they started the classes to teach us poor people to talk and write in English. The talk of the people in the settlement house was different entirely than what I used to hear. I used to love those American people, and I was listening and listening how they talked. That's how I learned to talk such good English. Oh, I was glad when I learned enough English to go by the priest in the Irish church and confess myself and make the priest understand what was the sin! But I never learned to do the writing in English. I all the time used to come to that class so tired and so sleepy after scrubbing and washing the whole day — I went to sleep when they started the writing. I couldn't learn it. They had the clubs for the children too; my little girls loved to go. And after a few years when they started the kindergarten, my Luie was one of the first children to go in.

That big and old building where Chicago Commons was in the

beginning was all full of rats — three pounds, five pounds, I don't know how many pounds to make those rats, but they were big! The residents used to wait in line by the bathroom door, and when somebody didn't come out and didn't come out, they'd push open the door, and there it was the rats playing tag with themselves. And when the residents were all sitting down eating dinner, those rats chased between their legs. And sometimes in the morning the dining-room girls came down and found big holes in the tablecloth. Those rats ate up all the places where the grease spilled! So Dr. Taylor begged the money to build a new building. He made it about six blocks away on the corner of Grand Avenue and Morgan Street. And me, I was the one to go in that new building and light the first match in the stove. I cleaned the kitchen the first one in the new Chicago Commons! In those first years the settlement house didn't have enough money to tell me to come every day. They were poor in that time. The residents — men and girls both — were going in the kitchen and washing the dishes themselves. Each one had something else for a paying job. They did the janitor work and everything like that free. Just once a week I was going there to do the heavy scrubbing and the washing.

Well then Dr. Taylor asked me if I wanted to go there in the old building and watch all the plumbing. The bathtub and all those plumbing things belonged to Chicago Commons and he was afraid somebody would steal them, so he wanted one family to live in there and watch. I said, "Well, I have to ask my husband."

He said, "You have to answer quick, because I want someone to be in that building."

So I told my husband and he was glad. He said, "Sure, we're going to go and pay no rent. It's good to pay no rent for a few months."

I said, "But I'm afraid. I don't feel like going."

He said, "Oh why do you want to be afraid? There's nothing to be afraid of. You go tell Dr. Taylor we're going to move in there."

Me, I was brokenhearted because I didn't feel like going. I ran by the Madonna Addolorata in the Irish church and I prayed. I said, "O Madonna, I feel so unhappy to go in that house! You put it in my mind if I should go or not go." Then I said a prayer. When I got up I felt in my heart, "No, don't go!"

So I went right away back to Dr. Taylor and I said, "No, Dr. Taylor. We don't go, because I'm afraid in a big house like that."

He said, "All right. When you're afraid, don't go."

When I came home and told my husband he was mad! He said, "Why did you tell him that? We want to go! Why not? Why you are afraid? We're going to go!"

I said, "No. You can go yourself, but I won't go there!"

Dr. Taylor put boards up to all the windows and he left that old house there alone in the middle of the lumber yard. And then it came one day after a week or two (I don't remember just how long, but just a short time) and an old man came by in a wagon. And nobody knew why that old man said what he did. He said, "I'll not give five cents for all the houses on this street!" (I guess he saw a little fire that started in the lumber yard, or something.) Just after he passed there exploded a great big fire. And there the old Chicago Commons went up in the air! If I had been there with my children we could not say "Jesus-Mary-Joseph," we'd have been killed so quick! The wind picked up that fire and it spread all down the street. All the lumber from the lumber yard, the wind picked it up in big chunks and it came down on our roofs all blazing — all fire. Those banana wagons full of hay in our alley, they caught on fire. My husband had his bananas in the basement, so they didn't burn, but all the swill boxes caught fire and the boards on the sidewalk. Everybody was carrying water and wetting the roof.

One lady, the boss of our house, she raised up her two hands and she hollered, "Oh, Sant' Antoni, help us! Help us!" She saw that fire coming. It was terrible. And just when she hollered like that the wind changed and went the other way! Sant' Antoni is the protector of fire. You can ask anybody that was in the Commons then and they will tell you too: that wind just changed around. Maybe it was not Sant' Antoni; but why did it change like that? The wind it turned around and it burned four blocks the other way. But all the houses by us caught on fire anyway.

My husband wasn't there when the fire exploded; he was downtown to send the ticket for his brother in *Italia* to come to America. But he heard down there that there was a terrible fire, and he right away came home. He had his wagon with the horse on and grabbed up some clothes and some quilts and trash from the bed. Then he took us and went out to the end of Indiana Street — a little further than Western Avenue. It was all prairie there then — all country. So me and the children were in that prairie, and my husband went back to look after the house. Our house, the carpenter had just made the new roof on, and it didn't catch fire. It had all that *resina* still in.

Me, I had a five-dollar gold piece I had saved. I had hidden it and I didn't tell my husband. And there I forgot it and left it in that house! Gionin came back ten o'clock night. He said, "Our house is saved. We can go back."

I said, "Oh, then I have my gold piece safe!"

He said, "You have the gold piece? You hid it from your husband, huh? See, that's what you get!" But he was glad too. He was a good man, Mr. Cavalleri. He was good to me. He didn't do nothing. Me, I didn't care for the house or nothing — I was only thinking of my gold piece!

We went back so happy and started eating the soup that was on the stove. There we had run away and left all the doors open and the soup on the stove. (I had the gasoline stove that time, I remember.) But I had the faith our house wouldn't burn, because I had prayed Sant' Antoni too.

I don't have to say it. You can guess yourself that the Madonna made a great miracle to save me and my children from the dead! My husband, probably he wouldn't have died because he was downtown sending the money to his brother; but me and my children died for sure if we'd been in that old Chicago Commons. It was some big boiler in the meat market next door that exploded.

That night the old settlement house burned those ladies from the new building didn't eat their supper — nothing — they were all watching. And after the fire they came over and picked up some little pieces of burnt wood. They said, "Sure, I recognize! It's a piece of my bedroom — it's a piece of the decoration!" They were so sad — they saved even those little pieces to remember.

26

THE year my Leo was born I was home alone and struggled along
with my children. My husband went away because he was sick — he
went by a doctor in St. Louis to get cured. That doctor said he must
stay away from his home one year and gave him a job to do all the
janitor work around his house for five dollars a month and his board.
So me, I used to go all around to find the clothes to wash and the
scrubbing. The city hall was helping me again in that time — they gave
me a little coal and sometimes the basket of food. Bob, the sign painter
downstairs, he helped me the most. He was such a good young man.
He used to bring up a big chunk of coal and chop it up right in my
kitchen and fix the stove.

I was to the end of my nine months, but the baby never came. So
I went by one woman, Mis' Thomas, and I got part of the clothes
washed. Then I said, "Oh, Mis' Thomas, I've got to go. I've got the
terrible pains!"

She said, "You can go when you finish. You've got to finish first."

"No, I go. Otherwise I'll have to stay in your bed." When I said
that she got scared I would have the baby there, so she let me go.

I went by the midwife, Mis' Marino, and told her to come; then
I went home. When I saw it was my time, I told Domenico something

and sent him with all the children to the wife of Tomaso. I told those people before, when they see the children come they must keep them all night — it's my time. It was really, really my time, and I had such a scare that I would be alone a second time. So when I heard a lady come in the building — she lived downstairs — I called to her. She said, "I have no time." And she didn't come up.

I was on my bed all alone by myself and then I prayed Sant' Antoni with all my heart. I don't know why I prayed Sant' Antoni — the Madonna put it in my mind. And then, just when the baby was born, I saw Sant' Antoni right there! He appeared in the room by me! I don't think it was really Sant' Antoni there, but in my imagination I saw him — all light like the sun. I saw Sant' Antoni there by my bed, and right then the door opened and the midwife came in to take care of the baby! It was February seventh and six below zero. There I had him born all alone, but Mis' Marino came when I prayed Sant' Antoni. She washed the baby and put him by me, but then she ran away. She didn't light the fire or nothing.

Oh, that night it was *so* cold! And me in my little wooden house in the alley with the walls all frosting — thick white frosting. I was crying and praying, "How am I going to live?" I said. "Oh, Sant' Antoni, I'll never live till tomorrow morning! I'll never live till the morning!"

And just as I prayed my door opened and a lady came in. She had a black shawl twice round her neck and head and that shawl came down to her nose. All I could see was half the nose and the mouth. She came in and lighted both the stoves. Then she came and looked at me, but I couldn't see her face. I said, "God bless you!"

She just nodded her head up and down and all the time she said not one word, only "Sh, sh."

Then she went down in the basement herself, nobody telling her nothing, and she got the coal and fixed the fire. Pretty soon she found that little package of camomile tea I had there on the dresser and she made a little tea with the hot water. And that woman stayed by me almost till daylight. But all the time she put her finger to her mouth to tell me to keep still when I tried to thank her. And I never knew where that lady came from! I don't know yet! Maybe she was the

[229

spirit of that kind girl, Annina, in Canaletto? I don't know. I really don't know! I was *so* sick and I didn't hear her voice or see her face. All the time she put her finger on her mouth and said, "Sh, sh." And when the daylight came she was gone.

About seven o'clock morning my children came home. And Mis' Marino, that midwife, she came at eight o'clock and said, "It's so cold I thought I'd find you dead!"

Then here came the city hall, or somebody, with a wagon. They wanted to take me and my new baby to the hospital. But how could I leave all my children? I started to cry — I didn't want to go. And my children cried too — they didn't want me to leave them. So then they didn't make me. They pulled my bed away from the frosting on the wall and put it in the front room by the stove. And my baby, I had him wrapped up in a pad I made from the underskirt like we do in *Italia*. But that baby froze when he was born; he couldn't cry like other babies — he was crying weak, weak.

My Visella was bringing up the wood and the coal and trying to make that room warm. But she was only a little girl, she didn't know, and she filled that stove so full that all the pipes on the ceiling caught fire. I had to jump up from the bed and throw the pails of water so the house wouldn't burn down. Then God sent me help again. He sent that Miss Mildred from the settlement house. She didn't know about me and my Leo born; she was looking for some other lady and she came to my door and saw me. She said, "Oh, I have the wrong place."

I said, "No, lady, you find the right place."

So she came in and found out all. Then she ran away and brought back all those little things the babies in America have. She felt sorry to see my baby banded up like I had him. She didn't know then, Miss Mildred, that the women in *Italia* always band their babies that way. And she brought me something to eat too — for me and for my children. That night another young lady from the Commons, Miss May, she came and slept in my house to take care of the fire. She was afraid for the children — maybe they would burn themselves and the house. Oh, that Miss Mildred and Miss May, they were angels to come and help me like that! Four nights Miss May stayed there and kept the fire going. They were high-up educated girls — they were used to sleeping in the warm house with the plumbing — and there they came and slept in my wooden house in the alley, and for a toilet they had to go down to that shed under the sidewalk. They were really, really friends! That time I had my Leo nobody knew I was going to have the baby — I looked kind of fat, that's all. Those women in the settlement house were so surprised. They said, "Why you didn't tell us before, Mis' Cavalleri, so we can help you?"

You know that Mis' Thomas — I was washing her clothes when the baby started to come — she wanted a boy and she got a baby girl right after my baby was born. When I went there the next week to do the washing I had to carry my baby with me. When she saw him she said, "Well better I have a girl than I have a boy that looks like your baby! He looks for sure like a monkey!"

In the first beginning he did look like a monkey, but in a few weeks he got pretty. He got so pretty all the people from the settlement house came to see him. After two or three months there was no baby in Chicago prettier than that baby.

When the year was over for him, my husband came home from St. Louis. He didn't send me the money when he was there — just two times the five dollars — so he brought twenty-five dollars when he came back. Oh, he was so happy when he saw that baby with exactly, exactly his face and everything — the same dark gold hair and everything — and so beautiful. But he saw that baby was so thin and pale and couldn't cry like the other babies. "Better I go by a good doctor and see," he said. "I've got twenty-five dollars — I'm going to get a good doctor." So he did.

But the doctor said, "That baby can't live. He was touched in the lungs with the cold. Both lungs got froze when he was born."

And sure enough he was all the time sick and when it was nine months he died. My first Leo and my second Leo I lose them both. Oh, I was brokenhearted to lose such a beautiful baby!

I have to tell about another good thing the settlement house did for me. That winter my Leo died we were still living in that little wooden house in the alley. All my walls were thick with frosting from the cold, and I got the bronchitis on the lungs, with blood coming up. So one of those good ladies from the Commons, she arranged and sent me to a kind of home in the country where people go to get well. They had the nice nurses in that place and they cured me up good. I had a good time there too – I was all the time telling stories to entertain the other sick ladies.

In those two weeks I was gone, Chicago Commons helped my husband take care of the children, and my family moved into a good building. That building in front of where we were living had the empty rooms good and dry. But when my husband asked the manager, he said, "No, I don't let no Italians in!"

So Dr. Taylor, he went himself downtown, or someplace, and saw the owner to that building. The owner said yes, the manager has to let my husband in. The rent was no more, and there we were in a nice dry building. I was no more sick after then. We were the only – or almost the only – Italian family in the neighborhood that time, and the Germans and Norwegians were afraid to let us come in their buildings. But Chicago Commons took care of us. In that time all the streets by the Commons were the Norwegians and the Lutherans. And on the next street were all the Irish. But then the Italians came and the Norwegians moved away. Most of those Italians, they were not Italians – they were Sicilians. Oh, the Irish and the Sicilians they didn't get along together! They were all the time fighting. The Sicilian downstairs put out the tomato sauce to bake in the sun – all the yard covered up with those boards for the tomato sauce – and the Irish upstairs she hung up her clothes above with the paper between so the cord don't dirty the clean white shirtwaist. When she took off the clothespins, the paper, and sometimes the pillow case, went in the sauce. Then they both got mad and started the fighting.

27

PRETTY soon after my first Leo died that darling Miss May got me the job to come every day to do the cleaning in the settlement house. Then Gionin got the good job sweeping the floor for the electric company. And after not long we got to be the janitor in that building where they didn't want the Italians. I had to scrub down the stairs once a week and do a little work like that, and we got the rent for half. We went along good that way. But I had a lot of worry too, because I was all the time gone to my work and my children were alone on the street. My Visella was eight or nine years old and she had to be the mother to the other children. And I had more trouble because the landlord in that new building was so mean. He was all the time beating the children. One day he kicked Visella and beat her terrible because she was playing house in the back alley and moved some boxes he didn't want moved. I was afraid to tell Gionin because he would start fighting with that boss. But I was crying one day when Miss May came in my house. I said, "If only I can have a little house of my own so those men can't lick my children."

She said, "How much do you think it would cost, Mis' Cavalleri?"
I said, "Oh, it costs lots — about a thousand dollars!"
The next week she came back and she said to me and my husband,

"If I borrow you the money to buy a little house do you think you can pay me back like rent?"

"Oh, no!" Gionin said. "That much money I can't take for a debt!"

And I said no too. I can't sleep with the debt. But she meant it, that good Miss May. She trusted us and wanted to do it. She was a rich lady but she used to love me. She was the one who slept in my house the time my Leo was born. And later she'd give me much pleasure when she'd come in my house and eat. She'd come in and see the onions and she'd say, "Oh, Mis' Cavalleri, I just love the onions! I want an onion sandwich." And she'd go out and buy a lot of butter and some bread and come back and eat with me.

The residents in the settlement house now are not like in those old days. Now they all have their own work and go their own way. They're all pleasant and nice. They come in the kitchen Sunday night and say, "How you are, Mis' Cavalleri? If we help with the dishes will you tell us a story?" But it's not like in the old days when everyone was one family.

Me, I was always one that liked to entertain the people. So every noon I used to tell a story to the other cleaning women in the Commons when we were eating our lunch in the kitchen. In that time I didn't talk much English but I acted those stories so good that they understood anyway. I made those women bust out laughing when I told some of those funny stories from the barn in Bugiarno. One day Mis' Hill, the housekeeper, came in and heard me telling. She was so crazy for the way I told the story, she went and told Dr. Taylor. Then Dr. Taylor found me one night and said, "Come in the parlor, Mis' Cavalleri, and tell the story to the residents."

Me, I felt like one penny the first time I went in before all those high-up, educated people, and I had to talk half in Italian. But I was so reverent and acted the story so good that when I was the sister seeing the Madonna come alive all those residents raised up from their chairs with me. And oh, I wish you could see how they laughed when I told the funny stories! After then I all the time had to tell the stories to everybody — to the Woman's Club, to the man's meeting, to the boys'

party, to the girls' party, to everybody. Sometimes when they had
the big meetings in Hull House they would tell me to come there. One
time that university in Evanston made me come there and tell stories
to those teachers who were going to school to learn the storytelling. I
went everywhere. But always some resident — one of the teachers
from the Commons — had to go with me, because I didn't know how to
go alone. I loved to tell the stories. I never said no.

Gionin, oh he was glad when I told the stories. So for practice I
used to test them on him first. If he listened good — if I made him
laugh or made his tears fall, then I knew I said them good. Sometimes
he went with me to those parties in the settlement; but when I went
up to tell the story, he went out of the room. He couldn't stay in, he
was so afraid I'd make a mistake. He was more excited than me. But
then after a while sometimes he used to stay in too. And he was proud
how the people were enjoying to hear me tell.

Me, I was always crazy for a good story. That's why I love so
much the dramatics. If somebody says to me, "Leave the supper and
take the show," I'll take the show every time and let the eating go. I
just love the drama! After I got the job to go every day to the
settlement for the cleaning, and Gionin had the job with the electric
company, we got along better. My children got bigger too. So then
I used to hide a little money from the food so I can go to the shows.
That one afternoon in the week I had home from the scrubbing I
hurried up and did my washing and prepared the supper; then I'd run.
But sometimes the show was long, and I'd see it start to get dark.
I'd have such a scare I'd run all the way to get home before my husband
came. I was going in the front door and quick put on the apron,
because Gionin came in the back door — from the back street through
the alley. Once he caught me. It was that time he was working in the
night. As soon as he started for his work, I put on my shawl and I beat
it. The snow was to my knees, but I didn't care, so long as I could
see the show. But Gionin came back again — he forgot his little knife.
He said, "Where's Ma? Where's Ma?"

Visella said, "Oh, she'll be right away back. Probably she ran to
the store."

I used to go to the drama on Clark Street. I walked way out on

Clark Street near Grand Avenue. The first drama I saw was *Hamlet.*
I always did like that drama. Laura Alberta, she was the actress that
made all those dramas in that New America Show on Clark Street. She
used to play good plays — only good plays. Oh, all the shop girls
were going behind by the stage door and watching to see her come out.
And she used to talk nice to those poor girls. Then she used to come
to our church. Sunday morning after the mass the people were outside
waiting and looking, like she was God coming out.

Once I begged Gionin so much to take me to a show, and I was
doing this, and doing this, and everything he liked to please him and
make him go. So when we came out it was late, and I was hustling up
so we can get a good seat. He said, "To other places you can't walk,
your leg hurts you so much; but to the show you can run."

The Folding of the Flag — something like that — it was a kind of a
war show, we saw that time. But my husband was not like me; he
didn't care so very much for the show. In that show they had beautiful
scenery — beautiful! I remember they had all that paper scenery. Now
no more. After that big fire the government won't allow it. Me, I
took my Visella and went to see that big fire — the Iroquois fire, where
the theater burned up. We didn't see the fire but we saw after, when
they were shoveling the dead people on the wagon. And then we had
the nerve to go right away to the show on Clark Street. (I'd like to
know what they did with that New America Show. It's not there
anymore.)

Yes, I was always a friend with the shows. I used to go over on
Milwaukee Avenue and see the nickel show. Oh, I remember one little
bit of a place with two rows of chairs and no air — but that was later
when they made the moving pictures. After five or six years the police
found out it was not a fit place to go in, and they locked it. Some of
those other places where I used to go the police came and closed too,
because they were dangerous for fire. Then there was one show near
the settlement house that was not right. There were some Italian men
that came out on the stage and said jokes to make everybody laugh. But
they said wrong things too — all kinds of dirty things that the men
like. Two of those teachers from the Woman's Club they told me one
day to come with them to that place. They wanted me to interpret

so they know what it was. They thought it was not right, but they had to know it to tell the government to shut it up.

But me, I didn't want to snitch. Those men were Sicilian, but they were Italian people anyway, and I was thinking maybe they didn't want to say those bad things — probably they had to say them to get the living for their children. So I said to those ladies, "Better you take somebody else, because those men are talking the Sicilian, and I don't understand very much."

So then I went to that Maurice myself — he was the boss of the show — and I told him he'd better look out and stop those dirty jokes. But he kept on just the same, and the government came and closed his show.

That Jew man that has the little moving-picture show across from my house now, he's good to me. When it's a nice picture he comes by my house and says, "You want to come tonight or tomorrow night, Mis' Cavalleri? It's a swell picture." And when he sees me come, he lets me buy the ticket and go right in the door ahead of everybody. He knows I can't stand in that line of people with my bad leg. When it's a bum picture, he doesn't tell me to come. He never tells me to come to those pictures where they won't let the children in. In those pictures I have to close my eyes almost the whole time to not make a sin.

Ten summers I took my children and I went to the Commons summer camp to cook for the boys. In the early time we had only the tents at camp. Every boy that came new had to go by the farmer and fill up his mattress with straw. When it rained those boys were in their bathing suits in the night. And in that big tent for the dining room, it was raining down in the sugar bowl in the middle of the table. And when it stormed with the wind, all the boys — about seventy boys — were hanging on that post in the middle so the dining room wouldn't blow away. Oh boy, think of the joy I had in that camp when they made the wooden house for the dining room, and the big barrel for the water! Oh, I remember one summer, such a trouble I had cooking for sixty boys when I had only two little gasoline stoves! I had to put the oatmeal on the night before to be ready for breakfast. Then I couldn't sleep because when the wind came it all the time blew out the light. Mr. Witter, he was so sorry for me he went in town to the company to find out how much it would cost for a gas stove. The company said, "If you dig the ditch yourself, it will cost much less."

So here Mr. Witter came back and called all the boys together on the hill. When he told them, they were so glad if they can help me. They said, "Yes, we're going to do it!"

When I saw all those boys digging the ditch I said, "Why you do that? Somebody can fall in."

Mr. Witter said, "Well, we make the ditch so the water will run off."

When the ditch was made, here came some men with the pipe and in one-half hour they had in a big gas stove — not a really stove, but four nice burners. Wasn't that a grand surprise! I went by Mr. Witter with my two arms out like a cross and I said, "Oh, Mr. Witter, if you were not a man, I would kiss you!" And all the boys busted out laughing. I was so happy! In one hour I had the whole supper made.

Those boys liked me so much because I told them the stories, and they were tickled to death to dig the ditch for me. They all the time were begging me. They'd say, "Oh, Mis' Cavalleri tell us the story! We'll help you get through your work. We'll scrub the barrel! We'll bring the water! We'll wash the dishes! Come on, tell us the story!"

One summer Dr. Taylor let some Jew boys come to camp with the Italian boys. In the first beginning those boys were like the Devil and the Holy Ghost together! And such a war they put up! They pushed out the clothes to each other from the tents. But in the end they were worse than sweethearts. When it came the end of two weeks they could even kiss each other — Jacob and Luigi, Tony and Sam. But whether they were Jews or Italian they all begged me to tell them the stories. And they all busted out laughing.

Me, I can't tell the stories so good like those men in the barns in Bugiarno. And the American people can't laugh like the people of Bugiarno. When I heard that a lot of my *paesani* had come to America and were living in Joliet I wanted so much to go there. But I was afraid to go alone. So one day that darling Miss May she bought the tickets and went with me. And we saw all those girls from the silk mills — Caterina too — and the men who told stories in the barns.

Miss May, she never forgets me. Whenever she comes to Chicago she right away comes and finds me. Oh, I have to tell how she came back in the wartime and preached against the war. She was a rich woman and she hired a hall herself to preach to the young men. She told all those young men that war is wrong, and it's better they go to jail than go and fight other young men. Dr. Taylor was signing the young men to go to war there in the settlement house, and Miss May hired the hall to do the preaching and tell them to don't go. Miss May knew my Luie so well, so she came and told him not to go. So he was listening to her, he liked her, and he didn't want to go anyway. He got the papers, but he didn't go. So here came the police to take him. Luie said, "No use for me to go, I can't shoot nobody. I'm a coward — I'm afraid to shoot somebody. They'll shoot me first." But the police took him anyway. They made him go.

When those boys with Luie went on the ocean many days, the boat stopped and everybody looked to see Paris. Some said, "You see all those high buildings? Now we'll get off the boat in Paris, France!"

But one said, "I think I've seen this place before. I don't think it's Paris. Sure, I remember that statue. It's New York!"

And sure enough, I guess they got the word the war is over when that boat was halfway across the ocean, so they brought all those soldiers back to America. But they didn't tell the men nothing — the men didn't know they turned around.

Oh, I was all the time crying when Luie went. I thought they would send him away and kill him. One night after we went to bed the telephone rang, and when Mr. Cavalleri answered, there it was Luie talking on long distance: "Hello Pa! Hello! How's Ma? I'm coming home pretty soon. I jumped off the train to talk on the telephone in the station. Hello, Ma! I've got to go or I get caught. Good-bye. I'm coming home pretty soon." That was the happiest moment I had in my life — the same happiness as when the baby is born. I hope there'll be no more war — never! My darling Miss May, I think she said true — it's wrong to send the young boys out to kill other young boys! I hope there never, never is another war!

Miss May, she's an old woman now too, but she never forgets to

[239

come and see me when she visits Chicago. Yes, the residents they are different entirely now than in the old time. Some they smile in my face and call, "Hello, Mis' Cavalleri, hello! Hello! How you are? Tell us a story," all pleasant and nice. But they don't get acquainted like in the old days. I just love Chicago Commons. I hope I'll never stop coming. But it's different now. The old Commons, when everybody was like one family, is gone.

28

TONIGHT the Madonna made a miracle to help me. Listen what
happened.

You know Mis' Bliss, the new housekeeper, she all the time comes
in the kitchen, and such a fussing she makes. She's a kind lady, she
never scolds nobody, but she wants everything made with such fussing
that she makes me really dizzy. For thirty years I've done the cooking
when the cook's away, and she thinks I don't know how? She has to
help me? Well she came in the kitchen tonight and she was fixing the
leaf on the salads, and fixing the dish for the potato with the parsley, and
decorating this, and decorating this. I got so nervous I forgot all
about those tomatoes on the stove. When I smelled them they were all
caught black on the bottom. I didn't know what to do! All those
tomatoes — lots, because we had forty people tonight. Oh, I was
brokenhearted. I put that kettle in some cold water, and I was tasting,
then Mis' Bliss was tasting. Those tomatoes tasted terrible burnt.
Mis' Bliss said, "Well, it's too bad, but we can't help it. We'll open the
can of peas, that's all."

I was almost crying — what a sin to waste all that good food. And
I started praying the Madonna. I prayed with all my heart, what I
can do to make those tomatoes come good again. All at once it came

in my mind to go in the pantry and get some of that black spice —
clover, cloves? I put some of that clove spice in a clean kettle with that
tomato, and some sugar too. Then I cooked it up a little and I tasted.
I could no more taste the burn — it tasted even good. I said, "Oh, Mis'
Bliss, taste now! Just taste!"

She tasted and she said, "Well I don't know, but I don't think I
taste the burn." Then she tasted again and she said, "It's good. It's all
right after all."

Just think how I was thanking the Madonna that she put in my
mind about that clove spice! I never in my life heard to put that stuff in
tomatoes. But when I told Mis' Bliss the Madonna made that miracle,
she looked at me funny, like she thought I imagined. But that was
true! The Madonna is the mother of us poor women. She helps us all
the time. In the old time there were more miracles than now, but I see
lots of miracles — in Chicago too. The Madonna and the Saints, they
all the time make miracles to help me out. I all my life keep the good
faith and the strong religion, that's why.

One time I saw a grand miracle the Madonna did. She didn't
make that miracle for me, but I saw it anyway. Oh, I told the whole
world that story — I told everybody. The residents in the Commons,
and the residents in Hull House, and the residents in a lot of those
other settlement houses in Chicago, and all the women in the Mothers'
Clubs know that story.

One society of Sicilians they were making the *festa* with the
stands to sell the pop and the snails and they had those gamble things
and the big fireworks and all like they do. Then Sunday afternoon
they took out the Madonna from the Church of the Addolorata and
made the procession all through the streets. It was that Madonna with
the Baby in her arms.

Well, that Sunday afternoon I came to the Commons to make the
supper for the residents like I always do. And one of those nice new
residents came in the kitchen after and dried the dishes for me. So I
got done early and I came out to go home. Right there by the corner
of the Commons the procession was stopped and the men from the
society were all running around to gather up the paper money to pin
on the ribbons of the Madonna. That Madonna was beautiful and

so big it took eight men to carry the platform. So the procession was standing there and here came the streetcar on the street in front. I saw it that the motorman had the intentions to go past — he didn't even slow down — so I said it's no use to run, I've got to wait for the next car. That motorman went half past the corner, then bang! He stopped that car so quick he made the people fall over themselves. His face was white like the ghost, and his eyes so big. He held up his hands together toward the Madonna. Then he was blessing himself, and he kept on fast making the cross and all the time looking to the Madonna. I looked too to see what he was seeing. And there I saw the Madonna all light and more beautiful than she was. Beautiful! And her eyes were looking at that motorman.

I said, "I'm going to take that car! I'm going to talk to that motorman!"

I ran across the street and climbed on that car. When I came on the front, there that motorman was standing with his arms hanging down still looking in the face of the Madonna. When I asked him about it, he said, "Did *you* see it too! Did you see!"

I said, "Well, I don't know if I saw what you saw, but I saw the Madonna all beautiful and shining, and I think she looked at you."

"Oh, me lady, me lady," he said. (Sure he was the Irish — he all the time kept on saying "me lady.") "You saw it? Oh, but you didn't see it like I saw it! She made me stop the car! She turned her head and commanded me! But those eyes — I never can forget!"

The officers from the society had to come and make that motorman go, or I guess he wouldn't go yet.

The *feste* and the processions in the old country, in Lombardy, oh, I used to love them. In Bugiarno everybody was reverent to the Madonna and the saints, even us little children. Our mothers hung out from the windows all what they had beautiful — the red shawl, the yellow silk bed quilt, the best sheet with the lace on — all what they had — to decorate the street. Then a lot of men came from Milano and put up the stands in the *piazza* and sold everything like a carnival. They had some gambling things too like in this country, and show people came and walked the tightrope. Everybody had a grand time.

But when they carried the Madonna out from the church, all was quiet — everybody was reverent. But the *feste* the Italian people make here in Chicago, me, I think with Father Alberto, it's not right. It's not right to take the Holy Madonna out in the streets of Chicago where so many people have not our religion. The American men smoke and chew and keep on the hat when the Holy Virgin goes by. That's not right! Father Alberto doesn't like it that they take the saints and the Madonna on the streets of Chicago. But never again will they take the crucifix. Never since that terrible punishment God sent the boss of the Sicilian society. Everybody was telling about that a year after. He's that big, black man with the pop-out eyes. He was living in the rooms behind when I was living in the front of that red building across from the Commons. Joe, they called him.

Joe, he was the president of one of those Sicilian societies. He was the whole thing, like a boss. And that man liked to make a big show. He wanted to make a grand *festa* on the streets. So the society had made a big, big crucifix, painted up beautiful — all red blood coming down the face, and the cross to look like gold, and everything beautiful. Those men took the crucifix by our priest in the Italian church and the priest blessed it. Then they made the procession. Oh, the streets were decorated wonderful — they looked like heaven, with all different colored electric lights. And there were the stands to sell the snails, to sell the pop, to sell the pieces of watermelon, and all kinds of gamble things. And the fireworks, I don't know how much those fireworks cost! You could hear them five miles away. The streets were chuckful, packed-down with people when they carried the crucifix. Twelve men it took to carry the platform, and three men did nothing else but pin the money on the ribbons. So much money! (But I guess the society spent all on the *festa*, anyway.)

So when they were through they had no place to put the big crucifix, and they asked Father Alberto if he wanted to take it in the church. Our priest said he would take it but they must not come back to take it on the streets again. So all right, all right. And Father Alberto put it up over the altar in front. But then Joe decided he'd like to make another *festa*. He went by the priest and said he was taking out the crucifix. Father Alberto said it was not right, but Joe wanted it anyway. "You take it out, you keep it," said the priest. "You can't bring it back here."

So they made another big feast, and when it was over Father Alberto said no — what he had said, he had said, that's all. So then they went by the priest in the Irish church. The Irish priest said he'd take the crucifix if they wouldn't come back and take it out again. So all right, all right. But next year, just the same, Joe came back and said he was taking the crucifix. The priest said, "You take it, you don't bring it back here. It's not right."

So after the procession those men didn't know what to do. The Italian church wouldn't take it, and the Irish wouldn't take it. Joe said, "We'll keep it ourselves, that's all." So they made a shed, like a big cupboard, beside one building in the alley. But a terrible storm came and knocked the shed down.

Joe said, "Now what'll we do? I'll take it in my own house."

Me, I saw with my own eyes when they brought that crucifix up the stairs and were trying to carry it into the little room in front. I even got the shock, Jesus looked so big! And here, even before they had it stood up, there came such a scream — the whole street below was one scream! And there they brought up the little boy of Joe — the only son he had — cut in pieces by the automobile. They laid that little boy dead on the table in front of his father.

Joe, his face went white like the blotting paper, but he shut his mouth tight. He didn't swear one word. He just grabbed up the cover from the bed and threw it over the crucifix. He knew that he deserved that punishment. But think what a terrible punishment — his only son!

So then Joe went by Father Alberto. Father Alberto saw he was converted and had suffered enough, so he took that crucifix in the Italian church and put it way up next to the ceiling where no one can get it down. (But it burnt up with the church now.) And Joe never again made the *festa*. And nobody, nobody can take the crucifix on the streets of Chicago.

Sometimes God punishes me too. He punished me when I did the fortune-telling in the teacup. I learned it from one lady that was working at the Commons, and I knew I could tell better than her, so I used to do it to make the entertainment. I just told the people to make fun. I said they're going to have luck, and I see a letter, and a little animal — maybe a cat — and this, and this. But pretty soon I saw it, some of those ladies kind of believed me. Even one of the residents used to wrap up her cup and bring it to me. So one time I was trying to think what I could tell the priest in the confession and it came in my mind that maybe the fortune-telling is a sin. When I told the priest I made the fortune-telling in the teacup, but just for fun, oh, he almost licked me! I can no more tell all he said. "Just for fun! For fun you put the thorns on Jesus' head! For fun you make him die! For fun!"

"But no, Father! I don't say nothing bad — nothing strong. A letter, a little money, a party. Why's that a sin?"

He said, "No, you must not do it! You have to stop!"

After a while Tillie, that Irish lady in the dining room, she came with her teacup again and teased and teased. She teased so much I told her just some little thing to keep her still. Then I told her she mustn't believe, because if she believed, it was a sin.

When I told the little new priest in confession, oh my, oh mercy! He said, "You're a woman and I think you have more sense than that! You make a mortal sin! That's a mortal sin! You're half in hell already!"

"Oh Father, don't say that! I didn't know it was a mortal sin! I didn't know."

"Yes," he said, "and you've got to swear to God at the altar that you never again will do the fortune-telling. You've got to swear." He gave me the absolution, but he made me swear to God by the altar that I never again would tell the fortune in the teacup.

When Tillie came with her teacup, I said, "Never again. I'm sorry, but I can't. I had to swear to God." She's not Catholic, Tillie. She's a funny religion I don't know, but I wish you could hear how she cursed the priest that he won't let me tell her fortune.

So then one day I looked in my own cup. I saw there some railroad tracks and a big fat woman. I said, "That looks like me fallen down. That's really me."

And sure enough that night when I started home from my work, I stepped down too quick from the sidewalk and one foot twisted over. I fell down in the street and I got the sprained ankle. I can't get up to go on the streetcar. A little boy came by with his wagon and he let me ride on that cart. He took me home, and there I had to stay two weeks. For two weeks I can't go to my work! You see it? That's the punishment I got from God. After I swore to Him by the altar, He wouldn't even let me tell the fortune to myself.

Another time I had such a terrible year — a most unlucky time. For many, many years all us poor women in the Mothers' Club in the Commons, we make the Christmas play. Twenty years I had been Saint Joseph in the Christmas play. Most times we went up on the stage and just acted those parts and some high-educated lady read the story from behind the curtain. But one year we had the talking play. So they wanted a king to talk in Italian and they gave that part to me. I like to do the talking on the stage and Saint Joseph didn't have any talking. They gave that part of Saint Joseph to Mis' Stefano. But that year I stopped being Saint Joseph and was a king, that was a most, most unlucky year! My Maria died, my Luie had the operation, and my husband was sick with the gallstones. I said, "Never again will I stop being Saint Joseph!" And I sure never did. Some of those new teachers that come to the Commons just to teach the Christmas play they get cross with me — they want to give somebody else that part — but I don't let them. I say, "No! Twenty years I've been Saint Joseph, you don't give it to somebody else now!" To heck with those new teachers! If God wants me to be Saint Joseph, I'm going to be, that's all. I don't want another unlucky year like that time. Never again.

29

AFTER my husband died, Luie and Visella they said, "Ma, you
don't have to go to work anymore. You're an old woman now and so
fat to go up and down the stairs and do that heavy cleaning. Stop
the work in the Commons."

"No," I said. "Chicago Commons is my home — thirty years
working there. I grew up with that place. I love it! I can't stop now."
So I was back doing my cleaning. But pretty soon I got the bad leg,
and then I had that other sickness — the time I was supposed to die and
didn't. After then I could no more go up and down all those stairs and
scrub and lift. The housekeeper said she had to have a younger woman.
But I didn't stop entirely — I kept a little job to go two times a week
for the cooking when Tillie has her time off. And I never miss the
Woman's Club, and a lot of times when they have no program, I tell
them the stories. That's why I like so much to go to the moving picture
— I learn a new story. The stronger they make it, the better I like
it. I never cry. Sometimes I laugh, though.

Oh, I never forget that time poor Ollie from the Commons
was sitting down next to me in the picture show. "You dirty brute!"
she hollered, and she was going right after the stage — she wanted to
kill the man in the picture. She was crying.

Me, I grabbed hold of her and I said, "Sit down, Ollie, sit down and keep still! The people will think we are drunk women! It's not a real man — it's a story!" And I had to hold her down. Oh, I miss poor Ollie so much!

One day the housekeeper invited me and Ollie to go downtown and have supper — she wanted to give us a nice, nice treat. She said we must meet her downtown at four o'clock on one certain corner by Marshall Field's. It was Thursday, so I had my day home, but I did all my washing and cleaning. Ollie, she worked all day scrubbing at the Commons. So I met Ollie and we went. We were kind of scared because we never went downtown alone; but we found the place she told us, and we waited. Ollie said, "Oh, I'm so tired!" She had such sore feet, with the bunion and the corn. She was even crying that she had to stand on them. And then those old shoes she got from somebody, they didn't fit either. Oh, her feet hurt her so much.

Then here came Mis' Bliss, looking like the queen — like the president — with white gloves, with flowers in her hat, and hair all in curls. We two poor women, we had on our best dresses, but we looked so poor and we were so tired from working. Mis' Bliss said, "I tell you what we do: we're going to walk all down State Street and look at all the store windows."

Poor Ollie, so tired with her sore feet aching, she looked to me, and I looked to her. But we didn't say nothing. Oh lordy, lordy! Mis' Bliss, she made us do all that walking on State Street. Me, I felt like crying. I didn't care for no dinner — nothing. She walked till she was tired herself; just think of us! Five o'clock we came back and she took us in the Chinese place. Oh, it was a beautiful place. But everybody was looking at her like a queen and us two poor women. (Ollie was dressed so poor!)

Mis' Bliss ordered chicken chop suey and all the grandest things. There was a row of silver by our place this big, but me, I was using just one fork so those poor servants wouldn't have to wash so many dishes. But when Mis' Bliss saw me — she was talking to us like we were babies — she said we must use this, and do this, and so, and so. Then she said, "Now you eat good and enjoy everything."

There was a special man in back of her chair dressed up like a soldier, with a blue suit and lines. He stayed right there and when he saw the water go down, he called another man to fill up the glass. "Oh, goodness," I said. "What for is that man?"

"He has that job to watch over us," she said. But how are we going to eat with that soldier watching how we do? Oh, lordy, lordy! It was funny, no? And Mis' Bliss, she was so happy with herself — she thought she was giving us such a good time. I was looking what she paid. She gave the man I guess it was a ten-dollar bill, and she got very little back.

Ollie and me, we were very, very friends together. She used to tell me all her troubles, and I told her mine. She used to go downtown and scrub the office building in the night. When she first came to do the scrubbing and cleaning in Chicago Commons she was so dirty dressed-up. She didn't even wash her face and neck or comb her hair, and she had the dirty sweater all pinned up with the safety pins. But she was the best one to do the scrubbing and the cleaning. And little and little, as she came to the Commons, she got clean. That poor woman, oh, she was happy when the teacher told her to come in the Woman's Club. She really washed herself and came to the club clean. She got the clean face and neck, and her hair combed neat. She had the nice yellow hair, and white, white skin. After she was to the Commons five, six months, she was a new woman entirely. And she was not so stupid, either; she was coming to the class in the night to learn the reading and writing. I remember now the big bunch of roses Ollie bought, when the Woman's Club made that nice party for Dr. Taylor's birthday. Ollie paid seven dollars for those roses! Her family couldn't eat for one week. But oh, she was happy she could give Dr. Taylor those roses!

One time when we were making the Christmas play in the Woman's Club, Ollie was supposed to say "infant," but she couldn't learn it. One high lady who came to the Commons to teach us the parts, she told her, and told her. But Ollie couldn't say "infant Jesus." She all the time said, "Infrant Jesus." So one afternoon when her scrubbing was done, she came where I was working, and she said, "What am I going to do, Rosa? I can't say it! What am I going to say?"

I said, "Well, Ollie, you say 'infrant.' You only must say 'infrant' when you die and go in the other world. *Porta infrant* is a Latin word the priest says when you close the door here and open to the next world. You've got to say 'infant.' 'Infant' means a baby." And I was making her say it after me, "Infant. Infant. Infant Jesus."

So then when the night came and we went up on the stage, I was listening to Ollie. Sure enough she said, "Infrant Jesus." In one month Ollie was dead. Something there was that made her say that word!

Ollie, her mother died when she was a little girl. When she was thirteen years old, her aunt made her marry an old man sixty years old. He was all the time drunk, and he beat her terrible. Such a life she had, that poor woman, with all those children and not one was right! Her husband, he was too old to work and he was awful mean. The Commons told Ollie better she leave that man. But she said, "No, he's my husband anyway." And she was not Italian; she was American-born in Chicago.

Ollie, she had the bad kidney sickness, and when she went to the clinic, the doctor pulled out her teeth. That day she came back from the dentist she looked white like the ghost. I was looking and looking. She looked like a saint! I was even jealous of her how beautiful she looked that night. Like an angel! I said, "Ollie, you're too sick. You sit down and I'll wash the floor for you."

But then, after dinner, the housekeeper said, "Ollie, you've got to wash the dishes tonight — I planned on you. I've got nobody else. A couple of teeth is nothing — you'll be all right."

So Ollie tried to do it, but she couldn't. She fell down on the floor. Me, I washed her dishes, and one dining-room girl took her home. When a teacher in the Commons heard about it, she went to Ollie's house to see. She took Ollie right away to the hospital. The next day poor Ollie was dead. Oh, I did cry for Ollie! I missed her so much. I used to love that poor woman.

The American doctors they ruin the people. I say, "People, don't go to the doctors! Let them alone!" Here in America everybody runs to the doctor. And those doctors! When you get a pain down here in your leg, they look in your mouth and say, "You have to pull out the teeth, that's all."

You get a pain in your stomach, and they say, "Take off the tonsils."

They tell you to take off all those things and they won't cure you till you do. They won't! In *Italia* we don't take off nothing – we keep everything, and we are not sick. God gave us all those little things: what for the doctors take them off? It's not right. And then they tell you to open the window to sleep and let in all the germs from the night air. The American people ruin themselves by running all the time to those crazy doctors. But I mustn't say bad about the doctors because sometimes they do good too. God made them, so we've got to have them, that's all.

When I had those eleven days the terrible pain in my leg, the sciatica, the doctor he wanted to pull out my teeth, but I wouldn't let him; that's why he wouldn't cure me. But the soul of purgatory cured me without taking the teeth.

Another time I was so sick I was ready to die. When the doctor said I was going to die, I was not frightened; I was ready to call the priest and have the sacrament. But I was wishing that I could live just for the Holy Year. Miss Taylor came from the Commons and stayed by me all night, and she was crying. I said, "Don't cry like that, Miss Taylor. I go to heaven and I'll pray God for you and for Chicago Commons."

The doctor was there listening to my heart and he said I have only a little while. But then he thought of something and he wrote it on a little paper and sent Luie running down to one drugstore that stayed open. In fifteen minutes Luie came back with some little pills. Six o'clock morning I began to get better and in one month I was up and well. And oh, I was thanking God that I got well and can live for the Holy Year. But my son-in-law, that new husband Visella got, he was mad at me that I didn't die when I was supposed to! He and Visella were figuring and figuring and running around to get all the money I had. And there I fooled them – I didn't die. They were so mad. The doctor told them before that it's better if they wait. My Luie didn't do like that: he didn't even ask about the money – he just kept saying to me, "You're going to be well again, Ma. You're going to be all right again!"

[252

Oh, I was glad that I lived for that Eucharist Year in Chicago! It was 1926. If you died in that year you had the plenary indulgence — all your sins were forgiven — you went right to heaven. But even then I was not wishing to die.

Me, I'm not afraid of the death, but I never can forget that snake in the cemetery. One day me and my Visella went to fix the grave of Gionin. Nobody was there — only far over were one or two men doing the digging. We were walking quiet, quiet, because all that silence in the cemetery made us feel kind of scared. But we had to walk some more and we passed a new hole where the dirt was just dug up. We looked in — I don't know what made us look in that hole — and there was a great big snake waiting to eat up the dead! No, I never can forget that day in the cemetery. But me, I'm not afraid of the death. I don't care if the worms and the snakes eat my body when the soul is not in. They can't hurt me then. When I come to my end, I won't need this old body anymore — let it go to the dust. Our body goes all back to the dirt but not the soul. The soul goes on. I'm not afraid, but I'm never wishing to die. I like to live.

Now I make for nine months the confession and Communion every first Friday for *una buona morte* — for a good death. I have only four more Fridays to go — I made five months already. Then I will have a good death. When it's my time I will die willing, without fighting God. I want to die quiet in my bed; I don't want to struggle.

But I don't wish that I die; I have it like heaven now. I'm really in heaven — no man to scold me and make me do this and stop me to do that. My Luie, so long he's not married, he lives with me, but he never scolds me for nothing. If I have his meal ready, all right; if no, all right too. I have my house to live and Luie pays the food, so I don't have to worry about the living. I keep my little job in the settlement house, so I have that money extra and I can go to the picture-show and see the good story. I have it like heaven — I'm my own boss. The peace I've got now it pays me for all the trouble I had in my life. I guess God says, "That poor Mis' Cavalleri, she suffered enough when she was a young girl in the silk factory. I'm going to let her have it easy now — she deserves it."

Of course sometimes I have a little trouble in my heart. It's like this, I guess: you know the mother, she all the time carries her baby on her right arm. When she puts him on her left arm he gets cross — he scolds and cries and doesn't like it. She can't hold him so good on her left arm. So God does to us. He always carries us on his right arm; when He changes and puts us on His left arm, we don't like it — it's not comfortable. But I always know where to go to get happy again. The Madonna is the one to take care for us poor women. You've got to have the faith in your heart — you've got to believe. But it's true and true: if you pray with all your heart and beg God and pray the Madonna you get help for sure. You get happy again. The Madonna, She helped me all through my life, and now She gives me peace.

Only one wish more I have: I'd love to go in *Italia* again before I die. Now I speak English good like an American I could go anywhere — where millionaires go and high people. I would look the high people in the face and ask them what questions I'd like to know. I wouldn't be afraid now — not of anybody. I'd be proud I come from America and speak English. I would go to Bugiarno and see the people and talk to the bosses in the silk factory. And to Canaletto. Those sisters would not throw me out when I come from America! I could talk to *Superiora* now. I'd tell her, "Why you were so mean — you threw out that poor girl whose heart was so kind toward you? You think you'll go to heaven like that?" I'd scold them like that now. I wouldn't be afraid. They wouldn't dare hurt me now I come from America. Me, that's why I love America. That's what I learned in America: not to be afraid.